CULTURES AND BEYOND

THE ART OF WORLD BUILDING

VOLUME III

RANDY ELLEFSON

Evermore Press
GAITHERSBURG, MARYLAND

Evermore Press, LLC
Gaithersburg, Maryland
www.evermorepress.org

Publisher's Note: This book includes fictional passages. All names, characters, locations, and incidents are products of the author's imagination, or have been used fictitiously. Any semblance to actual persons living or dead, locales, or events is coincidental and not intended by the author.

Publisher's Cataloging-In-Publication Data
(Prepared by The Donohue Group, Inc.)

Names: Ellefson, Randy, author.
Title: Cultures and beyond / Randy Ellefson.
Description: [Gaithersburg, Maryland] : Evermore Press,
    [2020] | Series: The art of world building ; volume 3
Identifiers: ISBN 9781946995056 (Amazon paperback) |
    ISBN 9781946995346 (IngramSpark paperback) |
    ISBN 9781946995117 (IngramSpark hardcover))
Subjects: LCSH: Fantasy fiction--Authorship. | Imaginary
    societies. | Imaginary places. | Creative writing. |
    Storytelling.
Classification: LCC PN3377.5.F34 E453 2020 |
    DDC 808.38766--dc23

Ellefson continues his masterful overview of worldbuilding, carefully and coherently dealing with every last detail...that...*Creating Life* and *Creating Places* haven't covered. All three are essential reference works...Ellefson is a master of this craft, and it shows. Highly recommended!

–ED GREENWOOD INVENTOR OF THE FORGOTTEN REALMS® AND DOZENS OF IMAGINARY WORLDS

CONTENTS

Table of Figures

ACKNOWLEDGEMENTS

Special thanks to Raoul Miller, Tom Farr, and
Vivian Syroyezhkina

Edited by JJ Henke

Cover design by Deranged Doctor Design

Introduction

With creating life and places covered in volumes one and two, we turn our attention to everything else about setting that characterizes our world, inhabitants, and storylines.

In this volume, we'll discuss:

- Cultural vision, scope, origins, and manifestations
- Organizations like organized crime or secret sects
- Armed forces (the army, navy, and air force)
- Religions and how to leverage deities we've invented
- The supernatural and its impact
- Items, whether supernatural, technological, or neither
- Languages and the impact they have on setting
- Names and techniques to invent them
- Educational, legal, commerce, health, and IT systems
- Approaches to managing world building development

Examples included in the text were created specifically for this guide and are not drawn from any setting I've created, or stories I've written or published.

Chapter 1 from *Creating Life (The Art of World Building, #1)* includes discussion of some principles referred to here, the main one being the use of analogues. This means inventing something that is based on an Earth equivalent but making enough changes to it that people are less likely to recognize the influence. This is known as the Rule of Three.

The book has a website where you can find additional resources, information on other volumes in this series, and other items as they are added.

Visit http://www.artofworldbuilding.com

WHERE TO START

The series and chapters within each volume can be read in any order but are arranged according to what might come first in a world's timeline. This volume is an exception; one chapter has little to do with the next. If you have an idea for something covered herein, write down everything you're thinking of before reading about other things you might consider. This will keep you from forgetting your idea or becoming overwhelmed with feelings of needing to get it "right;" there's really no such thing. Then you can read on for new ideas to enrich your setting.

So where do you start? Where your heart lies.

ABOUT ME

By profession I'm a software developer, but I've been writing fantasy fiction since 1988 and building worlds just as long, mostly one planet called Llurien. Yes, I am crazy. But I love what I do. I didn't intend to work on it for so long, but when life has prevented me from writing, I've worked on Llurien. I've done everything in these chapters and authored over two hundred thousand words of world building in my files. Llurien even has its own website now at http://www.llurien.com.

I've written several novels and more than a dozen short stories over the years, and began my publishing career with a novella that you can read for free (see below). Also a musician with a degree in classical guitar, I've released instrumental rock albums, a classical guitar CD, and a disc of acoustic guitar instrumentals. You can learn more, hear songs, and see videos at my main website, http://www.randyellefson.com.

FREE BOOK

If you'd like to see a free sample of my own world building efforts in action, anyone who joins my fiction newsletter receives a free eBook of *The Ever Fiend (Talon Stormbringer)*. Please note there's also a newsletter for *The Art of World Building* that is separate, though both can be joined on the same signup form. Just check the box for each.

Figure 1 Free Book

DISCLAIMERS

While some authors prefer the term "races" to "species," I've used the latter term throughout most of the series except for the section in the first volume discussing the merits of both terms. This book uses "SF" to abbreviate science fiction. SF is broadly defined herein as a setting with technology far in excess of current capabilities. Fantasy is loosely defined in this book as a setting using magic, knights, and lacking modern technology. As a stylistic point, to avoid writing "he/she," I've also opted for "he" when discussing someone who could be either gender.

THE CHAPTERS

What follows is a brief summary of what's included in each chapter in Volume Three, *Cultures and Beyond*.

CHAPTER 1 – CULTURES

This chapter discusses the differences between a culture and a custom, and that morals, values, and beliefs underlie everything. World builders can determine the scope of an invented culture, as some are regional or extend throughout a sovereign power. Cultural depictions can have visible, audible, and behavior aspects to define. These include issues such as body language, hair styles, gestures, clothing, and more. Greetings and farewells should be defined because characters will use them. Similarly, swear words, slang, verbal expressions, and colloquialisms can be created to characterize interactions. The daily life of a culture is depicted in dining, bathing, sleeping, employment, and transportation rituals and behaviors; pastimes, holidays and more create a respite for the everyday activities. Even architecture can be influenced by culture.

CHAPTER 2 – ORGANIZATIONS

Organizations for good or evil are a staple of both fantasy and SF. This chapter discusses both group types and their world views, plus common traits like goals, enemies, friends, and their source of (and quest for) power. How members join and leave such groups is an important element; some organizations might prevent or inhibit departure. Prerequisites can also bind a member to the group. The history and actions of a group are an important part of its reputation.

CHAPTER 3 – ARMED FORCES

Military groups such as the army, navy, air/space force, and knights are a staple of both fantasy and SF. We can leverage existing ideas or craft our own. Doing so means deciding how someone joins and leaves a military group, including requirements, tests, and training. Some species and races might be forbidden or assigned special roles. Throughout history, famous members can inspire pride or loathing. When devising military units and ranks, it helps to understand Earth analogues, so some basics are included in this chapter. The world view, locations, place in society, and symbols are all important elements of memorable armed forces and this chapters covers them all.

CHAPTER 4 – RELIGIONS

While some aspects of societies have history as a minor element, history is crucial with religions, so first we look at where and how the religion formed, including a prophetic figure and the role of a god, should one exist. Creation and end of world myths, and the afterlife, are important elements that potential followers consider, along with the requirements for worship and the penalty for failing to follow the rules. How someone joins and leaves a religion can be trivial or significant and includes the possibility of expulsion. We'll need holy sites, too, and a decision on holidays, customs, sects, relationships with everyone from species to other religions, and what members of the clergy are like and their role in society. Most importantly, we need the symbols and beliefs of this religion.

CHAPTER 5 – THE SUPERNATURAL

Supernatural elements exist in both fantasy and SF and can be used to add surprises. The audience may expect magic, for example, but not our version of it, so there's room for originality here. We can create energies that give rise to phenomena, beings, or places like magic pathways or alternate worlds and realities that impact our setting and stories. How much impact and prevalence these supernatural elements have, and how to determine this, are an important focus of this chapter.

CHAPTER 6 – A SYSTEM OF MAGIC

Magic systems can be simple or complex, but they should always be consistent. This chapter discusses the methods and principles of good systems and how to create them. This includes the importance of naming them, deciding if spells are needed and what those are for, whether spells can go wrong and how, and different types of magic we might want to include in our settings. We'll also look at how much training someone might need, what forms that training takes, and learn how to decide what's right for our setting. And no discussion of magic is complete without a look at how to invent spells.

CHAPTER 7 – ITEMS

Whether magical, technological, or more ordinary, memorable items exist in our setting even if we don't mention them. SF likely expects them, and fantasy often has at least one magic item someone has or covets in a story, but even ordinary items can be given significance through association with important people, places, or events. This chapter discusses how to invent their properties, origins, and form, and how to determine who is likely to use or want them. The creation of an A.I. is included.

CHAPTER 8 – LANGUAGES

Creating a language is one of the most challenging aspects of world building, but it's also one of the few that we can outsource; how and where to do so is discussed. Even so, some basic terms must be understood so we know what we're buying and receiving from our expert. If we choose to do it ourselves, we should consider whether it benefits our audience and how, or even whether it's a burden that we can save both them and ourselves. This chapter will not teach world builders how to invent a language because there are entire books on the subject, and those are referenced here, but it will discuss the pros and cons of constructing a language and what we lose by not having one (or more).

CHAPTER 9 – NAMES

Many techniques exist for creating names of people, places, and things, and all of them leverage our creativity to make the results and process more satisfying than using name generators, which are also discussed. Caveats and pitfalls abound, for while a great name elevates our story, bad ones turn off audiences, or keep them from talking about a character with an unpronounceable or unspellable name. We look at the differences between given names, surnames, compound names, and different ways to use parts of our invented world for all of them. The tips in this chapter will make this required activity fun and rewarding.

CHAPTER 10 – OTHER SYSTEMS

Other systems exist in our setting and warrant development. We'll examine educational systems and their impact on employment, plus where and how people are getting educated or being disqualified from it. Health systems include medical and mental, and they range from great to terrible, each having significant impacts on lives.

Information systems aren't just for SF, because fantasy settings need to disseminate information, too, and have their own ways of doing so. Understanding monetary systems and how to keep them simple is another focus of this chapter and includes how to determine the value of time, labor, and materials. And no world is complete without laws, crimes, and punishments, so developing a legal system is a critical world building task we breakdown into a manageable one.

Chapter 11 – Conclusion

In the series conclusion, we look at how to organize our files of world building notes so that the info glut doesn't become overwhelming; this includes some tools others have created, whether free or not, and the pros and cons of using them. We'll also look at different approaches to world building and how each affects our working methodology and results. Final thoughts include the merits of following our own rules and whether partnering with another world builder is a good idea or not.

Templates and Newsletter

Effective world building requires having written down details about the created world. To help you organize and jumpstart your efforts, each volume in this series includes templates in the appendices. This volume includes twelve: cultures, organizations, armed forces, religions, supernatural energies, supernatural lands, magic systems, spells, legal systems, monetary systems, education systems, and games.

Rather than typing these up yourself, you can download these templates for free by joining the newsletter for *The Art of World Building.* As each volume is published, whether you've bought the book or not, subscribers will automatically receive an email with links to download the templates as Microsoft Word files, which you can repeatedly use.

http://www.artofworldbuilding.com/newsletter/

CREATING LIFE (VOLUME ONE)

Everything we need to know about how to create gods, species/races, plants, animals, monsters, heroes, villains, and even undead is included in *Creating Life (The Art of World Building, #1).* Some basic techniques are also discussed, such as using analogies and deciding how many worlds to build. As with every volume, it includes reusable templates that can help you build better, faster.

CREATING PLACES (VOLUME TWO)

The life we create needs to originate from somewhere on a planet: an ocean, a continent, in a land feature (like a forest or mountain range), in a kingdom, or in a settlement. *Creating Places (The Art of World Building, #2)* goes into detail about inventing such locations and figuring out how long it takes to travel between them by various forms of locomotion: foot, horse, wagon, dragon, wooden ship, spaceship, and more. The overall rules of our world are also considered, along with inventing time, history, various places of interest, and how to draw maps. We can start our work with any one of those subjects and crisscross between places and life, for one often impacts the other.

WORLD BUILDING UNIVERSITY

World Building University (WBU) has online courses that provide step-by-step instruction on creating all aspects of great fantasy and science fiction worlds. Each includes a series of video lessons, quizzes to test your retention of what you've learned, and assignments designed to make your creation a reality instead of a dream. Courses are intended for authors, game designers, and hobbyists. A free course is available to get you started! See the website or mailing list for details:

http://www.worldbuilding.university/.

THE PODCAST

The Art of World Building podcast expands on the material within the series. The additional examples offer world builders more insight into ramifications of decisions. You can hear the podcast, read transcripts, and learn more about the episodes:

http://www.artofworldbuilding.com/podcasts.

YOUTUBE CHANNEL

The Art of World Building YouTube channel now has videos that also expand on the material within the series. Check out the growing playlists and subscribe. Videos include replays of webinars that feature a Q&A, lessons from the books, previews of WBU courses, and tips from the book, *185 Tips on World Building.*

http://bit.ly/AOWBYouTube.

CHAPTER ONE

CULTURES

There are so many customs and culture items that we could disappear down a research rabbit hole, so we'll focus on things likely to be useful as storytellers and gamers. In addition to working out details in advance, world builders can refer to this chapter when creating scenes.

While much of culture can be invented when we need it, the disadvantage is inconsistency if we're not careful and take notes. We can invent something earlier in a story or series, then forget and contradict it later. Generally, people (like our characters) don't care about customs until encountering ones different from theirs or when expectations are not met. In the latter case, judgment about the offender results. This is one value to us as storytellers.

If we need a reason for characters to not be accepted warmly, failure to follow customs is a solution. This can be individual characters or whole groups rejecting someone. It can be wise or fun to include a character who is more well-traveled than other characters and understands how to navigate other lands without offense. This requires at least two cultures: the one our characters are from and the one in which the story takes place.

WHAT IS CULTURE?

Culture is an abstract, complex concept. Most of us have a vague understanding of what it means, but when we're building cultures, we need clarity to know what elements to invent, why, and how. Culture is a social group's life-style. It is symbolic communication and often taken for granted, which is one reason we have troubling grasping the concept. It is a set of expectations. It evolves over time, though slowly, sometimes with bursts of social change. It not only differs across sovereign powers, but within regions and settlements. The culture of football players is different from that of rock musicians. Nonetheless, if they exist in the same society, they'll share other elements of culture; to coin a term, we might call this "cultural scope," which will be discussed further in this chapter.

The case can be made that values, beliefs, and morals are the origins of culture. These are ideas. And they manifest as rituals, habits, customs, art, music, and the use of language. When broken down this way, it becomes easier to determine what work must be done, and in what order: the ideas, then the manifestations. This is how we'll approach inventing culture, rounding out our concepts before deciding what they've resulted in.

Even if inventing the ideas first is helpful, we may have a few of the resulting manifestations in mind because we thought of them first, but this is fine. We can work backwards from them and try to determine what ideas they imply. For example, if rigid formality exists in greetings, we can infer that people feel oppressed or suppressed, or that open expression of feelings is frowned upon. This can help us create more manifestations, but it can also suggest some values: that emotion is considered weak, that dignity is prized, or that appearance is important. We'll look more closely at this.

CULTURAL SCOPE

Every culture exists somewhere: in a sovereign power (or several), a region, a settlement, a social group, or a race or species, to name a few. Every sovereign power has a form of government, which will greatly impact the cultures within it. We must therefore know what this is. Residents of a democracy have leeway to create culture whereas a totalitarian government may be forcing culture upon people; the culture will be very different.

Creating Places (The Art of World Building, #2) detailed our primary government options and, at a high level, what life is typically like for inhabitants of each. We want to consider how much freedom and control people have over their lives. The less freedom, the less variation in culture at the lower levels of region, settlement, and social group. And the more oppressive and rigid a government, the more likely residents live in fear and avoid any violation of expectations, which could result in imprisonment, torture, forced labor, or death. Before embarking on the invention of a culture, decide what the sovereign power's government is, even if you're creating culture at the social group level. It's wise to create culture in the following order:

- Sovereign power
- Regional
- Settlement
- Social group

The reason is that ideas and manifestations at the sovereign power level influence the regional level, and so on down to the smallest social group. If this seems like a lot of work, most of what we need to invent is at the top level and, being inherited by lower levels, only needs modification as appropriate if our tale or characters need it. Each person will belong to every level above their social one.

For example, Kier could be in the knight social group while Antar is in the archer one, but both are in the warrior one, the settlement culture, the regional one, all the way up to the sovereign power level. Some elements can be true in multiple cultures, such as nerds acting roughly the same way in Japan as in the United States; in reality, each will have its own nerd culture, but we'd still recognize some similar elements, in theory.

We may want to invent the most universal items early, then more localized variations. But we should always make a note about scope in our files. For example, "Throughout the Empire of Antaria (including sovereign powers and settlements that once belonged to it), wedding bands are worn on so-and-so finger."

Every species and race is likely to have variations. The elves and humans in Kingdom Illiandor will not have the same dining etiquette, but some similarities will exist, just as the elves of Illiandor will share some dining etiquette with elves in another kingdom. This means that we could scope certain aspects as being typically elven and others as being of Illiandor. For example, let's say that all elves drink only from the right hand, place a napkin in their lap, and never talk with food in their mouth, regardless of the elf's origin (never mind that individuals can defy these customs). But all species of Kingdom Illiandor swear an allegiance to the king prior to dining. While more involved, this is believable depth.

THE IDEAS

There are arguably three types of cultural sources: beliefs, values, and morals, with some overlap. Deciding which of each matters to a group depends on what impression feels right to the world builder=. Think about the group's role in society and its goals and motivations. We needn't feel locked into our decision. If we don't think of a manifestation of a specific value, that's okay. These are guiding ideas that we're unlikely to explain to an audience anyway, unless a character is monologuing their thoughts, which is a great way to reveal these ideas.

MORALS AND VALUES

An individual's values come from within, can change over time, and are personal principles. By contrast, morals are taught by society, are usually deep seated and slow to change, if at all, and guide us on how to live rightly. Morals sometimes result from a fictional or true story; the fictional ones are often designed to demonstrate a moral. While these differences between morals and values exist, we can treat them the same when using them to invent culture. Here are some traits we can leverage:

Acceptance	Gratitude
Compassion	Honesty
Cooperation	Integrity
Courage	Kindness
Dignity	Justice
Equality	Perseverance
Fairness	Politeness
Generosity	Respect

Responsibility	Tolerance
Self-control	Trustworthiness

A more high-minded society will value different traits (like dignity, equality, politeness, and tolerance) than a barbaric one, which might value self-reliance, courage, respect, and integrity. A society with more freedom might value most items on that list while individuals in an oppressive one might value courage, responsibility, politeness, and perseverance, while longing for things denied them, like kindness, dignity, and quality. The oppressive society itself might prize obedience, humility, and sacrifice, expecting citizens to adhere to these. The society's government may prize values that are different from its inhabitants.

BELIEFS

Many beliefs in culture originate from religions; those beliefs and how to invent them are discussed in chapter four in this volume, on creating religions. As we invent our world, we can take any religious idea and make it more cultural. An example would be Christmas; most would agree that the religious nature of this holiday has been taken over by the cultural aspects of it. There are other concepts from Christianity that permeate life in the U.S., including heaven, hell, the devil, and common swears. Religion's influence on culture runs from holidays to working schedules and beyond. Leverage the beliefs of a dominant religion to create parts of a culture.

For example, if one day a week is for religious observance, or a few hours are for prayer, then many will have work schedules structured around this. Even those who don't practice the religion will be aware of these times if widespread. We tend to expect fewer people at stores or on the roads on a Sunday due to church goers, just as stores are often closed on Christmas. Our world's inhabitants will be aware of these times and may plan for them, which is one way to sneak cultural elements into a scene.

As for non-religious beliefs, some are based in superstition. For example, walking under a ladder is considered bad luck, as is breaking a mirror, stepping on a crack, or a black cat crossing our path. If we've invented an animal, we can use it in the same way, choosing a physical trait that makes it ominous, such as one type being poisonous when the rest aren't (such an animal should be somewhat uncommon but not too rare or it never comes up).

Understanding the origins of such ideas can help us invent our own. Some are practical, like passing under a ladder being unsafe. Some may originate from a nursery rhyme. Then there's the talisman that can keep evil away, whether it's garlic and crosses for vampires or a rabbit's foot. Associate an animal with something good like a benevolent deity and a piece of one's body can become a talisman. Perhaps a plant has a root shaped like a humanoid and therefore any part of the plant, like garlic, is seen in either a good or bad light.

The black cat idea likely came from being associated with witches, so if we have a world with magic and a type of animal is often seen with wizards, who are also considered dangerous, a similar belief can arise; we can make this true in one culture and the belief may spread across others even if wizards elsewhere don't often have such animals with them.

The idea that bad luck comes in threes is an example of confirmation bias, where we believe something and then look for the pattern, such as two bad things happening, prompting us to look for the third item. There's debate as to the origin of this one, but the trinity is important in Christianity and we can do the same thing with a different number in our world. If we go with three, we earthlings will associate it with Earth.

Touching wood for good luck also has debatable sources. Some say it dates from when relics that were believed to be pieces of the cross Jesus was crucified on were sold. Some religions also worship nature and believe trees had spirits in them. Churches of wood were once used as sanctuary and knocking on them in a specific pattern was a signal for entrance. Perhaps pirates (who are notoriously superstitious) knocked on their ships before a bad storm. We leverage rationales but it's important to note that not only do most of us have no idea where these superstitions originated, we don't care, simply accepting them. Our characters will be the same, but our audience may wonder at the new ideas we invent, but explaining is best done in a single sentence, like this:

As she'd done since childhood, Tianna clapped her hands twice for luck, like the famous knight Kier had done to summon the horse he rode to glory at the famed Battle of Evermore.

The breaking of a mirror is another superstition, which arose after we stopped gazing in water to see our reflections. Technology provides ever greater possibilities for image capturing, and at my local Renaissance Festival, there's a running joke that photographers are stealing the souls of those whose picture they take. Such literal interpretations are less common in a more educated world like ours, but they can be fun and useful to remember for fantasy settings. Disturbing that which holds the image, such as breaking glass or causing ripples in the water, is seen as sinister portent. Leverage such a belief as desired, forecasting how many years of misfortunes are thus foretold.

Friday the 13th is considered bad for reasons that aren't agreed upon, but again, examples can give us ideas. Perhaps it's due to Christ having supposedly died on a Friday, or one of his twelve disciples betraying him (13 were around the table, including him). Some speculate that 13 full moons in a year caused calendar problems and was considered unlucky; if we have any similar pattern in our time keeping system, this is one way to attach meaning to it. Another way to make a number and day unlucky is to have a prominent group of good people treated badly (i.e., executed) on that day in the past. Confirmation bias can make people start seeing bad events on such a day, thereby "proving" the superstition.

As we continue, we'll see how beliefs like these can lead to culture's invention. They are a point of origin, just like morals and values.

CULTURE VS. CUSTOM

Confusion can arise about the difference between culture and customs. Customs are *part* of culture, are a way that culture is represented, and are expected behaviors in given situations. When we invent customs, we're also inventing culture. Since culture is a somewhat esoteric term, we'll be talking more about creating customs, with culture revealed *through* them.

The words "custom" and "tradition" are sometimes used interchangeably because the only real difference is the length of time that they're practiced. A custom becomes a tradition when it is passed down generation after generation. Customs are therefore newer. There's no rule on this, but if we're inclined, we can decide a tradition is over a hundred years old and a custom is more recent. Use "tradition" to refer to truly enshrined behaviors, the violation of which would cause a stronger reaction. Custom implies less formality, weight, or expectation – and less offense if violated.

CULTURAL VISION

World builders could invent various manifestations, like greetings, dining, and attire expectations, that contradict each other instead of springing from a common element. Imagine a culture where very formal greetings occur, with multiple bows, gestures, and elaborate phrases. At dinner, we might expect fine manners. Instead, we're shown people pushing unwashed hands into food bowls, eating off their hands and licking their fingers, and finally shoving the hand into the food again. While this is extreme, these greetings and dining etiquette examples clash and don't spring from a unified vision.

Before we get too far into inventing cultural elements, we should determine a vision that seems appropriate. These are related to values, beliefs, and morals. Some example visions are:

1. Formal: Refined, cordial, dignified, high-minded, controlled emotions
2. Exuberant: Hearty, boisterous, unrestrained, familiar, informal, crude, open emotions
3. Timid: Overly apologetic, not being a bother, polite to a fault, restrained in affections
4. Brash: Entitled, demanding, bold, proud, self-righteous, self-absorbed

5. Modest: Sincere, polite, down-to-earth, informal, compassionate, humble, folksy
6. Calculating: Friendly but distant, cliquey, rumor mongering, disloyal, fickle

If we wanted to be stereotypical, we might assume that royalty exhibit the formal one, while barbarians typify the exuberant. The timid one is based on a few 1980s comedies set in England, while the brash one is how some people describe Americans abroad. Those in small towns sometimes get the modest reputation, and teens sometimes experience the last.

In addition to those previously listed, a seemingly infinite number of cultures exist on Earth that we can leverage. As with every analogue, we should follow the Rule of Three – make at least three significant changes to it to prevent audiences from recognizing it. Otherwise they might recognize Japan, for example, when they see it by another name. There are so many aspects to culture that more than three major changes might be needed. How do we keep everything coherent? By following a cultural vision.

Regardless of our culture's source, whether an analogue, entirely invented, or somewhere between, we should choose a guiding principle or vision. Taking the first example, of formality, we need only imagine how people act based on these. If Kier is from this culture, he won't be chugging ale, slapping people's backs in congratulation, eating with his hands, being unkempt in public, or revealing his affection for a woman in anything but the most subtle of ways. But if Kier has a visitor named Torrin, who hails from the second culture (hearty, boisterous, unrestrained, familiar), we can imagine Torrin doing all of those things. If this is happening in Kier's homeland, Torrin may be judged as uncouth. If visiting Torrin's homeland, Kier would likely be seen as boring, stuck up, and arrogant. This is the sort of conflict we can leverage, whether we keep the impact subtle (as in a comedy of manners) or deadly (so much offense is given that execution or a duel is demanded).

RACE AS CULTURE

World builders are sometimes criticized for a mistake – making a race or species synonymous with a culture. This means each settlement of dwarves, for example, has the exact same culture as every other dwarven settlement. This is as unbelievable as humans having a mono-culture across a world. Avoiding this is easy; just create different cultures. That's time consuming and may explain why race as culture dominates the work of world builders, but all we need are variations.

We can leverage the cultural scope inheritance, where beards are prevalent on all males in a sovereign power, but those in one region or settlement braid theirs while others grow it to their waist, and yet another keeps it close cropped. This way, people can tell on sight where a dwarf is likely from. We don't need to justify differences because few people understand where cultural elements originate. But we could always decide that long beards are the norm and the short ones resulted from a deadly case of lice generations ago. Maybe the braided style came by emulating a war hero who did that. Just make these up. It's fun.

CULTURE DEPICTIONS

Culture could be divided into three types of depictions that storytellers and gamers might employ, singly or in combination: what's only seen, what's heard, and what's performed. This organization is mentioned for clarity as we investigate what to invent and what to bypass, which may depend on medium. We'll look at depictions that are subtle but which can permeate society. More pronounced depictions of culture, like greetings, clothing, and etiquette will be discussed later in this chapter, as most deserve their own section.

VISIBLE

The visible aspects of culture are seen but seldom commented upon by storytellers. This includes architecture, clothing, hair styles, and body language. Much of this can be quickly taken in by a viewer in a visual medium like film, TV, or gaming, where the set and costume designers will be charged with inventing most of it. This is not to say that storytellers can or should ignore it, but in the written medium, we devote most time to actions, dialogue, and thoughts. Some readers even dislike much descriptive writing as the story stalls while we describe something, unless we've learned the art of description as action or revealing of a character's state of mind.

With many visual depictions in the written word, it's often good to focus on the impression someone or something creates rather than going into details about how this is achieved. One reason is that most of us don't recognize terms for various clothing, hairstyles, or architecture, to name a few, and conveying these to an equally ignorant audience accomplishes little, while also making it seem like we researched this stuff so we could tell them. Don't name a hairstyle unless you're quickly able to describe it and what it's thought to suggest about anyone using it; that opinion will vary by other cultures.

AUDIBLE

The words our characters speak are most of what we need for audible depictions of culture, which often dictates what we say and how, or whether we say anything at all. There are times when we think it's not our place to comment on something because of how that's viewed. For example, if you say something rude about your absent spouse, am I expected to change the subject or wait until you do? Am I allowed to comment on it? Can I agree with or disapprove of your behavior? These cultural non-responses are due to perceptions about what a behavior means and the underlying value, such as minding my business or warding off a further venture into a personal subject. When inventing culture, we should consider what is expected to be said *and* what is allowed to pass without comment. It reminds me of the adage that sometimes it's not what we say and do but what we *don't* that is revealing of ourselves.

For example, humility is (at least theoretically) prized in the United States. If someone gives us a compliment, it's customary to politely acknowledge it before changing the subject, rather than gushing about how true their remarks are and encouraging more of the same. When determining what (or if a) response is expected, think about what moral value is exemplified by doing so, and what offense is avoided. Also think about the belief that is attributed to the action or inaction. If ignoring a compliment is *believed* to be rude, then it effectively is so, possibly because a *value* of modesty is violated. The quietness of a library or church is also respectful, but does it need to be in every culture? It's customary to mute a mobile phone when attending a meeting. Loud music in bars makes it customary to yell in someone's ear to be heard, causing a violation of someone's personal space that is accepted in that environment due to necessity.

Our voices, and the way we speak, can also be part of culture. Some languages are considered, by non-speakers, to be eloquent and flowing while others are harsh. But it can also be culture to speak softly/loudly, to speak at length or say very little, or speak with a prompting inflection so that even statements sound like a question; this is deferential and may reflect values of humility and respect. The "ums" and "ahs" of speech might be rampant or nonexistent; these can be unnoticed or frowned upon, maybe because they're believed to result from an unsound mind. Perhaps interrupting people is unusual because it's considered disrespectful, or commonplace as a sign of enthusiasm and sociability while remaining quiet is believed to show unfriendliness. We can spin interpretations.

Songs may be prevalent so that we write lyrics to print in a book. There are other sounds like the tone of alarms, phone rings, and even when applause occurs (in some cultures, there's no clapping between songs at a rock concert). We should consider the impression and quality of these sounds; for authors, that's most of what we can give the audience, whereas other media allow the audience to hear it. Other instances of audible depictions of culture will be covered later in this chapter in the form of greetings, curses, colloquialisms, and more.

PERFORMED

No culture is complete without actions people perform. We'll once again look at more subtle ones here. One of those is eye contact, whether this is maintained, averted, or avoided altogether, and for how long. This is influenced by attitudes about respect, deference, and domination. Use this as a guide to decide what people do. Some view maintained eye contact as challenging, while looking away is meekness. If a culture values personal strength, they likely approve of sustained contact and frown on looking away, while a culture that values knowing your place might feel the reverse. If an action is considered respectful, we don't need to explain why, but dialogue is a good way to do so if required. Consider this scene:

Kier burst into the throne room, bloodied sword in hand. "My lord," he began, addressing the king, "the ogres are minutes from breaching the defenses. We must leave at once."

The captain of the king's guard intercepted him. "You dare to carry an unsheathed sword before the king? Show some respect!"

Kier frowned. "You had better, too, or will you fight them with your pretty face?"

Amid the muted laughter from those assembled, the king caught the captain's eye and nodded. As one, the king's guardsmen ripped swords from sheaths and took up defensive positions.

The expectation to not bare a sword before the king, and the reason for Kier's doing so, is summed up in two short sentences that are relevant to the action. It also causes brief tension. This is why we need culture.

What side of streets, paths, and halls do people walk or drive on? The left side is preferred in countries where people are predominantly right-handed and physical combat (i.e., swordsmanship) was/is common. A swordsman wants his sword arm facing the potential opponent approaching him. The scabbard is also worn on the left hip and less likely to become entangled in anyone (people are walking on the other side of you). It's also easier for right-handed people to mount a horse from the left, which would be while standing in traffic if they're riding on the right of the road, so this is avoided.

But once wagons are in the picture, things may change. Picture a wagon pulled by two horses side-by-side. There was nowhere in early wagons for someone to sit, so someone is riding the left horse because it was easier to mount. As traffic comes toward him, he wants to keep his wagon wheel away from approaching traffic, which is easier to achieve if that traffic is on his left. The result is driving on the right side. If you want to prevent this, decide that even the earliest wagons had somewhere for him to sit. While this is interesting, we're unlikely to mention the reason for our choice.

Most of the actions we'll depict are incorporated into hybrid subjects (where what's done, heard, and seen are combined) like greetings, so we'll cover those after a word about social classes.

SOCIAL CLASSES

A social class can mean different things depending on the society, but it is a way of defining not only income levels but lifestyle generalizations and expectations. People of each class will think, dress, and act differently than those of other classes in the same society. They will also have different needs and therefore values. Everything from spoken expressions and body language to rituals will depend upon one's class, and it is typically quite difficult, even impossible, for one to switch between classes, which people are sometimes born into. We can do this with our invented classes.

In the United States and similar countries, there are five, each largely focusing on income. This economic indicator doesn't need development as we can leverage real world examples. These classes, with examples, are:

1. Upper Class (Elite): landowners, heads of companies and universities, "old money."
2. Upper Middle: professors, engineers, managers and directors, accountants, lawyers.
3. Lower Middle: clerical and support staff for the classes above.
4. Working: craft and factory workers, food and health service staff, repair shop staff.
5. Poor: the homeless or those on public assistance (welfare, food stamps, etc.), or earning just enough to rise above this, with full-time wages but still below the poverty line

Some suggest a sixth class, that of "new money"—when someone from a lower class becomes wealthy due to an invention, winning a lottery, or otherwise vastly improving their financial situation. If class is based on wealth, they have technically changed class, and yet they may act quite differently from those who've been in that class far longer. They may even be rejected as equals because their behavior doesn't morph overnight as their finances did.

In feudal Japan, people were born into one of three main classes, each with internal divisions. The highest was the royal class, which included the emperor and royal family only; the emperor was head of state, with little real power. Next came the noble (military) class, those who ran the country, which included shoguns (political and military leaders), daimyos (feudal warlords), samurais, and ronin (samurai with no daimyo). Roughly 90% of Japan was the lowest class: peasants (farmers and fishermen), merchants, artisans (entertainers, artists), and criminals. In a society dominated by a single group, such as the military or wizards, we might leverage Japan's model.

When inventing our own class system, we define a hierarchy and who belongs to each. We can see that in the U.S. model, the highest class includes those who are in charge, but in the Japan model, the highest class is partly figureheads while those in charge are at the top of the second class. As is often the case, there may be no getting it "right" in world building but getting it plausible; we're the one inventing the society.

Generally, the elite class members are rich, powerful, or of royal blood (or an equivalent), or some combination of these. They have the most prestige and power, unless someone like the feudal Japanese emperor is merely a ceremonial head of state, rather than the head of government; as covered in *Creating Places (The Art of World Building, #2)*, you may recall that the latter is the one with the real power. The elite class is very influential, often holding the purse strings within a society. They may only be symbolically in charge but could be those who are running the country, or the industries and institutions that drive it. These are the leaders who define policy, laws, and how life functions for themselves and the lower classes. In a constitutional monarchy, these would be members of parliament. In a military junta, they'll be warriors at the upper ranks, like generals. If corporations dominate as is often true in SF, then CEOs and other leaders of industry will be here. If wizards are widely accepted instead of feared, this could include the most powerful.

The second highest class will be the most important professions in the society. Those who produce food, such as farmers and fishermen, can be in this class in a fantasy setting, if they are revered instead of taken for granted; in SF, machines have likely taken over, and in some instances on Earth, these professionals are only peasants, the lowest class. In SF, scientists, engineers, and higher officers would be here, including many who build or command ships (regardless of what we call the rank). In fantasy with wooden ships from the Age of Sail, commanders might be here. In a fantasy setting, knights and other important warriors could be included, like the Jedi of *Star Wars*.

These first two classes will likely exist because the most elite will want to distinguish themselves from those just below them and upon whom they rely to run the country, even though those people are subservient to them. We can assume that roughly 10% of the population falls into the top two classes, which leaves us to decide on how to divide the remaining population. We can decide that it's multiple classes like the U.S. model, which is arguably more likely when industrialization causes additional groups of skilled laborers, who may need support staff (another class). Or we can leave it as one large class containing most of the population, which may be more likely in less technologically developed settings. The next table breaks down social classes in both fantasy and SF. What we see in fantasy is the three lower classes being merged into a single one.

Class	Roles	SF	Fantasy
Elite	Figureheads who direct next class	CEOs, presidents	Royalty

Class	Roles	SF	Fantasy
Upper Middle	Highly skilled, valuable, powerful professionals, those running country	Captains, engineers, doctors, lawyers	Nobility
Lower Middle	Supporting upper middle class	Admin staff	Serfs
Working	Entertainers, service industry, factory staff	See roles	
Low	Unskilled labor, poor, homeless	See roles	

Figure 2 Social Class Roles

It might seem like more work to define subclasses within these, but subdividing the groups can make sense. For example, an admiral or general has more prestige than a lieutenant, so while they're in the same overall class, each might have different expectations thrust upon them. On my Llurien setting, there are at least four distinct, named warrior types, and while they'd all be in the second class, there would be a hierarchy/subclasses among them due to their rank and what roles they serve. Before I decided on a class system, I already knew who was considered more valuable and the resentments this caused in others, and by understanding classes, I knew how to define and use this more effectively.

Once we define our classes and who is in each, we can invent culture for them (this is our cultural scope). We would decide on the morals, values, and beliefs of each group, and a cultural vision based on the hierarchy. It's safe to say that the elite class expects deference, though even in our modern society, they are often mocked (out of sight) by lower classes. The most rigid and elegant depictions of culture will be here. A trickle-down effect is in play, where lower classes are increasingly flexible and less formal, with their casual lifestyles an object of scorn from those above, who can be seen as elitist snobs. We should decide on these classes before inventing culture for any because the culture of each is partly in response to the culture of the others. Each class wants to distinguish itself, its members believing their way superior for one reason or another (because it supports their values, morals, and beliefs better than another class culture).

To determine a class cultural vision, look at the roles each fills in society and how important its members are, what problems plague them, and what traits allow them to overcome this. While the working class supports many people, individuals may be considered easily replaced as compared to an upper middle class admiral; there are only so many of the latter and yet anyone could probably become the former, like a waiter (no offense to waiters). A working class person is more likely to suffer certain kinds of abuse on the job than an engineer, but even the latter has problems, just of a different nature. A waiter must deal with poor tips, unexpected shift changes, and difficult customers. An engineer must deal with sloppy work by peers, shifting priorities, and clueless or obnoxious clients and managers. The waiter may value generosity, consistency, and kindness. The engineer may value diligence, planning, and patience. We don't need to work out every scenario, but if we have one that needs clarification, this is one way to achieve it among social classes. Try not to go too far down the rabbit hole on this.

CREATING CULTURE

Now that we've considered our guiding principles behind culture, it is time to invent the manifestations that reveal it. Our focus will be on elements we're likely to use, though some of us will need items others don't. This chapter can't be comprehensive because there's simply too much. However, the techniques behind the cultural manifestations presented here, and their rationales and considerations, can be applied to any item not included. Music and art are two areas we won't cover because they don't apply to the written word except as we describe them, and other mediums are likely to have dedicated composers or artists defining them.

Be aware that borrowing anything from Earth might result in accusations of cultural appropriation, a recent term implying that cultural elements can be devalued and insulted by use as something shallow when someone from outside that culture uses them in ways not considered respectful. Do world builders need to worry about this? Maybe. Whether they've thought about it or not, audiences likely don't expect storytellers to invent entire cultures because the work is vast and therefore, borrowing ideas from Earth can often feel like an homage. They can even feel pleased for it to be included. It helps to tie this manifestation back to our cultural vision so that it seems part of it, which we want to do anyway.

Remember the Rule of Three from *Creating Life (The Art of World Building, #1)* – make at least three *significant* changes to an analogue. If we don't, people may recognize it; I always think James Cameron swiped Native American culture wholesale in the *Avatar* movie; it's pronounced distracting, and regrettable. Other works often steal Asian cultures with little conscience. Moderation is often best.

HOW MUCH CULTURE TO INVENT

As with many items, we could spend the rest of our lives building culture, so we need to limit our work. Asking why we are inventing culture can help. The answer is threefold. We are inventing aspects that will:

1. Portray a more engaging, realistic world
2. Make our story appear to take place somewhere other than familiar (i.e., Earth).
3. Cause culture clashes, in the form of tension due to expectation and misunderstanding. There is a further question of degree. How much tension do we need?
   a. Minor, offended feelings to make characters dislike each other
   b. Serious breaches that lead to ruined agreements (like treaties), imprisonments, death, or alteration of story or character trajectory

This will help us decide how much culture to invent in any given location, and how much we need cultures to differ, and on what subjects. If bowing while greeting is considered a minor offense, we don't have a character thrown in jail for not doing it. But if it's considered major, perhaps we do. It will also depend on how touchy our characters are or if they're looking for an ulterior motive to imprison someone.

Rather than inventing specific cultural items before outlining a story, we may want to only note that we want a culture clash to happen in a given scene we're planning and the consequences of it. One advantage is that we can first plan our tale, then create cultural elements of great impact where we need them, then less impactful elements. We should also know how many locations we'll need. In a *Lord of the Rings* style narrative, characters travel across many kingdoms, each needing a culture. We might have characters from differing places that might also need cultural tweaks. Add up all the people and places and that's the number of cultures we might need. If we have three sovereign powers with very different governments and resulting lifestyles, such as a democracy, an absolute monarchy, and an authoritarian one, readily distinguishable cultures are easier to imagine than if we have three absolute monarchies. This can be a reason to vary the government types in our tale.

We can sometimes give the appearance of a culture being synonymous with an entire sovereign power, for example, even when differences exist within it. This may happen if we're only using one of several regions or cities, for example, and not showing the others. Some might say we've created a mono-culture, so just be aware that we can create this impression. If we care to prove we haven't, then we'll benefit from a character thinking a rude (or kind) thought about a style of clothing or hair they see someone wearing when that style originates elsewhere. A few ideas like this sprinkled throughout our narrative can at least suggest we know culture varies. Using this approach, we can minimize the amount of culture inventing we'll do.

THE BODY

The body may not seem cultural, but it is. Long ago, larger women were considered desirable due to a belief that they were more likely to survive pregnancy and childbirth. Today, many women face great cultural pressure to be thin. The rising obesity in the United States is seen by some countries as a decadent sign of wealth while other countries suffer malnutrition. Judgement is heaped upon the overweight and such nitpicking exists that healthy young women are shown doctored photos that make similar women appear even thinner, as a false standard of beauty that many consider harmful; this is cultural pressure and a *value* judgement.

Ageism is real and felt at all ages, while often targeting the old. A society which values youthful productivity might consider the elderly a problem that should be locked away in retirement communities and denied rights, like a driver's license and simple human dignity, because that society values youth and productivity. Another society might teach great respect and reverence for their elders because they value wisdom and experience. There's more to ageism than the body, of course, as mental capacity and maturity are related.

Someone's general appearance is also cultural. Social norms change with our location and even time of day. In business, we make ourselves more presentable while being more casual at home and on the weekends. But perhaps we have a culture where formality reigns so that even a trip to the drug store means not having a proverbial hair out of place. Or perhaps a culture acknowledges that people can be very productive at work despite casual attire. There's also the question of a bare minimum of make-up for women (or men), groomed hair/beards, and clothes that aren't wrinkled, for example.

BODY LANGUAGE

Facial expressions are considered universal across cultures, so that's one element world builders don't have to worry about, at least among humans. To make our lives easier, we can take the same approach to other humanoid species. We might decide that an ogre is smiling for a different reason, like the pleasure of imagining bashing your head in, but it's still pleasure. Changing a smile to mean what a frown does, for example, will not only confuse characters but our audience. There are other ways to have characters misunderstand something, such as seeing the smile as benevolent when it's not.

Posture, walking, standing, sitting, and even how we hold our head or carry ourselves can be specific to an individual but also part of culture. A dignified culture might espouse standing tall, with chin up. An oppressive culture might see that as arrogant and have dominated people so much that being hunched, with head hanging low, has become a cultural expectation. Sitting with back straight is a sign of a strict culture, whereas slouching might be accepted in a lackadaisical one. Walking might be brisk in a fast paced one, but slow shuffling or casual meandering might reflect oppression or peaceful relaxations. As with most cultural issues, we want to determine what's common so that we know when someone is deviating from it and how that deviation is perceived.

The concept of personal space is one that can vary among cultures and fictional species. Being close can express dominance, aggression, or signal intimacy. It can make people uncomfortable for all three reasons. Too much distance can be impersonal, standoffish, and dismissive. To decide how close is normal or unoffensive, think of the cultural vision. A more reserved society will want greater distance while a boisterous one might find that distancing an affront, as if we're better than them.

Eye contact can range from too constant to too fleeting. Some see looking down or away as appropriate deference, particularly when facing someone of higher station, whereas others see this as contemptible weakness. It can also suggest aggressiveness, whether that's simple meeting of gazes, a glare, or even refusing to look at someone at all. I've had some people stare at me so relentlessly that, aside from reminding me of a cat, they gave me the creeps. In a culture where status is highly valued and strictly enforced, deference is likely, but in a society where status is gained through conduct (whether social skill or achievement), a show of visual strength through maintained eye contact might dominate. We can tweak the length of expected gazing, but audiences don't want to be told that four seconds is fine, and anything less is not; instead, just state that a character looked away sooner than expected.

HAIR STYLES

The way in which hair is worn often symbolizes the social group to which one belongs. As fashions change, these associations can come and go; therefore, it is best to determine the fashion of a time rather than the past thousand years. Hair styles change more rapidly than that, generally, over the course of decades or a few hundred years. However, a more insular society might retain them longer. We often mock both current and previous styles as embarrassing as a way of distancing ourselves from the period or the perceived values of that group.

An association may be all that's needed to establish a hairstyle. In the 16th through 19th centuries, many men wore white, powdered periwigs. This spread from France to other parts of Europe because Louis XIII covered his baldness this way; the wigs became associated with power and eventually became quite elaborate until a taxation on the powder set in motion their demise. Women didn't typically use them unless they, too, had lost their hair, but men had their heads shaved so they could wear these wigs, which were considered cleaner than their own hair due to sanitary conditions at the time. In our invented world, we can ditch the powder, use something besides white, or make them shorter and more functional. We can also make wigs less or more ridiculous, but remember that we need to describe it to a reader unless we're in another medium.

In the U.S., long hair on men was once considered feminine and counterculture. In *Game of Thrones*, a Dothraki warrior with a long ponytail signified how long it had been since he'd known defeat. Samurai wore the chonmage style to help keep their helmets on during battle. This functional origin remained while also becoming a status issue. What country (and culture) do you associate dreadlocks with?

As this is not a treatise on hair styles, it's recommended to perform an internet search and make a note of what's been done or invent something yourself. Decide which group uses each style. In our world, we don't need to define the source of one and can assign them without a rationale, though if one occurs to us, we can note it. People generally accept that a style belongs to a group without questioning it; so will our audience, simply because we said so. If we want a species to have a style, choose one that has variations, such as most elves wearing periwigs but one culture going short, another long, and both use white while a different one uses green, for example. This gets us unity but avoids a species monoculture.

While hair color is not typically cultural, it can be. East Asians so often have black or dark brown hair that we can be surprised when someone's is different. Denmark, Norway, and Sweden have long been associated with blonde hair and blue eyes. Punk musicians have often dyed their hair colors that don't naturally occur.

Facial hair can also be cultural. A long beard may symbolize virility, strength, manliness, or health. A shaggy one can suggest someone is wild and crazy, while a neatly groomed one suggests refinement and civilization. We once again want to decide what's expected based on cultural vision: do we foresee people being meticulous or not?

BODY MODIFICATION

Regardless of type, all body modifications might take place before, during, or after an important ceremony or event, such as a wedding, childbirth, or age milestone. They therefore signify a rite of passage having taken place, and the absence of the expected modification indicates it hasn't happened. These can both come with judgments, positive or negative, about the *value* associated with the change. If the body is believed to belong to your god, then modification might be prohibited without permission from said deity; or the god might demand it.

Tattoos can be part of culture, whether that's the placement or style. We're talking less about individual expression here and groups denoting membership for their individuals. We can choose black or other colors, use symmetry or not. Women might have more feminine styles while men have bolder ones. A religious group can require them, as can social groups wanting a specific tattoo to show membership that must be condoned. In some cultures, it might only be criminals and gangs who wear them. Some tattoos, like henna, are not permanent. As for what's shown, these are typically symbolic, even if only being lines of some kind.

Piercings are another body modification that can be more than an individual's taste, but part of a culture. Many body parts are available, and invented species might have more, but ear and noses are the most widespread and ancient on Earth. Stretched ear lobes and lips are another form. The number, size, material, and style of piercings can all be expected and represent a value. They can be signs of nobility or wealth. Gay men used to wear only one earring to indicate their orientation. Beliefs and superstitions can result in them, too, such as an idea from the Middle Ages that a specific piercing improved long-distance sight, resulting in explorers having them. There can be practical ideas, such as sailors thinking a gold earring can pay for their burial if they wash up somewhere.

Branding isn't typically accepted on Earth in modern times due partly to associations with slavery; it not only marks property but can humiliate if the brand is always visible. It can be done as punishment, such as slaves who've run away, or military people who committed an offense like desertion. Any crime that we feel others should be alerted to can result in one. We can choose that those with inclinations deemed offensive by the state can receive one. We have leeway to decide where it is done (very visible or under clothing), how large, and its design.

Implants take on special significance in SF, where technology can become part of the body. These can enhance abilities and senses or simply replace lost or damaged areas. There may be backlash against this or full acceptance by all of a culture or only parts of it. Tension is always desired in storytelling, so it may be best for some groups to oppose while others adopt. Questions of authenticity may arise, in the sense that someone is no longer who they were born as, if enough changes have been made.

Are they still human? Do people feel augmented or like they're losing themselves? What is the psychological and philosophical impact of too much change, and where they draw the line at "too much?" What value is being offended or championed by the changes? This will decide how culture views it.

GESTURES

A sampling of gestures from Earth can give world builders ideas on what to leverage or invent; as long as we have a rationale, we can make up new ones or repurpose existing ones. Gestures that are a part of a greeting, for example, will be discussed later in this chapter because they include other elements, but some gestures stand alone. This includes one designed to show displeasure and give offense to the source of that displeasure. In much of the world, this involves raising the middle finger, a gesture that goes back to at least Roman times, with the finger representing a penis and the remaining finger knuckles representing testicles, though modern folks seldom know this.

Some cultures have alternate versions of this, such as two fingers (two penises) raised with the hand facing one way or another, or extending the arm before slapping the opposite hand into the elbow and bending the struck arm upward. Making a fist, with your thumb sticking out between your index and middle fingers, is called the fig and, to some, resembles a woman's privates. Putting your thumb behind your upper teeth, facing outward, and flicking the thumb is another variant called cutis. The "talk to the hand" gesture, arm extended, palm outward, all fingers spread, is called the moutza.

The "OK" symbol in the U.S., where the index finger and thumb form a circle and the other fingers are straight, means "asshole" in some countries. The thumbs up gesture can mean putting that up your rear instead of everything being okay. The devil horns can represent any animal with two horns but reminds some of a bull and suggests the target person's wife is having an affair (with the bull, i.e., a more virile man); we can do this with an animal of our invention. Another rude gesture is pointing to your other hand, where all five fingers are spread, indicating that the person you're doing this to had five potential fathers (a promiscuous mother). Crossing your fingers for luck can be seen as representing a woman's privates and is the same as calling someone a "c*nt."

Shaking your head for "no" and nodding for "yes" is not universal and is reversed in some countries. Crossing the arms is standoffish in some countries and arrogant in others; I personally just find it comfortable and wish people would stop reading into it! Punching your fist into the other palm is a threat of violence to some, but our fictional world's warriors might see it as wishing another warrior a good battle, whether literally or figuratively. Shaking two fists means good luck in Austria but could easily be seen as a threat in others. The foot can be considered very unclean and therefore, showing the bottom to others is highly offensive in some cultures; similarly, not taking shoes off inside is considered rude in others.

Sometimes our location while doing a gesture is an issue. Doing one over a threshold might be good or bad, or while sitting verses standing. A doorway is a transition, so a gesture that normally means peace could be seen as rude, meaning we hope the person's life changes for the worse. The opposite could be true if their life is unpleasant, in which case we're wishing them well? Think about what a location means and how we can spin the gesture's normal meaning. A church is a holy place to convene with gods, so being outside one, or in the doorway, and gesturing for someone inside to come to us could be interpreted as seducing them away from a god.

CLOTHING

Concentrating on clothing styles is time consuming; we're after a general sense of style. For example, the existence of buttons as a fastener, rather than as decoration. We take those for granted, but they didn't exist until the 1300s. What do people do without them? They wear looser, baggier clothing that may be tightened with a string of some kind; the clothes may just be wrapped around them (like a toga). This can impact culture; when buttons were introduced, so was tighter clothing, which could leave less to the imagination; resistance to the button could therefore happen because it causes a shift in culture, one that challenges ideas on modesty. Decide if buttons exist in this region or sovereign power and whether tight clothing is possible, and whether the existence of buttons is new or taken for granted (just like tighter clothing may be).

This is just one of countless examples, but it illustrates how the technological elements of our world impact and change culture. If we're thinking that only a fairly simple society may not have buttons as fasteners (decorative buttons are much older, to 5000 BC), such as a nomadic one, the Roman Empire didn't have them either, and yet they had aqueducts, dams, and ballistae. This surprising incongruity is real but if we do such things ourselves in a story, the audience might think we're making a mistake, so it may behoove us to meet expectations. Maybe we shouldn't have our star fighters not knowing what a button is.

Clothing can be used to indicate status, gender, rank, and social class. Plainer clothes suggest something lower while more adornment is for finer folk. Tunics in ancient Rome were adorned with colored bands, where the width, number, and color of these indicated standing. We can make up our own interpretations, such as wide and golden meaning better, and narrow, fewer, and more mundane colors meaning lesser. Decorations can be around the hem, neck, or wrists, but the front or back design was less common long ago on Earth, unlike today. Finer fabrics suggest wealth while coarser is for the poor. Richer colors, or even clean and bright ones, can indicate higher status. Consider how important status is to the culture and invent such expectations for cultures where status matters the most.

But even in cultures where visual indications of status are less important (possibly due to being a melting pot), situations will call for traditionally finer or more mundane clothes (church, a job interview, being on vacation). Those with the highest status might still indicate it with designer clothes, even if just wearing a skimpy bathing suit.

This means that we can still decide what constitutes higher fashion and a reason for this. Tailored clothing makes one look better, so this is an easy one. On Earth, even those of us who can't afford Louis Vuitton or Prada have heard of them, so we just invent a few names on our fictitious world, and we're done. We need only reveal its value in a quick line:

She strode in with a diaphanous Olliana gown flowing about her, the price of which would've fed a city block for a year.

Clothing can reflect what is important to the society, groups, or individuals. If hard work is admirable, then sturdy, dependable, simple, rustic, coarse, and unadorned clothing may dominate. Or is clothing ostentatious with embroidery, jewels, and richer fabric like silks? This might appeal to high society that want to wear the latest fashion, sacrificing comfort and durability for appearance.

Modesty is a major cultural element that manifests in clothing, not only in adornment, but how much of the body is visible. Are women allowed to show cleavage (but not "side boob")? How far up their legs can hemlines rest? Above the ankles, above the knees, mid-thigh, or can they wear a thong in public? Do bras exist and are they expected to hide any appearance of a nipple, or do they push breasts up, as we often see in medieval period films? Can the belly be shown? The shoulders? We should consider how sexually open or repressed the culture is; religions can and will impact this.

One option is to decide that culture is static, regarding clothes or anything else, and therefore newer, more revealing styles (possibly originating from another culture) can cause one culture to harshly judge another as promiscuous and not caring about family values. We can see how values lead to cultural ideas that manifest in clothing, in this case, and an observation of another culture's clothing leads to a (contemptuous) judgment about what they value. This is what culture is for with world building.

Do men wear pants? What about women? In the U.S., a woman wearing pants was once considered to be acting like a man, and this was frowned upon. It brought accusations of not acting like a lady, not knowing one's place, and being an unacceptable companion. We can do the same thing in our setting, regardless of what men's fashion a woman has chosen to adopt. Imagine the contempt heaped upon a man if he chose to wear dresses. In our designed culture, we can decide on norms for gender and then have characters violate it for reasons that are often practical; pants are more utilitarian compared to dresses, for example. A rebel will oppose norms just to do so, but such a character typically has attitudes that cause this.

Our cultural vision should influence these decisions.

The economy can impact clothing due to choices or lack thereof. Those who cannot make more sophisticated clothing must do without or barter/buy them. An isolated culture may have this problem, but so can poorer individuals in societies with significant trade. This can result in limited options and predictable styles for lower classes, ones that become part of culture so that someone who comes into significant money and upgrades their wardrobe might be seen as putting on airs. Note the value judgment.

Footwear can also be cultural. In warm climates, sandals or even bare feet might predominate, while fur-lined, leather boots may in cold locations. A traditional style can exist for either so that those who go against this are judged. While climate affects the choice of how much covering is typical (a universal consideration), the exact styles are not important to our audience and we have leeway to decide what's expected and what's a deviation and what the value judgment is.

ACCESSORIES

Accessories can also be cultural for having expectations associated with them. This includes what can be worn and when. Consider this partial list of items:

Arm bands	Jewelry
Bags	Neck wear
Eyewear	Shawls and wraps
Footwear	Watches
Gloves	Weapon holders

Head gear   Wearable devices

Types of hats can be customary based upon the event so that a baseball cap is incorrect at a polo match, for example. Some cultures insist that a hat not be worn indoors because it's considered rude, particularly in front of a woman. A woman's hat is often considered part of her ensemble and therefore does not need to be removed. In recent years, it's become customary for golfers to briefly remove their hat when shaking hands of the other players at the end of a round. These expectations fluctuate and we have leeway to invent justifications, which are often unknown to people from the culture. Just assign a value to a behavior's meaning. Other head coverings, like a scarf, can be treated the same.

Wedding bands being worn on the left ring finger is customary in many Earth cultures because the Romans believed that the vein in that finger led directly to the heart, but at least a dozen wear it on the right hand. We could decide a culture recognizes the importance of the thumb and therefore a ring signifying family (if not marriage) is worn on one thumb. Which hand? Just make something up. Maybe people are predominantly right-handed, and the left does less practical work, or one hand is reserved for ceremony and rare occasions, and therefore it is more sacred. Therefore, a man who resents his family, or if cast out by them, might wear the ring on the opposite hand in protest. Other types of rings or accessories are much the same. As with everything cultural, we don't need an explanation but can just make it up if we want one.

Some accessories result from function. A winged humanoid species working as messengers, rather than carrying scrolls in the hand, might attach them to a scroll case worn on the hip or a sash. Meaning can be attached to how it is worn—when carrying a message, it's worn on one hip, if not, on the other. Or perhaps it's not worn at all when off work, or it's simply left at home at certain times. Continuing to wear it at social occasions could be considered rude, as if saying, "I'm only here in official capacity, not because I care." Another species might be known for strong drink and always have a flask with them. While being drunk might be customary at rowdy moments, being sober at important events can be seen as respectful; perhaps still wearing the flask offends.

There are seemingly endless variations to accessories, so we won't cover more. Hopefully these ideas help you decide. As with all cultural issues, assign a value and its associated behavior and choose how that can go awry and what bad meanings can be associated with failing to meet the expectation.

GREETINGS AND FAREWELLS

One way to distinguish a culture is their greetings and farewells, but what all cultures have in common is the willingness to do them because it's a hallmark of goodwill, respect and civility. We can surmise that in a truly barbaric society (one that also has little culture), these greetings don't exist or are not much more than eye contact and/or a grunt, but most societies that world builders need to invent have more than this.

Greetings are typically more involved than farewells because they set the tone for the coming interaction, but when there's to be no real interaction (such as passing someone on the street), they're short. An acknowledgement is among the most basic of expectations, and yet some situations do not call for them and not everyone will comply even when they do (just as some will do them when not required). In a big city, people walk past each other on the street with no acknowledgement and it might even be considered weird for us to say hello to anyone.

As world builders, we should aim for brevity because the audience doesn't really care about these moments unless something goes wrong during them. Why waste a paragraph or five minutes of screen time? It's similar to an issue in *Game of Thrones*, where Daenarys had so many titles by the end that it took thirty seconds to rattle them off, and the show repeated this in every introduction instead of bypassing them. Never make the audience want to skip ahead.

Many potential failures exist in both greetings and farewells; storytellers can leverage all of them for tension. Some people will not respond to one at all; we don't need to first establish that a response is expected because our audience will assume so (it's implied), especially when other characters react to this. The unresponsive person likely knows they're failing in this, unless they didn't hear/see it or are distracted. Reasons for this are a storytelling issue, as culture doesn't explain a total lack of response or acknowledgment when doing so is universal across cultures.

By contrast, culture can explain responses that are considered inadequate, a fact that may surprise the one giving the inadequate response. It's almost a given that, without previous experience in another culture or someone telling us what to do, we will make mistakes. The degree of these will depend in part on how different the two cultures are (the one we're in and the one we're from). Ignorance is not the only reason for giving offense. Shyness can cause it, as can previous bad experiences that leave some fearing more of the same and performing poorly. Some people use too much or too little strength in gestures, such as a meek or crushing handshake. People are always interpreting the actions of others and some cultures might be more prone to finding offense.

We may want formal and informal greetings in our setting. In English, "hello" is more formal than "hi," which is not as casual as "hey," which still stands above "yo." Then there's "What's up?" or its shortened "'sup?" We don't need so many as this, and there are plenty more in America, but it's realistic that our traveling characters will greet comrades one way, strangers another, and those of a different station a third. Consider creating these variations.

Greetings sometimes have a practical origin, such as the handshake being designed to show that neither person has a weapon, or even to dislodge a dagger hidden up one's sleeve. A variation on this is to grab the upper arm. With alternate weapons in SF, we might think of a different greeting that has a similar purpose. Think of how a sneaky person would conceal an item and what gesture might reveal it and become commonplace.

In addition to greetings, some of what follows can also be done to congratulate others, thank them, say farewell, or confirm an agreement.

THE WORDS

Analogues are useful when inventing greetings and farewells, but first, a few observations.

• There's often a word that means "hello" and a more casual version like "hi."
• We can wish pleasant times on them, such "Good morning" and "Live long and prosper."
• We often inquire about their well-being, such as "How are you?" This can be rhetorical.

• We can state how happy we are to see or meet them, such as "Pleased to meet you."

• We can use a title, like "sir," "Lord Kier," "Mr. Smith," or "Grand Master of the Seven Realms."

• We can introduce ourselves first, last, or in between (when additional people are there)

• Using a given name is less formal than the surname

All we need do is combine these ideas while inventing variations that make sense for the context, which can be social, about station/rank, or both. Our cultural vision may have less impact on our decision because most greetings have certain values in common, those being respect, well-wishing, and a show of good and peaceful intentions. If an individual doesn't want to show those things, they don't make the greeting or include every part of it.

Some ideas are a bit religious, like "many blessings" or "may the Lord bless you." Then there are military ideas like, "May your sword never break," "May your bowstring never snap," and "May your arrows fly true." Just think of a peril that might befall a profession and we can invent an expression. Or we can avoid these slightly negative sounding ones for something more upbeat: "may your staff always shine," or "may your blade always gleam." A scout might be simply told, "many sightings."

Physical Gestures

In addition to (or in place of) words, both greetings and farewells can include gestures that may be optional, required, or at least expected. We should decide on this along with the gesture itself. That way, if something is required but our character doesn't do it, this is a larger offense. If it's only expected, it's a smaller offense. If it's optional, we pay little attention, and if it's highly unusual, we notice it being done and perhaps wonder why, though being offended isn't common.

There are different analogues we can leverage from both real Earth cultures and ones that other storytellers have imagined, but first, remember that touching others can spread germs. In a less technological society, like those in fantasy, people may be (and likely are) unaware of this. A prevalence for gestures that spread germs might exist unbeknownst to them, so we maybe shouldn't have them avoid it as if they know something they don't. In other words, don't project our knowledge of this onto them and have them prefer other greetings because of it.

Beings from different planets have different germs and immunities, which naturally arises more in SF. It's reality, but storytellers overlook this because acknowledging it could place a substantial restriction on character behaviors and plot developments. This is a personal call each creator must make. Just as European diseases infected Native Americans, killing many, planet-hopping characters would do the same. Those big SF movies where aliens need incredible weapons to wipe us out may miss the mark in that they may only need to drop even a mild pathogen (or several) here and come back later when most of us are dead; the exception would be when they can't wait for that.

THE HANDSHAKE

The handshake done on Earth in modern times is so common that we often want something else on our fictional setting, with good reason. This gesture is too much like here. Variations already exist and we can invent our own or leverage these, which is recommended for speed of world building. For all of them, we want ease of depiction; no one wants even two sentences describing it.

Some easy variants are:

- Forearm, bicep, or shoulder clasp
- Interlacing fingers
- Fist bump
- Two hands

The details of handshakes vary by country on Earth. They are typically done barehanded, meaning failure to remove a glove could be seen as disrespect. In some countries, only the same gender shake hands, or sometimes one gender is expected to be greeted first this way. A religion like Islam discourages gender-mixing. Children can be included or excluded. Some prefer a weak grip, others a strong. While some use right hands, they simultaneously use the left to grasp the other's right hand by the elbow. Sometimes a senior person is expected to initiate the gesture. One country considers it rude to have the left hand in a pocket during a greeting. While most handshakes are brief, some cultures expect people to hold hands for several seconds after the initial shake. In another country, that might be considered odd. There's a lot of opportunity for misunderstanding for foreigners. There are also combination motions that must be known in advance to perform. They're usually done by those belonging to a specialized group, such as athletes, musicians, wizards, or organizations, such as a secret society.

Speculation about the origins of handshakes is that soldiers did this to show they didn't hold a weapon, which could also have been a dagger hidden up one's sleeve. Refusal to shake hands could be a bad sign. We may find this useful in a scene.

THE KISS

As a greeting or farewell, a kiss on the lips would be too intimate for most cultures except among lovers or family, but it's an option, one that shows great comfort with physicality. It's easy to imagine other cultures viewing this as a sign of promiscuity or lasciviousness. It's also far more likely to spread germs. A kiss on the cheek is tamer and can either involve lips touching the skin or a cheek-to-cheek gesture with a kissing motion (or sound) from the lips, as if imitating. Sometimes a single kiss is done, but we've all seen each cheek getting the treatment. A kiss on the forehead is another option but can suggest patronization because adults sometimes do this to children, but maybe they don't in our world. We have leeway to invent the interpretations, too. Finally, there is the kissing of the hand, which has been presented for the purpose. This has often been done to women or those of higher station.

THE BOW

The bow seems more formal and may be appropriate in a culture where shows of respect are valued. It isn't just the important people who may need this deference, but the whole population. The degree of bow is commensurate with the level of respect shown; while it might be customary to kneel before one's king, if one is truly humble, prostration might feel appropriate. That might seem excessive to others. Even when one remains upright, there's still a degree of bow, such as a slight bend or much more. What is appropriate might depend not just upon the relative social standing of those present, but upon the occasion, as something more serious and formal requires a deeper bow.

In some cultures, people are exact about it and bowing too much is just as bad as bowing too little. We can decide for ourselves how touchy our peoples are.

A mere head nod would be the smallest gesture, followed by kneeling (one knee is less formal) and finally prostration (lying full upon the ground). These are levels of submission, which is why the more severe versions appear in religions. One version of bowing on Earth is Namaste, where we would place our palms together before our chest, bow slightly from the head, and say "Namaste."

The Salute

A salute is typically reserved for the military and can be any number of fingers, though it's typically all or the index and middle finger in a two-finger salute, with the other fingers bent and the thumb touching them. This can cause problems and has done so on Earth, as the Polish do the two-finger variety, like the Cub Scouts (children), and this led U.S. troops to assume the Polish were being disrespectful, as if implying they were kids. The result was Polish troops being arrested until the misunderstanding was cleared up.

In some places, a salute is only when a hat is worn. Others only allow it indoors when formally reporting to a superior officer. If enemy snipers are known to be nearby, no saluting happens (to avoid identifying an officer, who becomes a target). The palm can face downward as in the U.S. or toward the one being saluted. The downward version resulted from lower level troops working on tasks that dirtied their hands, and presenting the dirty palm to a superior during a salute wasn't considered polite. A closed fist can also be used, and the arm can be extended forward (instead of bent to bring the hand to the forehead).

The origins of saluting are suggested to be from knights raising their visor to identify themselves, which was partly a show that they weren't afraid of their foe, either. This can easily be used in the context of a knight who refuses to raise a visor and is taunted as a coward. In SF, salutes can be done with rifles. A salute can also be done with the sword, with enough variations in gesture that we can invent what we like. Pointing the tip at the ground is a sign of submission.

OTHERS

Sometimes we only nod at another person in passing, raise eyebrows, or just smile. We might say the briefest version of a greeting, such as "Hi." We may give a small hand gesture, like a wave, but without raising our arm. What all of these have in common is not so much a greeting as an acknowledgement that we saw the other person and we aren't pretending we didn't. This is more important when we know them.

The military salute manifested in the tipping of one's hat, by civilians, toward others as a greeting and gesture of respect. Sometimes the hat is touched, while other times it is removed, particularly indoors. Even today, some consider it wrong to leave a hat on inside. After some gestures, like a handshake, the hand is placed on our own heart, though secondary motions are less common on Earth.

We can borrow ideas from animals, as this might feel more appropriate for beast-like species, such as trolls, ogres, and dragons, all of whom might use sniffing like dogs. A winged humanoid species might stretch and/or shake wings. Maybe subtle ways of fanning those feathers mean something, like annoyance, impatience, or happiness. Folding them in might be a blow-off. Wrapping them in front of oneself might be seen as evasive or a sign of being uncomfortable; maybe they're just cold and this can be misinterpreted.

A species with a tail might raise it in a lazy swing, or crack it like a whip, making a sound. Some of this can be considered friendly or hostile. An Earth cat raises the tail in greeting, or slaps it on the floor when annoyed, and wags it when relaxed. Then there's the fluffy appearance when startled, though that requires fur. Cats can extend their claws at will, so maybe we have a species that does the same, even giving a friendly scratch or bite. A dragon might puff some smoke out, but a little fire is an offense.

A society where everyone has a bladed-weapon at all times might gesture with it, whether sheathed or not. Maybe the gesture is just to unsheathe it by an inch and put it back, and doing more so is considered a sign of aggression. "He bared his blade!" an outraged character might shout, drawing his.

In worlds with magic or technologies we don't have, wizards might make their staff give a pulse of light in greeting. A gun that has lights, whether a laser sight or just a flashlight, could be used for the same, especially if something like Morse Code signals are used on the field and have become a way to recognize allies. Maybe people position the staff or rifle a certain way almost like how a hat is tipped or a head is bowed. Since the powerful end of a staff is the top (usually), maybe it's considered rude for a wizard to tip the top toward someone they're greeting, but sliding the bottom forward can be seen as submission just as kneeling might be. Use your imagination.

LANGUAGE

Our use of language, which is covered in detail in chapter eight, is also cultural. Phrases enter the vernacular from common usage in a variety of ways, often from music and art, but world builders don't need to explain origins. What we do need and should invent are expressions, styles of speaking, and general tone, such as casual or formal, harsh or pleasant, etc. As always, culture is about expectations.

TONE

The way we speak carries as much meaning, if not more so, than the words we use, but those in auditory media can convey tone with greater ease than authors. Despite this, world builders should decide how people from a culture sound even when the words are not considered. Hollywood films are a good way to get a sense of how different cultures and their language come across from the tone of speakers. The French are depicted as haughty and pretentious in tone. Germans and Russians are gruff, hard, and cold. The British are overly polite, to a fault. The Japanese are elaborate, formal, and distant. Use these analogues as a guide.

COLLOQUIALISMS, SLANG, AND EXPRESSIONS

We can invent words and phrases that are often spoken in a culture, whether these are part of curses, greetings, or other elements we'll discuss further in this chapter. A colloquialism is usually understood regardless of any socioeconomic factors while slang is for smaller subgroups (like teenagers) so that those outside that group may not understand it. This can help scope expressions we invent, noting in our files if everyone "gets it" or just a subgroup. A colloquialism might contain slang.

A well-known example is the different ways people in the United States order carbonated drinks. This varies by the region. Some variants are "pop," "soda pop," "soft drink," "soda," and "coke." The latter doesn't mean "Coke." The phrase "chop your breakfast on a mirror" refers to cocaine use and may only be known by fans of Metallica, as the line is in their song, "Master of Puppets." The contraction "y'all" is associated with those in the southern U.S. For inspiration, Google is our friend and yields tons of ideas.

There are some basics we might want to focus on because they come up in conversation. For example, what do people say when they agree? In the U.S., we have "okay," "sounds good," "alright," "yeah," and "right" as some examples (there are more). Pirates say "Aye." When disagreeing, we tend to be less direct so as not to offend, saying "I'm not sure about that" or something similar. We don't typically say, "you're wrong." How do people tell someone they're a liar? You're "full of shit" is common in the U.S. Just think about things you say to people and invent alternates.

SF is infamous for technical jargon. To this, we mostly need to invent the technology and then refer to it. In both SF and fantasy, we can turn a noun into a verb to create jargon. Casting a spell on someone can result in them being "magicked," for example. If there's a common spell to cause changes to a person, this can be used the same way, such as a charm spell resulting in someone having been "charmed." If a common device gets the jitters, we can invent an insult that someone has been "jittered" one too many times, as if they're personally developed that trait. Names of devices can be used this way, too.

In our modern world and a SF one, the source is often media (TV, film, books, songs) and needs no explanation when a world builder invents them. Audiences come to realize it's such an expression when more than one character uses it over the course of a work.

SWEAR WORDS

Not all swear words are created equal. Some types are used far more often than others. Words for excrement are bound to exist in all languages and be in frequent use. We can just use Earth versions, because they're so common as to not cause a reaction, but it's better if they stand alone. By contrast, "I don't give a shit" is a colloquial expression and shouldn't be used.

The word "fuck" is unique and powerful. Some writers avoid having characters say it unless they're from Earth because it's too much like here. This is also true of "shag" from Britain. An infamous world building version is "frak" from *Battlestar Galactica*. That might bother people more, and if *Game of Thrones* used the f-bomb, so can we. A benign word in one language can be a swear in another, such as "bloody" in England; to create these, just use a slightly graphic word (like bloody) in a context where it otherwise doesn't fit (and is not simply an adjective) and do it several times in a row to get the point across that we're not being literal. An example would be, "I'm not bloody doing it. No way do I bloody pick that thing up." On the other hand, if we write, "I'm not picking up that bloody thing," it just seems like an adjective.

Invoking a god is often part of swearing. Sometimes it's literally just their name said harshly, or this can be combined, as in "Goddamn" and "Goddamnit." We can also merge words to create hybrids, like, "motherfucker," "dumbass," and "shithead." Animals can be leveraged, and if we've invented our own, this helps with uniqueness; examples include "sheepfucker," "bullshit," "horse piss," and "dragon spittle." All we need to do is find something objectionable, which is why bodily waste is popular, as are the body parts from which they originate, or other "private" parts. Other kinds of waste, such as something industrial in SF, can substitute. Perhaps magic leaves a residue we've named and can leverage.

DAILY LIFE

DINING

There's an etiquette to dining, which means there are values that lead to expectations. Does this culture value savagery and baseness (like lust and gluttony) or rising above animalistic instincts to one degree or another? This leads to a general level of hearty gusto, decorum and refinement, or something in between. It impacts everything from how people are called to a meal, how it's presented and consumed, and what happens when it's over. To keep things simple, we can decide that there are three defaults: hearty, refined, or moderate. Subtle variations on them become what we tweak for each culture we invent.

To be stereotypical, the hearty choice might best suit barbarians, nomadic peoples, and those whose civilization is in its early stages. Meals might be had at any time, while standing around or right after an animal is killed. No one washes up beforehand and they show up smelling however they smell, wearing whatever's already on them, likely dirty. Perhaps there's no table or silverware, and if people gather at all, they stand or sit on the ground or maybe a pelt. To call others to a meal, they might simply holler once and leave it at that; if you don't show up, that's your problem. Or they expect you to notice and come over. Food is eaten with hands. Dirty fingers and mouths are wiped on sleeves, if anything. Belching might be common, and loud songs, stories, and ale flow. Anyone who needs to step away just goes, possibly losing their spot if they've even got one. To relieve themselves, maybe people don't go far, doing it in sight. Those who want more of something just take it. Perhaps they eat too much, don't share, and there's no such thing as leaving some for someone else. When it's all done, no one cleans up other than to lick something clean or throw a bone elsewhere, like to dogs, who might be allowed to help themselves during the meal. This is a social event but mostly about eating.

Contrast all of this with the refined approach, again going for an extreme. Meals are likely had at a specific time that, if subtly changing from day to day, is still told to people in advance, usually politely; a guest might be asked to spread the word to others, and the meal doesn't start until everyone is seated and perhaps a prayer is spoken; there's no nibbling allowed before this. Hosts might also provide choices, such as stating that steak is the main dish and asking if corn or peas is preferred by the guest. The food is presented well, like a piece of art, with sauce dribbled over it and a sprig of parsley to one side. Everyone washes their hands beforehand and wears relatively clean clothes and is washed enough to prevent poor scents and appearance. Ornate silverware, china, and crystal goblets may adorn a beautiful table with napkins and possibly an elegant tablecloth, candles or soft lights bathing everyone. Food is not only eaten with utensils, but multiple forks, for example, are designed for use on specific dishes. Whether servants are present or not, food and drink are politely passed and/or served for dedicated bowls/trays and utensils no one's eating with. Even an unheard belch results in someone saying "excuse me," and permission is asked to leave a table for any reason, including the bathroom. Those who want more ask for it or go without if eating too much is considered gluttony, or perhaps they wait to be offered (and must accept?). No one ever takes the last of anything. When it's done, everyone concludes at the same time and departs together, helping (or letting servants) clean up and restoring order, pushing chairs back in, wiping mouths a final time and cleaning the hands, too. This is a social event where eating is almost secondary.

In between these extremes are what we'd typically experience in modern cultures. This means a roughly expected mealtime, casually announced. People are expected to wash up but often don't, and only blatantly dirty clothes get a reaction. There's one fork and knife per person; you get anything else you want/need yourself and come back. People serve themselves from plain dishes with either a serving spoon or something of theirs that hasn't been in their mouth (think knife, shoving stuff out of a tilted bowl or plate). Someone eats the last of something without much regard for anyone else wanting it. People leave when they need, without permission, and often only the adults who live there clean up anything. It's informal, satisfies a bodily need, and may not be particularly social.

These three basic scenarios can be altered, with more or fewer acts of refinement added/subtracted. In theory, a younger society might be rowdier while an older one could be more refined. Standards of cleanliness (which education influences) will impact the move away from the first example. There's more judgment in the refined scenario, where minor offense can be given for something as trivial as using the wrong spoon for soup.

Here are some additional questions to consider:

1. Can people invite themselves or others to dine? Are impromptu guests accepted?
2. Is there expected attire and what might it be?
3. Seating
    a. Who sits first?
    b. Are seats assigned an order or not, and how if so (rank)?
4. Are some tables reserved?
5. Does anyone enter or do something after everyone else is present or seated?
6. Serving
    a. Who gets served first and last? Is that based on gender, seniority, or do guests or the hosts receive the privilege?
    b. Are extra portions viewed well or poorly? Is it considered rude or wasteful to not finish what you've taken? Is it bad to not eat much as if disapproving of the fare?
7. Is it permissible or forbidden to brings weapons to the table?

We must consider how many meals are common in a day, when they're consumed, and perhaps what types of foods are associated with each. There are often traditional items. What comes to mind for breakfast, lunch, and dinner? Few world builders have the time to invent an array of meals or even occasion to show them in our work, so we likely want to be generic. For example, in looking at the food groups, are certain ones associated with one of these meals? Fruits might be consumed primarily for breakfast, snacks, or as a side dish, as often happens in the United States. But perhaps a fruit or veggie salad is a common lunch item instead. Fish might be eaten later in the day after it's been caught, but then fisherman are out early and maybe it's ready by breakfast, though that means fishing closer to shore. In fantasy worlds, there's no refrigeration and we can use this to decide what is often in a meal.

In the United States, the early bird special means eating a few hours before most people, at restaurants. This originates from the expression that "the early bird gets the worm" because rain causes worms to be on the surface and the first bird gets plenty of options. We can do this or reverse it, meaning most people eat early and restaurants are eager to lure people in later, after the rush. Here we might use the expression 'second mouse special', referring to an idiom "the second mouse gets the cheese" meaning a mousetrap kills the first mouse and, having been sprung, poses no danger to the second, who eats their fill.

A big family dinner (or other meal) where everyone sits down at the same table is a part of certain cultures, but in others, people might eat while on the go or standing in the kitchen after making the meal. The latter is often caused by necessity. If family togetherness is a value, however, eating together is likely as well. Dinner is usually the most important meal for this, with the day's events complete, but in our fictional world, it could be lunch followed by a siesta. Or breakfast with well-wishing for the day's events. Find a rationale to justify which meal is for family gatherings, while another, like lunch, may be with coworkers or friends. A character from a culture without this may place no value on the experience and not understand it; this can help create a culture clash.

There are cultural aspects to guests. If someone happens to be present near a mealtime, it's often courtesy to invite them, but perhaps our culture suggests politely showing them the door because this is a family occasion. We can spin these things. The guest might be expecting to leave and be embarrassed that they haven't already. Perhaps when they smell the food cooking, they become uncomfortable and begin to excuse themselves. But it could be reversed, where the smell has them assuming they'll be invited as in their culture, but it's not what happens, leading to offense. Perhaps a guest is expected to invite themselves or even help themselves to any food and drink in our house. Or a host is supposed to offer, the guest declines once, the host offers again, and only then does the guest accept. Doing so sooner might be considered hasty or greedy. Remember that culture has a lot to do with expectations, whether those are met or not.

FOOD

Cultures have their own foods. For inspiration, we can easily leverage Earth analogues. What do we think of with Chinese, Indian, and Italian foods to name a few? Even a city like New Orleans has associated dishes. There's New York style pizza and Philadelphia cheesesteaks. France and Champagne, Germans and beer, the U.S. south and moonshine. We only need to decide that something is particularly delicious somewhere or that they invented it. A drink or food can be notorious for its effect, taste, or smell.

But individual foods do not a culture make. Rather, there's a taste, aroma, and consistency often associated with a culture. This could be red or white sauce. It can be pasta or rice (Italy vs. Asia) with seemingly everything. What is often unique is the sauce and spice combination. Are foods bland, spicy (mild to hot), rich, creamy, tart, tangy, etc.? We could go on, but food is one area where the values we decided on earlier are of limited use in deciding what a culture's food tastes like. We can instead simply assign a style, though authors sometimes like to say something like, "Their food was as spicy as their lovemaking." This can help us decide.

Its presentation, however, is another matter, as culture influences this. Japanese culture is often refined in appearance, manners – and how food looks on a plate. There's a design aesthetic. Another culture might heap everything onto a plate, or pile meats and veggies atop a rice bed. Every approach can exist in the same culture, but we have the option of creating expectations. The dining style likely accompanies the presentation. How stately do chopsticks look, and the little white bowls of rice, soup, or tea?

When inventing foods in world building, it's often the impression we want, as the audience will never get to eat them. We want to comment on the reaction to be served, not to mention consuming, anything. Why reaction? In the United States, fish is served without a head, but in other countries it will still be attached, a fact that bothers many American diners, to cite one example. There are also body parts some cultures eat and others won't, like pigs' feet. The existence of rice, noodles, various meat types, and vegetables will not change much on even imagined worlds, even if the details do or we create analogues, so we should spend more time on impressions and reactions.

Specific foods are often consumed at traditional times, such as turkey at Thanksgiving in the United States, or ham for Christmas and eggs for Easter. Believe it or not, KFC is a traditional Christmas food in Japan since the 1970s. We likely need a few of these items if a holiday is occurring amidst our story; we can take common foods and simply decide they're had that day, possibly prepared or served a certain way.

Crops are harvested at different times of the year. This can result in seasonal foods that are also part of culture. Absent refrigeration or being stored somewhere cool, most fruits and vegetables only last a day or two without quality loss, but they can still be eaten days later, though there is risk of bacteria having grown on them, depending on the item. There's a lot of variation to this, but some plants can still be associated with a whole season because not every apple tree, for example, needs to be harvested at the same time, and in our fictional world, with invented variations on plants, we have leeway for our decisions. In *Creating Life (The Art of World Building, #1)*, we covered creating plants like Earth ones, with minor changes. We can learn when a food is harvested and mimic this with ours.

BATHING

In a modest society, bathing is in private, but some cultures have people bathing together, whether coed or not. We typically mean using soap, but a Korean Bathhouse has people soaking in a variety of pools of varying water temperate, even saunas. These can also be coed or not. A culture clash on modesty is easily done for this, with value judgments being made.

How often do people bathe on average? This often reflects a society's understanding of hygiene, with SF worlds tending toward better education. Our fantasy characters may get one bath a week, taking any reasonable chance to swim in the interim. And a bath it likely is, not a shower, due to technology. Rarity may promote the use of perfumes as deodorants, with higher society possibly overdoing it, though they likely have more frequent bathing, a fact that easily distinguishes them from commoners; better kept clothing does the same.

Parents bathe children, but at what age does this stop? When do kids go it alone? If self-reliance is important, this may be earlier. If a child is rare (due to something like overpopulation that means a couple only gets to have one), then perhaps the parents fawn over a child and bathe him until he's older. Does one parent or both assume responsibility for this? A child may also join either parent in a bath, meaning the parent is bathing, too. We might also see a family bathe together, all genders. If hot bath water is a luxury, decide who enjoys it first and last. We can use this when a character who got it last as a child, for example, gets the rare chance to go first as an adult and thinks about this during the scene, thinking back to childhood. Even without the luxury of warm water, who gets to go first when bath water in a tub must be shared?

At what time of day do people bathe, morning or night? It's seldom midday but could be, particularly in a culture with a midday siesta due to heat. Those who are apt to get dirty during the day will likely pick night to avoid getting their bed dirtier than necessary, so this may apply to blue collar workers more than princes, for example.

SLEEPING

A culture can be known for varying degrees of sleep, which the species/race makeup of that society can impact. A race that needs little sleep might have an active nightlife. One that needs a lot might have afternoon naps as commonplace. If that race dominates the culture, the impact will be felt. If it does not, then other races may judge them for how much or little rest they need.

In many cultures, it's standard for a couple (especially if married) to sleep in the same bed, but that's a custom. It isn't necessary. Consider keeping this in a society with low temperatures much of the year; in *Game of Thrones*, some women are referred to as "bed warmers." This is unlikely in a hot climate and people may prefer their own beds, which don't need to be in the same room, either. Imagine a race where the males always snore; the females may be used to it, or they may insist on different rooms.

Some other questions to ask are:

1. Do children sleep with their parents, either in the same bed or room?
2. What age is this frowned upon, if ever?
3. Is the culture aware of Sudden Infant Death Syndrome and preventing it?
4. Do babies have traditional items slept with, like a teddy bear? We can mock an adult character who retains such an item or simply has one around for some reason, such as intending to give it to a niece.
5. Do people sleep with a light on or total darkness? Perhaps a scented candle is traditionally lit on some occasion. If the environment is typically bright or daytime naps occur, maybe masks are worn just then or all the time.
6. Do window coverings exist because of this and allow for easy manipulation?
7. Do people sleep nude, in undergarments, or specific bed clothes? Naturally, regional air temperatures influence this.

The shape of beds is assumed to be rectangular due to our bodies being longer than wide, so no one will question this. But we can imagine that a bed for two does not anticipate them lying side-by-side. How about feet-to-feet, or head-to-head, in a very long bed? Circular beds are an option, as are those inspired by a culturally significant symbol, such as a heart for a honeymoon suite. There are also bunk beds, water beds, air beds, pods, ones that can be retracted into a wall, those on the floor (without legs), or even suspended ones, like a hammock. Something is likely to dominate. Decide what it is, what's traditional, and what's the latest craze. Don't forget to mention those useless, decorative pillows, should they exist.

Employment

Unless independently wealthy or living with their family, most people need a job. On a cultural level, what we're looking for is a typical number of hours worked in a day and how many days per week. A related question is whether positions pay enough or whether people need additional employment, or to combine income with a spouse, extended family, or friends who share living expenses. Working out this detail for every position would be very time-consuming without much payoff for us or audiences, so focus on what's most common. Do most people at a given class level need to work two jobs or is that uncommon? If it's very common, it can become part of a culture and is therefore expected.

The 40-hour work week is a decent average for humans, who work more in some industries. But consistently going beyond an 8-hour day, 5 days a week leads to worker burn out (and to make our world different, we should alter this). If we need many characters with lives that are miserable in our setting, exceeding this is one way to achieve it. Laws sometimes forbid such a thing, which can lead to secondary jobs, though perhaps there are laws against that as well. But the state often mandates minimum pay rates, though such a thing is more likely in SF than fantasy due to increased government. Some companies allow variations, such as 4 10-hour workdays a week, so perhaps this is common in our fictional world. Maybe people must work almost every day but only 4-6 hours. Do they have long days mixed with short ones, with a name for each type?

Another employment issue is how early or late people tend to work in a day. Perhaps early rising is standard, or working into nightfall (or both). Taking a break during the afternoon, such as for an extended lunch break of hours, might be common in the culture. This is called a siesta and results from a combination of a big, heavy meal at lunchtime and excessive heat, both of which can lead to drowsiness. Consider adding this to any culture near the equator or other hot areas; that culture can spread to other regions that don't have the heat. Many businesses will close for 1-2 hours during this period, a fact that characters will take into account when they need supplies. A siesta also lets people stay up later, extending social life. Is a siesta so common that sleeping chambers are part of the office environment? Imagine the privacy and security concerns subsequently raised and steps to mitigate them. These sleeping rooms might be coed or not; imagine the combination of coed and nudity.

Are children allowed to be brought to work? Can a woman breastfeed at work at all, and is this openly or is a room set aside? Are daycare facilities available in this society and do they provide adequate care? Maybe it's so expensive that some mothers or fathers don't work and stay home to raise children while the other spouse works.

On that note, are women in the workforce? Are men? What about children, and at what age? Is any gender or age group discriminated against, given better pay and benefits, or denied certain types of employment? Is there cultural shift underway or is the status quo rigidly maintained? When rights are restricted in a supposedly free society, there's often a "two steps forward, one step back" shift toward more freedom, due to resistance. Decide if such a movement is needed in the setting and how it might impact the story. We don't need incredible details on this unless it's a major story element, but a decision about employment opportunities will certainly impact the outlook of all genders. For example, a woman who can't get a decent job might take to adventuring (or piracy) if she's got the skills and personality for it.

We can consider many aspects of employment, such as whether people get vacations or holidays at all, health and other insurance benefits, pay raises, and what type of abuses must be endured from management, coworkers, or the public. We can model a SF world similar to but more advanced than an Earth society, but fantasy might require reimaging employment; on the plus side, with less formal organization (i.e., companies), there are fewer policies, for example, to decide upon. That someone has a great or crap job, in their opinion, can sometimes be enough, and all we may need is their comparison to a better or worse life that someone else has, with a few details that amount to discrepancies between what is and what could be.

TRANSPORTATION

Transportation may not seem like a cultural element, but it is. Some cities, like Los Angeles, are known for their cars, while another might be known for motorcycles. Venice is known for gondola boats. Cities are known for pedestrians, bicyclists, and traffic jams, not to mention extremely limited parking. Residents and visitors take this into account; sometimes, they plan their lives around it. A science-fiction setting might similarly be known for certain types of craft.

There are subcultures that trick out of their cars with all sorts of aftermarket accessories. The same can be done for motorcycles or spaceships if those are personally owned. With a little imagination, perhaps we can do the same with wagons, horses, or even dragons and the gear we use to ride them.

The existence and state of public transportation can have cultural impacts such as whether a settlement is known for people having to walk because public transportation doesn't exist. Or maybe it's free, or really expensive, either extreme impacting the willingness to travel. Crime with public and even private transportation (think of unlicensed taxis or services like Uber) is also on everyone's mind. What kind of security is typical in the culture we're inventing? It depends partly on the wealth available for police and infrastructure to deal with criminals.

Long distance travel is another concern. In SF, this is almost a given, but in fantasy settings, many people can't do long-distance travel. Here, the horse or wagon are the typical methods of getting around, but they're not the fastest or most comfortable way of doing so and necessitate either camping or staying in an inn. Both offer dangers depending on how safe the landscape is. In our modern world, we tend to assume that we can go on a hike without being mauled by an animal or killed (depending on where we live), but this isn't true in a fantasy setting. Traveling over land poses risks, which come from other humans, species, monsters, animals, and possibly even plants, whether those are predatory or just poisonous.

If only a few people do have personal experience with distant cities or lands, those people might be admired. This can also cause people to lie about it. Significant ignorance or simply false information about faraway places could be prevalent in society. This can mean that word-of-mouth and rumor predominate. It can also mean that those who officially travel in some capacity, whether sanctioned by the government or knights errant, are looked to for news of the outside world. This, in turn, could lead to "street criers" hanging out near the city gates, collecting information from incoming travelers, and then going to the town square to disseminate that at specific times, like morning or evening, when people are drawing water from a central well.

In volume two, we covered calculating travel distances and times, but here we're looking at the impact on culture. In a fantasy setting, many roads and paths are dirt—mud when it rains—more so in a village, less so in a town or city. The likelihood of muddy feet can impact footwear, dress hems, and pants cuffs in an entire region if rain is common; details of where steady rain is likely is part of *Creating Places (The Art of World Building, #2)*. This, in turn, can impact culture, such as people staying indoors during the rainy season. Perhaps going barefoot becomes common and it is part of culture to wash one's feet on arrival inside somewhere, and locations are expected to provide the opportunity. The same could be done in dry climates, but now it's the removal of dust that is a concern.

Is it customary to have somewhere to stable a horse for visitors? What about a parking space for vehicles? Do people double park and is that expected or an irritation? Imagine what sorts of issues might arise with SF vehicles that can hover or outright fly. Then decide what is considered customary and courteous; the ways people react to violations are likely similar to road rage here on Earth.

PASTIMES

How people spend their free time is a cultural element we can develop. If they are out adventuring and saving the world, they may lament not enjoying their usual pastimes, or find ways to inject them into their adventuring life. Using the United States as an example, men stereotypically watch a lot of sports on TV and may attend sporting events in person. Women shop, talk about their feelings, and gossip (or so men believe). Those with dogs must walk them or take them to the park. Both might take fitness classes or enjoy exercise like swimming, jogging, or biking, to name a few. Some people enjoy cooking while others enjoy eating out and can't cook a thing. There are countless activities like fishing, off-roading, or travel.

We don't necessarily need to invent pastimes for our world. Many of those just listed are universal, as are countless others. However, we can put a new spin on them. If we have a pet dragon, that presumably comes with different responsibilities than a dog. Decide what they are; this can be used on multiple worlds, with some minor variations. If hunting is a pastime and we've invented new animals, we can decide how challenging each animal is and what trophy typically results. New plants and animals may impact cooking (such as very long times at a low simmer to make something edible), but this is the sort of thing we can invent on the fly. Any plants, animals, magic, or technology that are involved in a pastime gives us leeway to decide how it influences that hobby.

It's recommended to create a handful of activities for a novel-length work, less for something shorter, more for a longer work. With a novel, one or two can be shown during a scene, such as characters hunting or playing a game of cards or dice during an important conversation. The others can be mentioned in passing; a character can lament not doing one or mock another for their hobby. Two people can look forward to doing something upon arrival at a destination known for that pastime (or not). A character can be made to feel like they don't measure up because they spend too much time on a hobby. These briefly mentioned ideas don't need long explanations about rules or anything else. Consider this example:

> *Kier remarked, "I can hardly wait to reach Illiandor and play valends with someone who doesn't lose within minutes." He smirked at those around him.*
>
> *His companions rolled their eyes and one replied, "If you spent half as much time on swordplay as on card games, we wouldn't have to save you every other encounter."*
>
> *"Right." Antar flashed a grin. "Maybe next time we'll just let you be killed and take back your winnings that way."*
>
> *The captain strode in. "No time for gambling ashore boys. We've a hanging to stop!"*

What may take longer is the invention of games or sports, if the details are to be shown. Smart world builders will take existing games and modify or combine them. This is easier when the existing Earth game features an animal and we're substituting one we've invented. It's differing abilities might mean new rules, especially if it has abilities that create unique advantages; we only need to decide what those are and place restrictions on whether they can be used at all, under what conditions, or how frequently. Most Earth sports involving animals feature horses, elephants, or camels, as these are the few ridable options. Some games involve animals fighting each other, but there are likely few rules in such a case because animals, by their nature, are not going to understand or obey them, unless our invented ones are smarter.

Our invented species may also have attributes that are forbidden or restricted in use. Perhaps a team can only have one elf, for example, due to their skills. Maybe dwarves aren't allowed at all because they can't compete due to height. We can just decide how the game is played (by humans) and consider the pros and cons of others and what problems their attributes cause; these problems will result in rules to deal with them. All of this applies more to sports than something like card games, as physical attributes greatly impact the former but mental ones the latter.

RITUALS, FESTIVALS, AND CEREMONIES

BIRTHDAY OBSERVANCES

Many celebrate a birthday on the day they were born, but all birthdays in a given month could be officially the same day in an authoritarian regime that restricts and standardizes such events. An important religious day could affect this, especially if the god is believed to have come into existence that day; everyone is sharing a birthday with a god. We can make up other scenarios.

If we do this, people could have two birthdays: the actual day and the universal one. The former might be privately and quietly celebrated by family and friends; if the universal birthday is state sponsored, other celebrations may frowned upon. We can even use this to get our characters in trouble for celebrating their actual birthday.

There are other religious holidays that might be observed across multiple cultures, but only if that religion is prominent in all of them (think of major religions on Earth for inspiration). In a later chapter, we will look at creating religions and these events, but for each, we should decide how these impact culture. The simplest variant is that people take the day off from work to observe the holiday; a formal government, likely in SF, might sanction this so that people are paid that day. In a fantasy setting, this is less likely, as the concept of paid holidays might not exist.

HOLIDAYS

Most of us look forward to holidays because we're paid and get a day off, especially a three-day weekend. This is something that'll be on the mind of characters in similar situations. Others may know that a day is coming up and expectations need to be met for prayer or family gatherings. Even characters who are off adventuring will be aware that they're missing a holiday and loved ones might be wondering what happened to them. An exception would be when they're so busy running for their lives that they not only forget about holidays but what day of the week it is. Still, can you remember the last time a character thought about a holiday in a story? Authors tend to ignore this altogether.

Some holidays are reserved for civil rights leaders who impacted culture, a political figure like a first president, the military (especially in a military junta), or even wizards if wizardry is commonly accepted. Major wars, disasters, or first contact with an alien species (that become allies) are potential holidays. More events were discussed in *Creating Places (The Art of World Building, #2)*.

There may be several holidays, or even a season of them, that strongly impact the culture, like Thanksgiving in November through New Year's Day in the United States. Retail has turned this into a major shopping opportunity, but themed movies and decorations abound, too. Such a scenario is arguably more likely in a modern or futuristic world than in fantasy, but we can still have sales of smaller magnitude at festivals. Some cities might be known for better festivals, causing widespread travel to reach them.

Some countries may refuse to acknowledge a holiday or ceremony for ideological reasons. An authoritarian regime is unlikely to appreciate people celebrating a holiday from a democratic country even on their own time, particularly if that holiday celebrates a political figure who pushed for greater rights. Conversely, those in a democracy are unlikely to appreciate someone celebrating a holiday from a regime that promotes civil rights violations, even if the celebration is tolerated due to something like freedom of speech laws.

CEREMONIES

Ceremonies are often religious in nature and we can leverage a religion we've created to invent them. Some ceremonies dominate a culture for weeks, such as Ramadan in Islam, but only if that faith is widespread or even state sponsored. People may plan in advance if a pilgrimage is needed, meaning this impacts them before and even after the ceremonial period.

If people have left this culture for another land where the ceremony isn't acknowledged, they may return home for it, possibly meeting resistance to the idea. Their parents might have originated there and instilled the faith in them, though they've never returned; it's still on their minds even if their current homeland ignores the ceremony/holiday. Imagine needing to take a day of vacation for Christmas day because your country doesn't acknowledge it. Adding a small detail like this to a character's thoughts can make our world look more believable.

When inventing ceremonies, decide how widespread they are and if everyone is aware of one due to unusual prevalence. Some of us might've heard of one but know nothing about it if it's less practiced. The details of a ceremony only matter if we're going to show it, and in this case, we don't have to explain each moment. If we say anything, it's often best revealed quickly as a character's thoughts. Have them think about what each step means, such as consuming a liquid that represents a god's blood, or food that equates to their benevolence, or kneeling to show deference and humility.

FESTIVALS

Festivals can be based on holidays, ceremonies, or the reasons *those* exist, but they can be seasonal, such as a harvest festival, a spring one, or a solstice. These need fewer explanation. Festivals are easier to create in the sense of justification, but if we have little reason for inventing one, the details of what take place can be harder to imagine. Fortunately, we can leverage Earth festivals for ideas.

Sporting contests are common, whether these are lighthearted (such as bobbing for apples) or potentially deadly, like a joust. Races are particularly rousing if our characters gain something important by winning. Food and entertainment, whether plays, singing, or other contests are bound to occur. If we're out of ideas, we can also visit a Renaissance Festival for inspiration. For those writing SF, just replace everything with modern equivalents. A race would be in space craft. Fighting against holograms might replace jousting. Games may employ technology.

FOLKLORE

Folklore can include jokes, stories, songs, and proverbs that help establish and maintain collective identity with a culture; types of toys might be included, particularly if they represent a character from a legend. These are elements not taught in school, but which are picked up via word of mouth by living in the community. They aren't created by individuals with copyright privileges, which means we don't have to worry about the origins other than understanding what value system gave rise to one, to make it feel appropriate. The folklore must always be relevant to the group or it wouldn't exist, unless it has achieved a significance beyond its original meaning. An example would be Halloween, which shows us that holidays or events can result from folklore.

Given this, story characters who exemplify a value, and those who don't and paid the price, are good ones to create in folklore. Hansel and Gretel, Cinderella, and more teach a lesson, and in a fantasy world, they are likely to still be relevant ways of instructing the young in community values. These tales often include a simple premise and setting, one or two characters with one goal, and a villain in the way. We don't get things like backstory, and even character motivations might be missing. A character wants something, and the more universal that desire is, the less it needs explaining.

Folklore can be divided into verbal, material, and customary (i.e., behavioral) elements. And each may be present in a single manifestation of folklore, such as birthday parties where a song is sung, a material item is presented, and guests, hosts, or a person being honored perform actions like blowing out candles. We don't have to explain them, though a quick line about it is often better; meanings may be lost in more developed societies like ours or in SF, but simpler societies may remember.

Folklore must be performed because without it, an item like a birthday cake is just a cake. This is known as "framing," which is a cue to the audience that we are entering a moment of fairytale. Both performers and audiences understand that it's not intended to be real, but symbolic.

This is one way that folklore is separated from witchcraft, for example, though one could be mistaken for the other. These performances are partly to remove us from daily life for a brief time and may involve going to a specific place, such as a shrine in the woods, or be done at a given time, like midnight. Verbal folklore may begin with a phrase that reveals it is folklore, like, "Once upon a time..." We can invent our own, but the audience will not recognize it and we'll need more improbable moments in the story to indicate this. For example, "In the land of mist and spice" can be a common opening, followed by, "a man with two heads" because we know that's not normal and this story isn't real.

ARCHITECTURE

If we haven't traveled to other regions or countries much, we might not think architecture is part of culture, but it can be. We take the architectural style of where we live for granted but notice it in places that look very different. In some rural regions, a wrap-around porch is very common. In towns, bright pastel colors may dominate exterior walls, or everything is bright white stucco. In still others, murals or graffiti abound. Each of these influence the impression architecture creates, and this impression may be what we're most after.

Saying construction is brooding and menacing, or quaint and homey, is more useful than using technical terms for building styles because many of us (including audiences) don't understand those terms; authors should use them sparingly if at all. Materials can be commented on, such as clay, wood, stone, and metal, because these imply sophistication, sturdiness, and overall impression, and are easy visualize. The vibe that materials impart can influence how we feel about a place.

A log cabin with a thatched roof, or one made of bamboo, gives a very different impression than a steel and glass building. In between are buildings made of stone, tiles, and synthetic materials. The hue of these contributes to the impression of a location as drab or colorful, but this becomes cultural when such a style is not just in architecture but clothing and more.

Regardless of material, we can leverage the reality that villages often have narrow streets from when people only walked or rode a horse. Many roads aren't wide enough for a wagon. Anyone who's traveled to Europe has likely seen an "old town" where everything about the architecture is smaller, including the space between buildings.

One way to decide on styles is by government type. An authoritarian regime may be reflected in menacing, dark architecture that intrudes upon the psyche. A democratic one may favor bright colors and greenspaces. One that prizes order is likely to have well-designed spaces, possibly with geometrical layouts that include how gardens are structured. A poorly run or chaotic government might have housing that has sprung up wherever it could, where little planning has taken place; this could be true if war has taken a heavy toll, causing governments to rise and fall in quick succession over the past hundred years, leaving people on their own to "make do." Even when a more successful government takes over, it may leave such slums as they are, even if crime and disease run rampart there. Such places intrude on culture because people consider the safety (or lack thereof) of them. It isn't just homes that are affected, of course, but public buildings that are likely financed with taxes. Private businesses built and paid for by a company are impacted less in a fantasy setting where these companies don't exist.

Necessity often dictates culture. Those in a medieval town may dump a chamber pot out a window into the street. Is this considered standard in our culture or are these people breaking a local law? The stench of many doing this could lead to people wearing a perfumed scarf over their lower faces; this becomes cultural and can outlast the original cause when society advances and people stop dumping poop in the street. Urban, suburban, and rural areas often have different styles, sometimes due to necessity or industry.

Culture affects the interior of buildings, too. In the United States, for what's called a single-family home, we expect certain rooms. On the first floor, it's the kitchen, dining area, formal dining room, formal living room, casual family room, an optional garage, and the laundry room (which might be on the second floor instead). On the second floor, we mostly expect multiple bedrooms and associated bathrooms. There may be a basement, and this could either be finished or unfinished with multiple rooms. Two stories with the optional basement is common in many areas, while single story, rambling houses appear in other areas and times. We can add expected rooms, such as ones dedicated to magic, religion, target practice, or weapons play. Rooms can also be designed with certain activities in mind but converted to another, such as a spare bedroom being used for a nursery. If our culture has a siesta, there is likely to be a room for this, or part of one, if people don't always do this in their bedroom. This room might be closer to the front of the house for not only themselves but a guest to use.

Consider whether there are species and races of different heights in the setting and whether this is considered. For example, do dwarven homes have a front door tall enough for humans, and social room, too, but father inside, where guests are rare, the doors and rooms cater only to dwarves? If this is true in a society, people will expect and reach a conclusion about a dwarf whose home is exclusively dwarven-sized. Is he anti-human, for example? Or was this the only one available, prompting him to apologize to human guests all the time? Do people talk about him being anti-human behind his back?

Something we can leverage from history is the existence of utilities such as running water, power, and appliances. These impact the cleanliness of our inhabitants and their general fitness and longevity. Technology and medicine are the primary reasons that those of us alive today live much longer than in the past. In SF, we may just assume these (and better versions) exist, but certain things may or may not in fantasy. For example, running water actually can because it doesn't depend on electricity.

WHERE TO START

The order to create culture in isn't hugely important, with one major exception: decide on ideas and beliefs, and then a unified cultural vision early on. This doesn't have to be first, as having a few ideas of culture can inspire the vision, but try not to go too far until an idea is achieved. If we still can't decide on one, we're risking incongruity.

It's important to create the social classes to know where the group for whom we're creating culture falls, since this impacts many aspects, including their formality. The rest can be done in random order, but we'll get the most from greetings, farewells, clothing/accessories, dining, past times, and daily life. It can be wise to keep ideas we don't use for one culture but associate them with another instead. This helps set them off against each other. Or we'll use that other one in another world altogether.

CHAPTER TWO

ORGANIZATIONS

Organizations for evil or good, like the mob, Avengers, X-men, Arthur's Knights of the Round Table, or Robin Hood and his merry men, help us create a dynamic setting. These groups are less formal than military ones discussed in the next chapter, and are less structured, being more loosely held together by common beliefs.

GROUP TYPES

FORCES FOR EVIL

Most groups arguably don't think they're evil, even if the majority of outsiders think otherwise. Even terrorist organizations seemingly believe that they're doing good things when blowing up civilians, killing children, and worse. Their worldview is at the heart of their machinations and is therefore among the elements to focus on first. If we don't know what our group wants, how can we decide what they'll do to get it?

Whether religious, social, or philosophical, evil organizations often justify their actions, and it is their behaviors that make them evil, not their beliefs. Such groups often disagree with that, however, and frequently murder others for having different ideas, which are a threat to them and their goals. This is one justification for killing "innocents," people who don't deserve death. Evil groups can declare others are evil and try to destroy them. Some such groups seemingly attract members with little conscience.

Either way, decide what the group's guiding principles are. Do they want to spread a religion? To topple a kingdom whose way of life offends them? To get revenge in the name of a fallen idol or cause they appreciated? How far are they willing to go to get it? Did the group start off less "evil" but due to circumstances we'll name, they've lost their way and become something more abhorrent? Are they justifying a means to an end, such as killing civilians because they're in the way?

Forces for Good

An informal group that's a force for good is unusual in the real world because we have police and organizations like the United Nations to oppose wrongdoers. This is different in fantasy because police forces aren't as formidable as they are on modern Earth. Evil organizations may also engage in activities outside of a jurisdiction, which is far worse in SF, where it can extend planet-wide and beyond. A formal group that is bound to a sovereign power may lose the right to counter the evil group's actions outside the power's jurisdiction. But a force for good can be devoted to doing that very thing.

A good group can have a mix of high-minded and realistic reasons for existing, such as upholding certain virtues and stopping the spread of nefarious regimes that will impact them or loved ones. The ideas can be inspired by religion, philosophical justifications, and a sense of fairness. These people are virtuous but grounded in humility, compassion, and other positive traits that inhibit a slide into being an evil organization dominated by idealism, lack of reality, and selfishness.

We'll need to decide what guides this group and if it's written down or just an understanding. The latter gives way to misunderstanding and assumptions, which might result in bylaws being written. Perhaps there's an oath people repeat at meetings, to remind of what they stand for. These groups will also try to forge a positive relationship with not only those who can help them, like city leaders, but with the public whom they help and protect. Reputation is important and can be aided by charitable actions. Fantasize about what sort of group you'd like to form yourself if you were a powerful wizard or knight with equally strong friends who agreed with your world view. Tired of certain kinds of atrocities in life? What would you do about it?

COMMON TRAITS

Whether evil or good, group members have certain things in common. Invent a symbol or traditional colors, and whether anything is given upon joining, such as a tattoo or medallion. These can cause quick reactions among characters and are a fast way to reveal who someone is.

GOALS

Every group wants something. Knowing their objective is crucial. We must also define the current state of their goals, so we know how far or close they are and how they feel about this.

OBJECT CONTROL

Sometimes a group's goal is an object they can hold in their hand, like treasure or a device, but only a few may be able to literally do so. If the object has religious or supernatural significance, then obtaining, recovering, or protecting it can be a goal, but additional motives may apply.

What will the group do once the coveted item is obtained? Use it for something or just possess it? The latter isn't particularly interesting. Money is typically used to buy other things, but members could have different plans for their share of the loot, assuming it's not seen as belonging to the group. If it's divvied up, the group may disband unless a desire for more keeps them together. If it's an item to only possess and not use, why will the group stay together after getting it? They might need other reasons, such as undertaking missions. This is true of a good group that wants to confiscate dangerous items and prevent usage by evil groups.

LAND POSSESSION

Land can be great appeal for security, strategy, or to control assets like a mine. A religion's followers may seek to control and preserve a holy site or use it to interact with a god; a real-life example is the Middle East conflict over Jerusalem. Using territory as a group's goals is problematic because disputes over land are typically between sovereign powers or settlements, not groups that, by their nature, might be more mobile. The solution is to having them working to benefit a power through that acquisition. They can be officially sanctioned (or not) by that power, able to perform acts the power can't do openly. A group can also deliberately destroy diplomacy to cause war.

POWER

While power can be a group's goal, it's usually a means to an end. It's a cliché of poor storytelling for a villain (or his henchmen) to want nothing more. It makes them cartoonish. Make sure there's a more complex goal than this, as power only works in the short-term, such as ensuring the survival of the group or individuals within it.

UPHOLDING IDEAS

Many groups have philosophical or religious reasons for existing. They want to uphold the virtues they've learned. This can mean either promoting those ideas or destroying those who defy them. Intolerance is a staple of humanity; an invented species can be different, which can allow us to comment on this aspect of humans. Whether good or evil, such groups and their members are often willing to risk their lives for the cause.

We may need gods and religions for this, but general-outlook philosophies can work. Examples of the latter can include believing in equal rights (for all genders, races, and more), abolishing slavery, spreading democracy, and ending the abuse by aristocracies. We may have philosophers like Plato or Socrates who have imagined ideal states that inspire groups. The advantage of using gods as inspiration is that each will have a vision their followers support and which can become the basis of multiple groups, which is easy with a pantheon where the gods are divided by their chief areas of concern. But consider how many religions and groups arose on Earth, with a single god.

ENEMIES AND FRIENDS

Whether individuals, species, kingdoms, or other groups, the one we're inventing will have friends and enemies. We might need to draft several groups before deciding their relationships, but whenever we're deciding what they support, think of who that might upset into forming an opposition group. Sometimes one group will indeed inspire another's formation and, if the second destroys the first, it may no longer have a reason for being unless it has found more purpose elsewhere. Creating multiple reasons for a group's continued existence is wise as organizations have more usefulness to us and seem more well-rounded than focusing on the destruction of another group.

An organization with more than one purpose can result in multiple friends and enemies. At times, a hostile group might even become an ally, which makes for dynamic settings. Doing this requires having a clear understanding of the group's goals, passions, and beliefs. A list of gripes about the misdeed of others, and actions to right those wrongs, or uphold positive ideas, will suggest people who oppose or support them. Do they thwart or respect authority of nations and other groups? What does the average person in their region think of them? Other regions? Are they a symbol of something? Are they feared or respected? Much of this is about their history.

POWER STRUCTURE

Knowing how the group operates has much to do with the power structure. World builders and audiences gain much from having clarity about this. While some groups have a leader, others are run by an inner circle and others might have member votes. Nevertheless, a single leader, even a figurehead, can be useful, speak for the group, and do things like break a tie. Power struggles within an inner circle can be useful for tension; they may arise from the lack of formal structure we'd see in the military.

Power comes in many forms, such as physical or supernatural might. This may be more prized in evil organizations, a leader possibly chosen by killing a previous one. That might cause fear that keeps people in line in an evil group, but likely causing dissention in a good group, where intellect might be more favored.

Wealth can be power when properties are acquired, such as a group's headquarters. For the rich, this can confer power over the group unless it can choose another HQ. Money can also purchase supplies, whether weapons, armor, transportation, or basic necessities. It can buy spies and corrupt officials. But others might covet it, putting the individual at risk. Some groups won't respect it. And wealth can be lost.

Connections and influence are impossible to steal and difficult to acquire. Influencing those outside the group, such as political leaders, tends to be for older people, who've had time to forge relationships over decades.

Within the group, anyone could forge influential connections, making others see them as a leader, despite not being an official one.

Mental acuity can be prized in leaders, especially in good organizations, where leaders rely on input, showing respect for those they disagree with and giving kudos to those whose ideas help, which increases loyalty. They can become the leader even if someone else has more money, connections, or physical strength. This power cannot easily be taken from them. They conceive great plans that further the group's goals and foresee flaws in others' plans.

Aside from leadership roles, the rest of the group may have no defined structure beyond an inner circle, who earn that place through the influences just discussed. New recruits may be treated differently, but once accepted beyond a probationary period, the new individuals may be on their own to form allies within the organization. Unless we have a specific reason for being detailed with group structure, such as writing a story about someone's time joining a group, participating, and eventually departing, a non-structured group is a good choice.

History

While the group can be new, a history creates depth. This should include the formation story of how, why, and where the group originated, and what actions they've attempted to do, why, and the result, both for themselves and those impacted by their existence and efforts.

ORIGINS

A group's location will influence their origins. We can use any regional conflicts to inspire their rise. If two sovereign powers are at war, for example, we should know what each wants, why, and the tactics used to pursue it. Do they force people to serve in the military? Do they commit war crimes? Are they harming people and livelihoods? Is injustice being forced on the population? Are riches (like access to a mine) being withheld by one power to the detriment of the other? Any of these and others can inspire opposition that leads multiple individuals to ban together and form an organization.

Another option is a weak king who lets forces overrun his kingdom, or an evil warlord threatening destruction, or a supernatural phenomenon to contain. These are events that thrust people into action, and when they realize others want to take the same actions, the group arises. War might trigger groups' creation in other ways; for example, if it ends, leaving something the group considers unfinished business. For example, maybe the "evil" army is defeated, but many groups that comprised it are still extant. This group will go on a search and destroy mission, the first of many. Others might admire this and join the group.

The group may arise from a shared philosophy about what is right and wrong in the world, whether that's inspired by specific events or not. Each individual will largely agree with the group's outlook. Such a group may form in peaceful times, where social injustice is in their sights to correct. The group may exist informally before an event triggers them into becoming a more serious organization.

ACTIONS

No history is complete without attempts, successful or not, to achieve their goals. Create a half dozen attempts with a mixture of failure and success. Have they fought in battles with others? Just on their own? What famous incidents are attributed to them or foiled by them? Both failure and success should result in the death of members, only a few of whom might be noteworthy. Others outside the group will also have died, including members and leaders of opposing groups, warriors, wizards, and civilians. The latter may be inspired to join this group's enemies. All will have left a mark on someone, somewhere. Lives might also be saved and cause similar recruitment or supporters.

Some actions may only partially get their ultimate goal, which allows us to grant some success without eliminating the need for their continued existence (if that goal makes them disband). For example, an organization dedicated to keeping powerful magic items out of the wrong hands might perpetually be recovering and storing them. If there's a wizard cabal that keeps causing trouble, this can cause multiple events. If we want the group gone, killing them is one way, but a more peaceful end means their goal might've been realized, but sometimes a new group arises from the ashes of the old.

IN AND OUT

Once the group exists, we should decide the circumstances under which it may accept or reject members. The larger the role this group plays in our story, the more we benefit from this. A character from one will be aware of possibly being ejected for a failure while another may be determined to prove he's worthy to have been accepted. A more established character may be involved in the inner circle or aspire to be. All of this helps us create depth.

JOINING

Accomplishing deeds in line with the group's goals may prompt an invitation to join, with possibly repeated recruitment attempts. The organization will need a sales pitch, so decide what benefits they're offering someone. Is it safety (in numbers), intel, prestige, allies, or better rates of success? Some are material concerns, but there might also be philosophical benefits of a world view strengthened by joining with others of like mind. Is there a problem someone seeks to alleviate by joining? This can be lack of supplies, high failure rate of their own missions, great danger, or anything that being alone in a pursuit exposes oneself to. We'll have people joining an organization for different reasons, which can also create internal conflict when some are more interested in one aspect than another. We can imagine someone stating that they're here only for the money while another character scorns them for not supporting the group's grand vision more.

Existing members can recommend new members, though this may require having their own membership settled; a new member's recommendation may not carry much weight. This provides an opportunity for conflict if the suggested person behaves poorly and casts a bad light on the guy who vouched for him.

What causes someone to be accepted or rejected? Informal groups often don't have formal tests, so someone may join on probation of a certain length, and a certain number of missions. They may be assigned to work with one or more people who have responsibility for them, any of them able to give a recommendation to the group's leaders about membership. During that time, it's likely that the organization's secrets will remain unknown to this person, and even upon acceptance, only the inner circle may know certain things.

What happens if candidacy is rejected? This may depend on how quickly this happens and whether the group is benevolent or nefarious. We can see an evil organization killing a failed recruit or sending them on a suicide mission; in the latter case, what if they survive? They may be forced to commit serious crimes and failure results in expulsion or death. A good organization is more likely to let someone walk away peacefully and have tests that amount to matters of character, judgment, and ability to support the group, including following orders. A group intending to physically fight might require skills tests. A supernatural group might need a display of talents.

LEAVING

People will leave an organization for many reasons that we don't need to invent here. We only need to decide how the group handles departures.

For evil ones, we can make this simple in that exiting means death. This might be a well-kept secret or one visibly demonstrated. This is an easy way to characterize them early in a story, such as showing a minor character earning this fate. It can shed light on why a more important character intends to disappear instead, possibly faking their death. Or maybe the important character tries to kill everyone else in the group, knowing they'll be hunted forever if they don't. We can also have their mind erased or a similar act that safeguards the group's secrets.

With good organizations, such tactics are highly unlikely. Members are free to depart at any time, though they may incur a debt that needs repayment or which the group could waive. If they're truly valuable, they may be talked into a temporary departure, but informal groups likely aren't insisting that someone's decision is irreversible.

Regardless of group type, a member may not have been important enough to warrant much concern about their exit. An inner circle member is more likely to face scrutiny. This could include inquiries into their motivation. Loss of life or limbs is a risk to groups. A member can become disillusioned with the group's stated goals, or exhibit behavior that goes against it. A change in leadership can result in unwanted changes, especially if it's a coup. During these, factions might appear, leading to infighting. These are some issues to consider when creating a history.

WHERE TO START

The first decision is to determine whether most people view them as basically good or evil. We should decide how we intend to use them, such as being allies or foes of our main characters. Are they on the same side of a conflict but with different value systems, or in genuine opposition? Decide their goals and the tactics used to achieve them, as this determines reputation. We can then envision past actions and start creating the history, including an inception point. The power structure and how members join and exit can come later, as can a decision about who else is their friend or enemy. Be sure to decide on a symbol and use other considerations found in appendix two.

CHAPTER THREE

ARMED FORCES

Military groups like knights, cavalry, and star fighters will exist in our setting whether we invent and mention them or not. However, not creating these is a significant oversight. Some will become an army, navy, or air force (or space force), each possibly comprised of multiple specialty groups. We might also need to create them for other species who have very different ideas. World builders often resort to generic groups that are not well-defined, even if characters from those groups are major characters.

Well-crafted groups can add believable tension and detail to a setting and achieving this is the goal of this chapter. As with many subjects, it's possible to invent far more than we can realistically use, but as with character back story, inventing some items helps us portray the world. This chapter includes a set of items to develop, but world builders are encouraged to decide on which aspects to invent, based on story needs or preference.

We must decide what type of group we're defining. Is this the navy, air force, or army, for example? We can ask what purpose they serve, but the military is typically for both protection and conquest, as needed. Once we know which type we're creating, this will help make other decisions discussed in this chapter.

Virtually all armed forces work for a sovereign power. This means that, in a story with two different kingdoms, for example, we might need two armies; this is needed if we'll use characters from either and those details inform our plot or characterizations. This could become overwhelming to invent, so we must be realistic and only create what we need.

The type of government will impact much about this group. An oppressive one will provide a strict environment, including mandatory service, while another might have far more freedom, at least when people are off duty. It's a mistake to create a military group without understanding the government that controls them. *Creating Places*, went into details on many government types and it's recommended to become familiar with them and their likely impact on all aspects of life.

LOCATION

Specific relations with settlements and sovereign powers, or even regions of land, can be determined in the world building files devoted to those. Large forces like an army are comprised of people throughout a power, but they'll have military bases in specific communities. This will be strategic locations and often large population centers, so if we've created a map or otherwise decided where major settlements are, this decision can be made for us.

Smaller forces like a knighthood may exist anywhere there's a need, including in or near smaller settlements. It is these that we may be able to decide on a case-by-case basis for which communities have them in quantities beyond the lone person. Assess the threats posed by animals, monsters, and species found in each land feature (such as mountains and forests) near a settlement; armed forces are designed to protect against such threats.

TERRAIN

Creating Places (The Art of World Building, #2) taught about the different varieties of terrain: open land, forests, hills, mountains, deserts, and swamps/jungles. Few military groups operate equally well over these terrains, and not at all in some. This helps us decide how commonly encountered they are. Terrain also impacts their transportation choices. For your files, state what types of terrain they're found in or what sort of encumbrance they experience if traveling there, such as being slowed down or having to go around.

For example, horsemen would be stopped by a jungle, but a savannah would be more like open land; the difference is underbrush. We don't need to note how they fare in every forest type. Instead, state that underbrush and low branches slow them and that the latter can also impede the use of certain weapons like the sword, leading them to use shorter blades. We may need to remind ourselves of their reduced effectiveness in certain conditions so we can more realistically portray and use them. They may become known for one, which may have led to their development. Horsemen excel at open land, whereas a force that rides dragons or large birds might specialize in mountains because they can fly over the terrain that hampers others.

Multiple species help us because each may be helped or hindered by different terrain. Imagine armed forces reaching a jungle and stopping because the humans on their horses can't continue, which prompts a recruitment effort seeking out members of a species which can. This is unlikely to be a secret, leading to open acknowledgement of the need and role these species fill. Maybe every squadron of these horseman is expected or required to have them.

These terrain decisions help us determine where the armed forces are found. A city surrounded by jungle won't have a cavalry at all, but one with open plains in every direction certainly will. A mixed-terrain settlement will utilize the most appropriate group based on circumstance. This can also lead the population to think more highly of one group than another, namely the one seen as more responsible for protecting them. That can cause tensions and resentment among rival military groups. All of this adds believability and layering to our setting. It's easy to create a character who belongs to one group and has an attitude about anyone from the other group. The amount of each territory within their jurisdiction aids the decision.

SPECIAL SITES

Our military group may have special sites, such as training facilities with unique instruction in weapons or even withstanding types of pain. Members may be sent to areas where a foe they're expected to specialize in are found in high numbers to gain practical skill fighting. Giving these places names, like "The Citadel" or "The Dark Abyss" adds mystique. Characters can remark on the time spent there, inspiring audience curiosity. More mundane training centers will exist, typically at major settlements. The best teachers can impact the most people there.

If they are religious or highly ceremonial, sacred places that come under threat can upset the military group or cause periodic pilgrimages. Destroyed or damaged places help us create history even if we don't comment much or at all on what happened. Who doesn't love a ruined or abandoned site? Traditions can impact reverence and trigger long-standing animosity toward whatever creatures or sovereign power was responsible. Sites of great battles can also achieve relevance. We're looking to invent some lore for our group.

Are there places where they store weapons, defenses, ships, or other equipment? Some of this could be ordinary, some unique or magical and rare, and others acquired in battles, as gifts, or from deceased members. All may be guarded by various means, physically, magically, or technologically. The more valuable, the less likely they openly admit to the locations or types of defenses.

We may need to solve practical problems for our group with special sites. For example, a group which specializes in riding flying animals embarks on a journey too long for a single flight, requiring an overnight stay. Maybe they've planned ahead and built a series of towers in the wilderness, each inaccessible from the ground. This aids with keeping the riders (and animals) safe while asleep. Try to think of realistic problems and their solutions.

TRANSPORTATION

In this section, we look at what the group provides or is expected of members. They may not provide steeds, machines, or training, though that doesn't mean our members cannot acquire and use them. How members of this military group get around might not seem important, but it can generate decisions. This is especially true in fantasy, where riding animals on the ground or in the air can impact where this military group can operate and how they're used for scouting or in battle. In SF, this aspect of transportation might matter less if everyone is getting around on flying craft. Everyone must disembark eventually, but in such cases, we typically see people on foot or in another vehicle. When was the last time you saw someone exit a spaceship on a horse, for example? This could be plausible, however, if they know the terrain they'll find and think this is superior; perhaps machines scare local people or wildlife, or cause harm they wish to avoid.

WALKING

Walking, running, or even rolling along the ground (for our ball-shaped humanoids, should they exist) requires little invention. However, the number of legs impacts both speed and endurance. For anything humanoid, we can decide they're not much different from us unless we're altering a characteristic by at least 10%. Maybe they can reach somewhere in 9 or 11 hours instead of our 10, or travel 9 or 11 miles or kilometers in a given time frame instead of 10. For anything with four or more legs, we should base its capabilities partly on a similar animal, so if the species is essentially a large feline, base its speed and endurance on lions, tigers, and similar cats. Quick research will turn up numbers, which we can modify. The goal is believability. Reasons they use their own locomotion include terrain that inhibits other options, they only operate within a settlement, or a lack of alternatives. The latter may mean not enough horses or equipment (like saddles) to equip them.

RIDING ANIMALS

Especially in fantasy, riding animals is an option that facilitates speed of scouting, spreading information, and maneuvers, the latter being especially advantageous in combat against unmounted forces. This is so decisive that wars have been won this way. Riding animals may be expected if the military group operates outside a settlement's walls; it speeds travel, scouting, and other acts in emergencies. However, terrain may inhibit this, from trees to steep, rocky inclines; specialized groups might be needed and operate primarily by foot.

Think about why we're inventing this group. If their role is to protect a settlement, they'll bear resemblance to cavalry or knights and we can leverage these. If they're messengers or patrollers who must be able to fight their way out of trouble, then they'll act alone or in small groups and require self-sufficiency and light encumbrance; they'll have a known response to encountered trouble, such as calling for reinforcements that will take the form of more serious military might. If creating knights or cavalry, they fight from horseback (or a similar animal) in an organized manner. The existence of both groups is horse-centric, but other military groups may mostly use the same animals for transportation or hauling supplies. In these cases, decide how prevalent the riding skill is and what degree of mastery is expected.

A flying animal poses a similar problem as a ground-based one: encumbrance. Loading them down with supplies, plus our rider, limits speed, endurance, and maneuverability, all placing the rider at increased risk of defeat by opposing forces. If problems with that are avoided, the great advantages are speed, perspective from above, escape from all land-based threats (unless flying low), and the ability to bypass difficult terrain.

Any military group typically furnishes animals that are required, but if not required, members may still be expected to have a fundamental skill. Consider a town guard that operates primarily on foot, but which occasionally needs to guide riders through town, or escort them to somewhere out of town. Would their leaders want the limitation of knowing some of their guards can't ride a horse? Probably not. Decide which animals they're expected to master and to what level; basic proficiency is the bare minimum. Perhaps they can ride but not fight particularly well from atop this animal.

RIDING MACHINERY

Whether cars, motorcycles, tanks, planes, space craft and more, SF worlds are more prone to ridden machinery than fantasy ones, where it is mostly wagons that might be used to haul supplies. We can invent machines, including their pros and cons. The limits we create for a machine can give us ideas for other machines that were developed to compensate for that weakness. Variety makes settings more believable and creates chances for the characters to settle for less than ideal equipment, with consequences we control. As with other transportation that can be used for making war, decide what vehicles are typically available to members of this armed forces, what they're trained in and to what degree, and what they are given and expected to have.

THEIR WEAPONS

Military groups and their members are often known for their weapons, skill using them, or both. A distinctive choice makes them more memorable and entertaining. Think of the light sabers Jedi wield in *Star Wars*, or the phasers from *Star Trek*. There are special weapons in fantasy, too, though seldom by an entire military, presumably due to manufacturing limitations, but we don't have to abide by that. And weapons don't have to be spectacular to be associated with the military.

Do they all have a two-handed sword because they specialize in fighting something like giants? If they're archers, we can decide whether bows are always made the same way, using wood from one type of tree or another. It sounds better when we've invented the tree and can write something like, "Kier lowered his solanaen bow as the loosed arrow slammed into his nemesis." With repetition, naming the type of material helps associate it with a mythic quality. Audiences begin to wonder why we mention it and how such an item is special, even if it's really nothing.

At a minimum, we should decide what weapons are required and bestowed by the military (and replaced by it if broken or lost in the line of duty). On Earth, members were sometimes required to supply their own weapons and armor; not having them would prevent inclusion.

We can also determine their preferred weapons, such as a long bow instead of crossbow despite having proficiency in both. Do they prefer a short sword to a long sword? What weapons do they rarely use? Are there any for which they have contempt? Snobbery exists in all things and a master swordsman might find a bashing weapon crude. A sense of their outlook and missions help us determine these. If we can't decide now, return to it later when we understand this military group better.

THEIR DEFENSES

Defending against threats is a basic reason for military groups. While a settlement may have fortifications manned by this military group, what we're looking at here are their ways to protect themselves.

ARMOR

Regardless of genre, a military group typically mandates a minimum requirement for armor. When was the last time we saw a knight wearing only leather? It could happen if he's on light guard duty deep inside a well-fortified city that hasn't been attacked in a decade. Even then, his superiors would have approved this before it happens unless he's headed for disciplinary action. This sort of detail brings our world to life.

IN FANTASY

We don't have to invent armor types in fantasy. Unless adding magical properties to it, everything we need probably already exists: leather (studded or not), chain mail, plate mail, plate armor, and variations on these. Understanding the differences helps us decide what they wear, including cost, how cumbersome they are to don, fight in, or wear for extended periods.

For example, chainmail is heavy but can be donned by one person, so a character prone to solo travel might prefer this. By contrast, full plate armor generally requires help, which is one reason knights have squires. Plate mail, which can be light and easier to put on, is a compromise. Since we're talking military groups, it can be surmised that they often work with others, but perhaps not. Form an opinion about their likelihood of working alone as part of deciding that they use plate armor. Similarly, if they go many successive hours on duty, perhaps chainmail isn't their usual garb due to the fatigue it causes.

We may want to decide that those of a given rank have superior armor; after all, commanders are more valuable. Consider the chart, using army ranks to demonstrate.

Rank	Typical Armor
Private	Leather
Warrant officer	Studded leather
Lieutenant	Chain mail
Captain	Plate armor
Colonel-Generals	Plate mail

Figure 3 Armor and Rank

If you're wondering why a captain would wear the heavier plate armor and the more senior generals would only wear plate mail (arguably less protection), captains are the highest rank that's in the field and expected to fight. Plate armor is unwieldly and impractical, so there's little reason to believe a general would wear it; plate mail is easier to deal with while also conveying supremacy due to an appearance like that of plate armor. Throw in an elegant cloak or sash and the generals can look more regal.

In SF

In SF, ranged weapons like guns (regardless of what sort of projectile they fire) reduce the need for the sorts of armor we expect in fantasy. Even so, body armor does exist. The mundane Kevlar and similar materials in real life can be used, but we can invent armor that deflects or lessens the damage of our invented SF weapons. We should think about protective clothing so that everyone isn't only wearing their uniform. Some range weapons will work on the principle of a projectile, meaning the force of it striking causes damage. Other weapons like a laser can cause burning wounds, so heat resistant armor is more effective. Another beamlike weapon may emit radiation, whether a known kind or something of our invention. Either way, just like real world clothing offers limited protection against radiation, we can decide that some protection is incorporated into body armor but that it has limits.

Skills

Our members might be trained in hand-to-hand combat with and without weapons. Is boxing part of training or do they only brawl? Our sense of their refinement and dignity can help us decide. The kinds of missions they go on can, too. Covert work often leads to close fighting – so close that swords (and longer) aren't feasible. If such work is reserved for special forces like Marines, then perhaps the special skills are, too, with only basic fist fighting practiced elsewhere. Never being disarmed is unlikely.

There are various forms of martial arts on Earth and we can invent hybrids or our own. We'll want a new name regardless of how much we borrow from one either in philosophy or form. It's okay to describe one in such a way that people recognize what it is but realize we've changed the name, because most people won't identify it anyway and the names of many are specific to Asian countries that don't exist in our fictional world.

THE ROAD TO ENLISTING

PREREQUISITES

While most if not all military organizations will train recruits, some skill and/or aptitude is typically required before training so that less time and resources are wasted on training someone who won't be up for the job's rigors. If we've already decided the expected skillset of accepted members (or ones that have completed training), this can help us decide on the prerequisites. For example, if advanced horsemanship will be acquired during training, basic horsemanship is a prerequisite.

Some level of proficiency with various weapons is likely required, and these can be divided into broad categories: long and short bladed weapons (swords and knives), blunt force weapons, and range weapons (bows, guns). Elite groups may require more skill across a wider array of weapons. We can decide that if there are six requirements and someone only has four but shows great promise in those, that they are provisionally accepted. There are no rules except for those we invent. Some organizations will churn out elite fighters while others may only produce average warriors who are half-expected to die within two years of enlisting.

Not all prerequisites involve something physical. Knights may require noble birth. Perhaps they must show strength of character, which may either be tested or vouched for by reputable sources. There might be educational requirements or the ability to read and write certain languages. This can make characters more believable, especially if they aspire to belong to this group and must prepare for an initiation test. If they've failed once too often, maybe they cannot be considered anymore and have feelings about this, ones we can exploit. Remember that some underprivileged people might try to join the military precisely to gain access to things they can't otherwise acquire, such as food, lodging, clothing, and pay.

Characteristics

In *Creating Life (The Art of World Building, #1)*, we looked at intelligence, wisdom, charisma, strength, constitution, agility, dexterity, and morale as traits to define for species like humans and others. While writing a description of each and how it manifests in a species is preferred, we can also assign a number from one to ten as a quick indicator of what is typical. We can do the same with the characteristics that a member of this military needs in order to be accepted or successful.

Officers will require higher mental traits, while enlisted troops, expected to do most of the fighting, need better physical ones. While deciding the latter, think about what weapons they prefer. It takes greater dexterity to use a sword or bow than a cudgel. Superior dexterity is needed for skilled swordsmen, but a crushing weapon depends on strength. Knights aren't known for their agility due to wearing heavy armor, at the least, but if we're creating a group that wears less, perhaps agility is expected. Wearing heavier armor might require greater endurance, too.

For wisdom, are they skilled at battle plans, or do they make foolish mistakes? Can they learn from history, keeping and reading old plans? Do they have military and advanced training for officers in matters of running a large military? Officers must pass tests, which are designed partly for measuring intelligence, not just education.

Morale is highly prized but is not the same thing as courage. Rather, morale is partly the ability to maintain formation in the face of peril, instead of everyone running away. Militaries require this and do things like court-martial those who run, but a specialized group that doesn't operate in formations might have less regard for it (and value courage instead). Morale is a hard trait to determine beforehand, however. We can still jot down a note about their reputation for it.

While working out the details, we may be unable to decide on everything. Returning to rework items is part of the process, so do what you can and move on for now.

INITIATION TESTS

A candidate may face tests to verify prerequisites are met. The exam also allows someone to demonstrate how good they really are at a skill. If they're already advanced, maybe they can skip some training, have a superior trainer, or be singled out for honing into a finer warrior; we can also use this to make peers resent that person. We should decide what weapons are tested and what level of skill is required for each, with some preferred over others.

Tests can also focus on how a candidate reacts to failure or challenges. Someone who whines about unfairness is likely frowned upon. Does a combatant get back up or otherwise shrug off a blow? Some of this is to be expected, but consider if a trait like unusual perseverance is required. Must members of this military stand for a day without fatigue? If so, this might be tested, but development of it might be expected during training rather than being there from the start. Imagine ways we'd use this military and its members and then concoct tests to demonstrate potential.

An example of what to write for a knighthood might be: "The minimum requirements are: demonstrated skill with the sword, average proficiency with a horse, average skill with at least one missile weapon, a willing desire to learn weapons skills, and honorable conduct at all times."

TRAINING

A military group without formal training makes for one that is easily defeated due to inconsistent skill levels among personnel. Knowing what weapons, steeds, machines, and knowledge they require helps determine what training they receive. Some basic ability to make minor repairs might be needed, especially in SF. Are they expected to know certain languages, and does that include reading and writing them? What about understanding some neighboring settlements or sovereign powers, whether allies or enemies? The latter points are almost a given for officers, but the lowest ranks can be captured and find themselves trying to escape enemy territory. We might also decide that they're expected to know or utilize whatever is handy and be generally resourceful.

Officers receive advanced training, typically, being college or something similar. We don't need to specify details but can assume it includes superior knowledge of language, societies, customs, tactics, politics, and anything else that helps them run an organization better.

We should keep all training simple unless showing a character going through the details of becoming a member. But we may want to decide how long training lasts in months or years. Base this on their expected skill level but don't get too specific unless you've researched what's likely. We might say someone can become an expert swordsman in six months when an educated audience member knows better.

Decide where training takes place. There may be cities or universities that do much of it before people are deployed. This will impact the culture of a settlement due to the number of recruits there.

FINAL TESTS

If we've done the previous work in this section, determining final testing is largely done, but we can add drama by claiming two candidates must fight to the death, for example. Maybe they must defeat a monster. Tests can be spread out over days and be an ordeal designed to test their mettle. Are these tests feared or are relatively benign? Are people tempted to cheat and can they get away with this? How strict is the governing body? In a lawful place, good oversight might exist, but a barbarian horde may allow cheating under the premise that you'd accomplish a mission no matter what must be done. Officers will have written and oral tests of knowledge.

IDENTIFIERS

The identifying marks of the military are on clothing, items, skin, buildings, and vessels. Consider the impression the group wants to make. Some example options are listed and grouped to create a brand:

- Noble, proud, strong
- Bold, intimidating, forceful
- Elite, precise, elegant
- Covert, deadly, efficient

COLORS

Choosing colors for our military group can be challenging. It is therefore best to go with no explanation or with something obvious, like silver for steel if favoring blades. Black suggests stealth and nighttime operations, or those in space. Red is obviously for blood. Gold, silver, and bronze can suggest wealth and elegance. A good source of ideas is to research flags of Earth countries and find the explanation for the colors, then leverage these. Rationalizations only matter if someone's really going to care about the color choice; few in our audience will. However, military members will be taught the significance and can think about this during a scene.

SYMBOLS

Armed forces both protect and conquer. A symbol can inspire ferocity from its members or a willingness to sacrifice for an ideal. They can intimidate opponents and impact their morale. Sometimes it takes a reputation to go with these symbols. Consider their sophistication. Expert swordsmen have more refinement than those who bash people; their symbol can reflect a fighting style. Education matters, too; if ordinary people can join and find a calling, perhaps a symbol reflects a universal appeal, whereas a highly trained group might want to appear elite.

Animals and weapons of war (especially one that the group is known to use) are frequent symbols. If we've invented animals, we can leverage their reputation. Using Earth examples, what comes to mind for a lion, snake, eagle, or horse? Symbols that require explanation are less powerful, so if we're using an animal the audience hasn't seen, show it and establish its reputation before revealing it's part of a symbol.

SYMBOLS OF ACCEPTANCE

Medals, pins, clothing, armor, weapons, and transportation can also show that someone is a member of this military group. However, the purpose of medals and pins are often to denote rank, whereas clothing signifies membership. A uniform is often head-to-toe, but in fantasy, it may be less comprehensive. We sometimes show them wearing their own attire but with an item like a cloak to denote service, as if uniforms don't exist, possibly due to limited manufacturing.

Militaries have requirements for armor and weapons, the style of which can reveal service, though this assumes mass production more likely to be found in SF but not fantasy. Either genre can cause symbols to be added. In fantasy, just as clothing might not be supplied, weapons or armor might not be provided for some soldiers so that they're using their own. In addition, a soldier might own something unique that they might not be allowed to use, whether it's weapons, armor, or their own steed, because uniformity is encouraged. Getting special exception can be problematic if others resent it.

For transportation, if they require something to do their job, like a highly trained animal, they may be given this. It still belongs to the military, who is responsible for its stabling and care when not in use. Do they form bonds with an animal so that it's considered theirs despite this, or are they expected to use whichever one is available? People are sometimes sentimental about ships, which have their quirks, but these almost always belong to a military, sovereign power, settlement, or wealthy privateers due to sheer cost.

THOSE WHO SERVE

MEMBERS

We should decide which species can join. Humans may comprise the majority, with others in specialized roles or in locations where their skills assist, such as elves stationed near a forest military base. But a military group for another species might work very differently, with humans a minority or not allowed. Use the world view of both the species and this military to decide if it's a good fit among them. As mentioned in *Creating Places*, joint settlements and sovereign powers can exist, implying a species melting pot and leadership is shared, which can lead to joint military groups, too. If elves revere life but a group doesn't take prisoners, preferring to kill them, we can assume elves don't join. The prerequisites may be designed to eliminate them, either for world view or physical reasons. A knighthood might require using a lance, eliminating a dwarf.

This raises an important point: not all members of the military are fighters. Those in a modern Navy on Earth are unlikely to engage in hand-to-hand combat, but in the Age of Sail, they were expected to if boarding or boarded (or on land excursions). In the case of our life-revering elves, perhaps they are the equivalent of doctors. Such details add believability to a military, where good uses can be found for species with specific traits and concerns. Isn't it good to show that the elves are there but in a typical role, and perhaps the dwarves are, too, operating artillery like catapults? They can be officers, too, as they seldom fight. There are plenty of support personnel who also don't.

Consider whether members of any religion are part of the military, in what capacity and what rank they have. They might be fighters, healers, counselors, or all three. Today we're all aware that soldiers become traumatized and need psychological support, but even if our world is too barbaric for that sophisticated level of support, soldiers die, and many will desire last rites.

IMPORTANT MEMBERS

Whether they're still active, alive, or long dead (and revered or despised), notable members are figures that our characters can aspire to be like, or dread being compared to. All we need is a name, a reputation, and the deed that caused their fame, plus maybe a sense of how long ago and well-known this is. We benefit from at least one good and one bad member, one to cause pride, another to cause shame for members. It's realistic. People can simply fail to do a job, or they can do something deliberate, such as betray their fellows and run from battle. If we have a specific set of job functions this group performs, have someone fail in that, as this makes the character more memorable.

RELATIONSHIPS

Our military group has a relationship with the rest of our world and it's smart to at least quickly decide what those are like.

WITH OTHER MILITARY GROUPS

A world without rivalries is less entertaining and realistic. In any region, sovereign power, or settlement, it's possible for two or more military groups to exist and be called upon for different reasons. This can lead to resentment. If the knights are always given the toughest jobs of fighting the most feared creatures, it's reasonable that another group might wish for an opportunity to prove themselves capable of this task. The knights could also be condescending towards others. Our multiple groups don't have to suffer discord, of course. Perhaps they complement each other well and look forward to working together.

Bear in mind that two groups who don't get along in one location might be great comrades in another. This may mean deciding on a city-by-city basis, but as that's time consuming, we can decide on several typical relationships that happen and then just assign one of these to each settlement as needed when we're using that setting. The usual reasons for this discord or cooperation will be found in our file about the military group. In our settlement files, we'll only say which version is happening and possibly a specific incident that triggered the current (or usual) status of relations. This keeps us from repeating explanations in one settlement file after another, beyond, "They resent and bicker with each other here."

Below is not an exhaustive list of options for how they could get along, but it can give you some ideas, all of which might be true on your world in different locations, between the same two groups. These might not be mutual, or one group could be more at fault than another.

1. Mutual admiration and respect, cooperation and appreciation on joint missions, seeing themselves as collectively part of a large picture
2. They work fine together but disrespect each other privately (usually)
3. On joint missions, they contest the other's authority and are difficult to work with
4. They avoid joint missions and are known to openly sneer at each other
5. Brawls between them are common in bars
6. They sabotage each other's missions
7. They are in open conflict (for control?)

WITH SPECIES

Not every species will view our military group the same way. Clearly, knights who destroy an evil species won't get admired by their victims, but even a species that receives protection from said knights might take it for granted. Even so, we should decide what every species' typical attitudes are toward this military group as a whole and its individual members (these can be different).

We should also decide what this group officially thinks about each species, as attitudes are often shared. Sometimes an organization promotes a viewpoint that its members are indoctrinated with, whether this is good or bad. This will depend on the dominant species. Some members might disagree with that attitude but learn to keep their mouths shut, while others speak up and get themselves into trouble. To decide attitudes about each species, we can leverage the relationship they have.

Using the knights as an example, if they're always saving the dwarves in a region, they might have either contempt for dwarves or amused condescension. This might be true even if they admire and like the dwarves for other reasons. They might enjoy saving them, but they might also resent it, particularly if their friends sometimes die in the process. It's easy to imagine the less noble among them thinking that their friend would be alive if the dwarves could defend themselves. While we associate knights with good deeds and bravery, etc., that doesn't mean some of them aren't asses. But we wanted to decide what the entire military thinks, so why does this matter? Because this sort of experience can cause many to share this attitude.

A supposedly evil species that our military group is routinely defending against, or driving away from a settlement, is sure to cause a uniform attitude among the group. They likely think disparaging things, perhaps rightly so. Maybe they want to exterminate them altogether.

Another possibility is someone holding attitudes from his home organization, getting involved with soldiers from somewhere else, those who don't share this stance. Maybe a knighthood in a different region needn't rescue the nearby dwarves, who can fend off nearby threats. When these knights air opposing views, an argument can ensue.

WITH SETTLEMENTS

Most military groups will be based in a settlement they are charged with defending. Unless they're poorly performing their duties, they probably have a good relationship with the town's inhabitants. There are shops, bars/taverns, and more that cater to them, offering discounts, supplies, or social activities. We need only point out especially friendly or hostile establishments in our files. The military may get too rowdy, starting brawls, resulting in confiscated weapons upon entry. If two military groups don't get along, an establishment may cater to one and ban the other, or make them sit in designated areas. Strict militaries will have better behaved warriors, generally, at least at home, but some forces are less so. Decide what makes sense for them.

How well behaved they are in other settlements will depend on several factors, including, how they're viewed and treated, and whether that settlement is considered an ally and has its own military. If the settlements are in the same sovereign power, they may have a rivalry that falls short of physical altercations leading to death. Consider whether they've saved the other settlement in the past or failed to and earned some discontent or worse.

WITH SOVEREIGN POWERS

If our settlement exists inside a sovereign power, the military groups are associated with the power more than the city in which they're based. This is especially true if they have more than one location. Each power could have a different relationship with their knights, as well. They could be nonexistent in other places, known only by reputation. We could think that an authoritarian power is unlikely to have knights because the latter is noble and the former can be brutal, but it's not always the case. A republic could, but we most often associate them with monarchies. All of this may be true with other military groups.

WITH ANYONE ELSE

We may have created organizations as per another chapter in this book. If so, we can decide how that organization gets along with this military group. The military may be an obstacle to avoid or overcome, or allies who protect and help the organization's members. Such interweaving of our inventions makes our world stronger.

There can also be types of people who are collectively viewed a given way. In a world with magic, are there any generalizations we want to make about how wizards and this military group view each other? Are wizards included as special ranks, like the Marines? Are they forbidden? Does this military feel like wizards are often causing problems that lead them into battle, such as raising an army of the dead (or living) to conquer lands this military is charged with protecting?

These are generalizations, but take the time to mature the outlook of this military and then compare and contrast it with everything else in the setting to determine relationships. This task is one to return to often for a few minutes at a time, tweaking our decisions. Always be thinking of how to cause tension, even among allies, who might fight on the same side but bicker over minor differences in form or substance.

MILITARY UNITS

Large forces are organized into military units, each led by a commander. When combined, these units form larger groupings that can amount to an army, navy, or air force (or space force). The armed forces we're inventing now may not exist in such large numbers; maybe they're more of a specialty group, like the U. S. Marines, who have special training and may accompany members of larger military units. Decide which type you're creating as this determines whether you need to organize them into military units or if they accompany the units of other forces.

The following chart shows typical army units, numbers of individuals comprising each, and the rank of the usual commander. Each unit is comprised of multiple small units. For example, a platoon is composed of multiple squads. This means that a lieutenant (in charge of a platoon) has several subordinate sergeants (commanding those squads at his direction). We can alter these numbers. This can be a guide or used wholesale.

Units	Number of Soldiers	Commander
Fireteam	2-4	Corporal
Squad	5-14	Sergeant
Platoon	15-45	Lieutenant
Company	80-150	Captain/Major
Battalion	300-800	Lieutenant Colonel
Brigade	1000-5000	Colonel/Brigadier General
Division	10000-25000	Major General
Corps	30000-50000	Lieutenant General
Field Army	100000-	General

Units	Number of Soldiers	Commander
	3000000	
Army Group	2+ field army	Field Marshal
Region	4+ army groups	Commander-in-chief

Figure 4 Army Units

The following chart shows several air force units and how many aircraft are in each and the usual commander. Regarding groups and wings, significant variations occur across countries, making it harder to generalize, but these names can be used interchangeably.

Units	Numbers	Commander
Flight	3-6 aircraft and support crew	Squadron leader
Squadron	3-4 flights	Squadron leader
Group/Wing	3-4 squadrons	Wing Commander/ Group Captain

Figure 5 Air Force Units

TROOP NUMBERS

Those wishing to write war stories often struggle to determine how many troops are in a settlement, sovereign power, or in an army facing another army. This will depend partly on things like forced military training, expectations, the level of threat in recent decades and today, and even the sort of government that exists. This allows some leeway, but a military junta is likely to have a high per-capita number of available soldiers compared to a monarchy, which might count farmers in its ranks, as opposed to trained warriors.

For perspective, the United States has almost 7 soldiers (combined military branches) per 1,000 people, or nearly 7 per 1000 capita. A city of one million can therefore produce 7,000 soldiers. It's not quite that simple, of course. Army, Navy, and Air Force bases create concentrations of personnel where those bases are located. But the soldiers may have joined the military from a broad area. Some cities or regions will contribute more or less than others, partly for cultural reasons.

We don't need to get this detailed, and we can fudge the per capita higher or lower based on our needs, with no one able to argue with us. This number varies considerably across Earth nations, from about 2 per 1000 capita to over 100, with many below 10. We can choose a typical per capita and assume this as a default. Then state in each settlement or sovereign power file whether these armed forces produced from here are at, below, or above the typical per capita. If we ever need a war and want troop numbers, we can add the total population of cities and towns in a power and arrive at a likely army size.

Formula: Population * Per capita = Troops
Example: 1,000,000 * .007 = 7,000

This becomes useful when determining who has the bigger army. We can change the numbers if we want Kingdom 1 or Kingdom 2 to have the larger number of troops. There are more towns and settlements on our map than we've likely drawn, so we can also raise the number upward by 10-20% for all of those unaccounted for settlements. Recent battles or famine are just two of many scenarios that could've reduced one power's available forces. Such details add believability and are arguably better than just deciding one army is bigger than the other because we said so.

RANKS

Using ranks makes our armed forces more realistic. The simplest approach is to use a standard naming convention from Earth. It's familiar and already understood (especially by those in a similar military branch here) while creating the necessary and believable structure that would likely exist. But we can also strike out on our own, carving out specific roles and their associated ranks. Renaming existing roles creates the sense of another world, but the audience won't know what we mean without some minor exposition. If we choose to rename them, it might be wise to keep track of what they're normally called for our internal world building files. Preserving the rank name lets us research more about them should we need to later.

The following chart lists ranks in order of highest to lowest and compares the titles of similar ranks across the army, navy, and air force.

Army	Navy	Air Force
Commissioned Officers		
Field marshal, or General of the army	Fleet Admiral	Marshal
General	Admiral	Air chief marshal
Lieutenant general	Vice Admiral	Air marshal
Major general	Rear Admiral	Air vice-marshal
Brigadier general	Commodore	Air commodore
Colonel	Captain	Group captain

Army	Navy	Air Force
Lieutenant colonel	Commander	Wing commander
Major	Lieutenant Commander	Squadron leader
Captain	Lieutenant	Flight lieutenant
Lieutenant (first)	Lieutenant junior grade	Flying officer
Second Lieutenant	Ensign or midshipman	Pilot officer
Officer cadet	Officer cadet	Flight cadet
Enlisted Grades		
Warrant officer or sergeant major	Warrant officer or chief petty officer	Warrant officer
Sergeant	Petty officer	Sergeant
Corporal	Leading seaman	Corporal
Private or gunner or trooper	Seaman	Airman

Figure 6 Military Comparison Ranks

Aside from those in the military (or their loved ones), most people have a limited understanding of or interest in relative ranks. Authors need to navigate this ignorance during storytelling. What the audience most needs to understand is who is higher and lower in the chain of command during a scene, not what their day-to-day responsibilities are; the audience can infer major duties from a scene involving the character carrying out some duties, such as during a battle scene. Ranks don't accomplish this because most of us don't know what someone with a given rank does. So why do we care about rank? Because soldiers refer to each other by rank in dialogue.

If we're writing a story that is heavy on the inner workings of a fictional military group we've invented, then we'll need to invest more time in working out duties. This can also be easier than researching all of these ranks and trying to determine what they do. When I've investigated this, I've often come up empty, which is why there's no chart listing every rank and its responsibilities. This also changes from country to country, meaning we have leeway to invent. Plausibility is the bar to get over; we are inventing a fictional group, not correlating it exactly to Earth military. Obviously, we don't want to call an army private a general, and we should form a sense of hierarchy, but beyond that, little is needed by most world builders.

COMMISSIONED OFFICERS VS. ENLISTED GRADES

In the previous table, ranks are divided into commissioned officers (CO) and enlisted grades. The former is appointed by a formal document issued by the head of state (the individual running government; *Creating Places (The Art of World Building, #2)* discussed heads of state in detail). The generic word "officer" typically means "commissioned officers" even though it could refer to non-commissioned officers. COs are trained in management and leadership and often have college degrees, which are required at higher levels. If such education doesn't exist in our world, we can decide that experience matters more. If they have little to no experience or practical knowledge of being in the field, they'll have trouble understanding the life of the enlisted grades they command.

By contrast, enlisted grades means any rank that is not a commissioned officer (who also outrank them). These are the bulk of any military—the fighting men and women and those who support them, such as pilots, engineers, technicians, and more. They can be promoted to higher enlisted grades and sometimes become a non-commissioned officer (NCO).

An NCO hasn't earned the commission yet, and is promoted from the enlisted grades due to experience and seniority (as opposed to being an officer from the start). They aren't paid as well, are less educated and trained, and have fewer legal responsibilities. Despite this, they are considered crucial to the military for several reasons: they're the most visible leaders (higher officers are seldom seen by most soldiers); and the senior NCOs are the main link between enlisted grades and COs. Because they rise through the ranks, they have practical experience as soldiers, as opposed to COs, who may have none. They outrank lower enlisted grades. An army sergeant is an example.

COMMANDING AND EXECUTIVE OFFICERS

Commanding and executive officers have different positions that are quickly summarized here.

A commanding officer (CO) is responsible for planning strategy and tactical moves, finances, equipment, duties, discipline, punishment (within military law), and more. Available positions are limited, with seniority determining who is promoted into an empty spot. Any unit that's expected to operate independently can have a CO but the term is generally reserved for major units like an army, regiment, and battalion; smaller units have a commander, who is an officer, but is not a "commanding officer" with the rank, pay, or responsibilities/duties of one; they are often referred to as a leader, not a commander, as in "platoon leader." As an example, a platoon leader cannot administer judicial punishment, but a CO can.

An executive officer (XO) is responsible for running a military organization and reports to the CO. By running the day-to-day activities, the XO frees the CO to concentrate on his own tasks. The XO is typically second-in-command in navies, but in other branches, they may not be in command, only overseeing administrative functions. We can change this, of course. Companies, battalions, regiments, and brigades each usually have an XO.

RANK AND ROLE

While the details of what roles a rank has can change, there are some high-level leadership positions we benefit from understanding. In other words, who leads a battalion? What's a rear admiral do? What about a wing commander?

For each military branch, the ranks and roles are listed next. By necessity, these are generalizations due to variations on Earth. Use these wholesale or as a starting point for customization. In some cases, you'll see the role repeated for two adjacent ranks, which suggests either rank could perform that role, or both individuals at once, with one subordinate to the other. Use your imagination.

Rank	Role
Commissioned Officers	
Field marshal or General of the army	5-star rank, commands a sovereign power's army, sometimes honorary or only used during wars
General	4-star rank, commands an army, highest peacetime rank
Lieutenant general	3-star rank, second-in-command

Rank	Role
	(of an army corps)
Major general	2-star rank, commands a division
Brigadier general	1-star rank, commands a brigade
Colonel	Commands a brigade
Lieutenant colonel	Commands a battalion or regiment
Major	Commands a battalion
Captain	Commands a company, or second-in-command of battalion, can be entry-level rank for those with advanced college degrees (doctor, lawyer, wizard?), highest rank that's still in the field (as a fighter)
Lieutenant (aka, First)	Commands a platoon, often second-in-command/deputy to a captain
Second Lieutenant	Entry-level rank for officers. College graduates can skip this rank, and even others are often in it less than a year
Officer cadet	Trainee rank
Enlisted Grades	
Warrant officer or sergeant major	Warrant officers are typically technical experts, pilots, military police, etc. Sergeant major is highest enlisted rank
Sergeant	Commands a squad or fireteam
Corporal	Commands a squad
Private or gunner or trooper	Entry rank of 4-6 months duration (rank can be skipped if given awards). Troopers are cavalry, while gunners operate artillery

Figure 7 Army Ranks

Rank	Roles
Commissioned Officers	
Fleet Admiral	5-star rank, reserved for wartime, commands multiple fleets
Admiral	4-star rank, often the highest rank in peacetime. Commands a fleet
Vice Admiral	3-star rank, commands the vanguard of a fleet
Rear Admiral	2-star rank, the least experienced of three admirals (at the rear of a fleet)
Commodore	1-star rank, commands more than one ship at a time (flotilla or squadron of ships that is part of a fleet), temporary rank (usually a captain)
Captain	Commands the largest ships, highest rank to command a ship
Commander	Commands smaller ships like a frigate
Lieutenant Commander	May be the CO of smaller stations/ships, or XO of larger ones
Lieutenant	Senior-most junior officer rank, formally second-in-command of a ship (behind captain), multiple lieutenants on a ship used to be numbered by seniority as "first," "second," etc.
Lieutenant junior grade	May require two years of service
Ensign	Commands squadron or team. Entry-level rank for officers. Named for carrying the flag.
Officer cadet	Trainee rank

Rank	Roles
Enlisted Grades	
Warrant officer or chief petty officer	Requires passing special exams and with high scores, plus enlistment time
Petty officer	Often specialists
Leading seaman	The senior-most seaman
Seaman	Entry rank

Figure 8 Navy Ranks

Rank	Roles
Commissioned Officers	
Marshal of the air force	5-star rank, typically ceremonial (like those from the royal family) if at all (it's rare)
Air chief marshal	4-star rank, commander of the air force, highest rank
Air marshal	3-star rank, commander of a large formation/vanguard of fleet
Air vice-marshal	2-star rank, commands large formation/rear of fleet
Air commodore	1-star rank, commands multiple groups
Group captain	Commands a group (aka wing)
Wing commander	Commands a wing or squadron
Squadron leader	Commands a squadron or flight, most junior of senior ranks
Flight lieutenant	Manages team of airmen/specialists/NCOs, can be second-in-command of squadron
Flying officer	Applies to ground crew too
Pilot officer	Entry-level rank for officers, can be skipped for those with training

Rank	Roles
Flight cadet	Trainee rank
Enlisted Grades	
Warrant officer	Warrant officers are typically technical experts, pilots
Sergeant	Commands a squad
Corporal	Commands a squad
Airman	Entry rank

Figure 9 Air Force Ranks

History

While we don't need an extensive history on our armed forces group, some details make them realistic. We don't have to say what caused them to exist; people will assume that a need led to it. If the military group and need is quite specific, such as dealing with a type of creature with unique abilities, then we might want to decide when and how it formed. What were these creatures doing en masse, and repeatedly, that made people realize a standing force of trained warriors to deal with them would be needed? The obvious answer is threatening a settlement/power or critical resources; there's no reason to get fancy.

Decide how long ago they formed. We have three options: very recently (the last ten years), a long time ago (five hundred or more), and somewhere between. The latter is our default option when a formation period doesn't matter to us. Truly old organizations are likely widespread, with strong history, meaning they've been influential in multiple major battles and wars. They have proven their value and are held in high esteem, with numerous legendary characters along their long history. By contrast, a very new group might not have been tested even once. They may be less trusted or relied upon. No heroes exist, or maybe one, who might be considered an anomaly. If going this route, our story likely features the formation of this group, so do this when the details of a group forming are of interest to you and you can make it a good story.

We may also want to decide where they formed. This is useful when trying to decide where they've spread to since inception, how long ago, and therefore how ingrained in society they are in different places. This allows us to create a little variety without much work. They will have spread out from this origin point in one or more directions. Using general population and the United States as an example, Europeans settled first on the east coast; as a result, despite hundreds of years passing, population is still denser than farther west, north in Canada, and even south – the directions people spread. A similar phenomenon can happen with a type of armed forces becoming popularized.

In worlds with flying or water-based ships, this spread over the land may be supplemented with the relatively sudden appearance of these armed forces in locations far removed from locations already having them. The idea of them will have been brought with the travelers. Designate somewhere as "The birthplace of the knighthood," for example, and then decide to where they spread. If we have a file for every sovereign power or kingdom, and have used the templates provided with these books, we'll see an entry for "Armed Forces" for us to jot this down.

With the number of world building tasks before us, creating a history for a military group is one to keep brief. If we already have wars invented for the past, add a mention of their role. Some examples:

• "They entered the Battle of Evermore late due to the distance to traverse, but they turned the tide and helped ensure victory, leading to their celebration as an elite force."

• "At the Battle of Evermore, they led the vanguard and were destroyed to a man in the first assault."

• "In a position of leadership throughout, their forces controlled the pace and tactics of battle, leading to yet another victory and an increase in their reputation as masters of warfare, without whom many evil regimes would dominate the land."

We may also want to invent specific missions they undertook and whether they were successful. We need their objective, which can be stopping someone, recovering or destroying an important item, or rescuing someone. We'll also state what they overcame, such as enemy, supernatural, or science fiction forces, and the ultimate outcome. If the mission augmented or damaged their reputation, say so. Remember to focus on what you can use in your work, what makes the group more believable, or both.

FAMOUS DEEDS

Unless our military group is less than a decade old, there's a likelihood that some of its members, while on official missions or not, have been part of famous exploits. This can be admirable or not, depending on our goals. Even if we have a group, like knights, that are esteemed, we can still have them be part of an ignoble event, possibly because they made mistakes or failed, not because of nefarious intent that we don't associate with a knighthood. Such discrepancies can humanize them. Conversely, a group known for bad deeds may have helped stave off a disaster because it might've affected them, too, adding dimension.

It bears mentioning that a group considered heroic by some will be despised by others, sometimes even by the people they help. For example, jealousy of knights could lead some to think they're arrogant, causing disrespect by the people they protect. Esteem is never universal; nor is loathing. When we decide and describe their relationships with others, we can comment on these aspects of them. Create a story with thought given to how both sides view the deed. We can invent a nickname that different participants assign a character, such as "Kier the Valiant" and "Kier the Butcher of Illiandor."

LORE AND MYTHS

New groups are unlikely to have much myth behind them unless they formed as the result of a momentous occasion or achieved prominence during one. They might have been the elite force that finally killed someone who promoted great evil, for example, possibly during a prolonged war or battle. Such a deed, heard around the world or across the cosmos, can give quick mythology to a group or its members.

Older groups are more likely to have multiple instances of heroism or impact in their past. This is where having invented historical events aids us because we can decide someone from this military unit did something important in one battle or another.

Some military groups also like to create a mythology around them. It typically includes an historical person who does something that embodies a trait the group admires, such as sacrifice or courage. This is an opportunity to create a mythical figure and a deed that our present story's characters may reference as a hero or role model. We can create a 2-3 sentence blurb on what they did like this:

"At the Battle of Evermore, Kier led a band of knights to rescue the elven high priestess, but found himself surrounded by ogres. Knowing it was certain death, he ordered his men to carry the elf to safety while he remained behind, fighting to his end. A statue in his honor stands among others at their compound in Illiandor, and the elves improved their relations with humans in the aftermath, a tradition that continues to this day." I wrote this in about the time it took you to read it. These are easy and fun to do, while adding depth and history. These stories can be a bit off from the truth, as often happens, but unless we have reason to mention that the narrative is off, it may not warrant inventing it.

WORLD VIEW

LANGUAGES

We may have little need to specify which languages this military group can speak. Instead, we can take a predictable but believable route and decide they know enough about the language of any nearby species that they must communicate with regularly in the performance of their job. This will change from sovereign power to sovereign power, even city to city. It's a fast decision that makes sense and gets the job done. It provides flexibility to decide on a more case-by-case basis that they don't live up to this somewhere, or are particularly fluent in a language somewhere else. We can leave a note about this in our files and be done with this.

We may want to specify that they're expected to know, and be trained in, the languages of species with whom they have frequent interaction. We'll need to decide if this is only speaking it or also reading and writing. In SF, a universal translator may negate the necessity of this learning, while a language considered universal, like "common" in fantasy, can also make this requirement unnecessary.

PLACE IN SOCIETY

How does society view this group and its members? With reverence? Fear? Suspicion? Or are they taken for granted, their protection and sacrifices hardly noticed? This will impact their place in society. Respect can result in being present at ceremonies, gifts bestowed on some occasions, and people gathering to see them leave or return. Contempt will not. Fear will cause avoidance; perhaps they can only dine in back rooms so people don't feel uncomfortable, or maybe they refuse this restriction and end up chasing away other occupants of a tavern with their presence alone. Are there shops that cater to their needs and inclinations, even if it just means having their favorite items ready? Or are such things absent altogether to avoid tempting them to enter? In many cases, unless we have a need for one extreme or another, moderation will be best, meaning there's nothing special about how they're treated or welcomed. Remember that their place in society might be slightly or even dramatically different in one settlement or sovereign power from another.

CUSTOMS AMONG THEM

As with all customs, we want to focus on the ones we're most likely to use: greetings, farewells, and in the case of military groups, toasts, burial rituals, and pre-battle customs. Think of an expression and gesture they use on meeting, and what physical and verbal response is expected. Farewells are less formal or ostentatious and an expected one is arguably more likely to be absent altogether. Such actions of familiarity, shared among only their group, strengthen the bond between them; this is useful in battle, where people die or are scarred for life, physically, mentally, and emotionally. These bonds help with morale, which we touched upon in *Creating Life*: the willingness to stand firm, together, in the face of mortal peril.

Toasts are likely to focus on body counts, skilled performance in battle, and things like weaponry or armor withstanding the forces at work, the idea a kind of well-wishing visited upon those being toasted. Some examples:

- May your arrows fly true
- Break heads but not blades
- A blow for Kier! (a hero)
- May Sinistria (a goddess) favor your hand
- To hell with our enemies (use an afterlife of your invention, not hell)
- May heaven bring you peace – many years from now!

WHERE TO START

Our first choice with creating armed forces is to decide whether it's a smaller, specialized group like the U.S. Marines or a larger force, and what kind it is: army, navy, or air/space force. This will determine where they typically operate, which will impact every subsequent decision. We should then envision what role we see them playing, particularly in a large conflict such as the world wars that are so common in speculative fiction. If our story only needs a high-level depiction of them in action, we can skimp on many details of invention, but if our characters (even minor ones) are current/former/future members of this force and are impacted by this, we'll need more. Decide on the scope you need. Most other aspects of their invention can be done in any order.

At a minimum, we must invent symbols, colors, and any slogans. If they wear or utilize specific armor or weapons, we'll be showing this and must decide on it. Envision their place in society as this will inform what and how they do things and how those actions are viewed by other characters; this includes working out relationships with others, at least at a high-level. We can skip a complete history if we don't need it, but an historical figure or two is recommended. Another area we can skip is how such individuals become one or creating ranks that differ in any meaningful way from the standard ones listed in this chapter.

CHAPTER FOUR

RELIGIONS

To create organized religions, we'll need our god(s) worked out in some detail (refer to Chapter 1 of *Creating Life, The Art of World Building, #1*)). Many religions focus on a single god, even if others exist, but some will worship several gods together. The techniques and considerations in this chapter apply to both. It also helps to have our species created so we can decide which ones tend to be part of which religions and even if those religions exclude one or more species, for example.

HISTORY

Major religions on Earth are thousands of years old, but minor ones are sometimes new. In either case, we don't need a detailed history, but some significant events are worth inventing. Many aspects of a religion originate from its inception. It's therefore recommended that we begin creating one at its source.

CREATION

The story of a religion's founding is crucial to how it is viewed and often what is expected of converts. A prophetic figure is an expected source. This person speaks in (or receives) the words of a god and brings those messages to people. To create this, some basic ideas are helpful:

1. Their name (previous and potentially new)
2. Their occupation before becoming a prophet – they are typically transformed by the experience
3. When it happened – a calendar may use this as a starting point
4. Where it happened – this can result in a holy site
5. How it happened – this can generate relics, symbols, and rituals

We can keep this brief, like this example: "In the year 12 A. K., the horseman Vicen rode into the Dark Peaks in what is the modern day Empire of Amarysh, emerging as the prophet Kier, Chosen Voice of the God of War, Arian, whose golden sword he pulled from a petrified Lluvien tree, whereupon he heard Arian's voice commanding him to return and form the Blades of Arian, an elite force of mounted, religious warriors." In a sentence, we have two potential symbols (the sword and a specific tree type), plus a generally holy area (the mountains) and possibly a specific location, assuming anyone can find the petrified tree.

This can result in pilgrimages at an interval of our choosing. While that can be a literal returning to a site, it can also be figurative when being literal is too challenging for many (due to distance, cost, etc.) or even impossible (the site is lost or destroyed). Religions make use of symbolic gestures. Instead of traveling 5,000 miles to Kier's petrified tree, perhaps someone would travel to and pray at a replica that is only 100 miles away, and which is said to have grown from seeds of the same tree or grove as the original. We've all heard of "guilt by association." Religions practice a kind of holiness by association.

That tree type is probably planted at other holy sites like churches or even the front yards of converts; sighting it while on missions might be seen as a sign from the deity. Maybe furniture is made from it, or a wooden practice sword. Priests might wear a wooden talisman of a sword around their neck. While on his journey into the Dark Peaks, perhaps our prophet survived on a kind of fruit found there. Eating this then becomes part of rituals. The juice from it can be a drink consumed only at holy times. The spilling of that juice can be seen as an offense.

What these ideas have in common is the finding of ordinary details and assigning them significance because they're part of our prophet's experience and story, either at the moment he became a prophet or in a subsequent moment from his life. Or death.

Decide how long this prophet lived and when he died. To create these, invent these details:

1. Did he die naturally?
2. If killed, who did it, why, how, and when?
3. How did the religion react to this?
4. What did the god do?

New religions are seldom met with affection by rulers, who want the hearts and minds of the population to be theirs rather than with a religion, which is often seen as competition. It is easy, natural, and believable that a prophet meets an untimely demise. Martyrdom also raises the prophets' importance, as dying for your beliefs is considered by many to be the ultimate sacrifice and proof that those beliefs are valid. A wise world builder kills their prophets. This can also result in holy sites (where they died), artifacts (based on what killed them), and rituals to commemorate the occasion. It can also create enemies, at the time or in the future, where the people who killed the prophet are long considered enemies of the religion and its followers, leading to tensions.

DESTRUCTION

A religion can cease to exist without the end of the world happening, too. In a world without real gods that interact, all we really need is people to stop believing. This is arguably one of the reasons that religions insist people believe in the god and the religion's practices. Why would they stop believing? A foretold event not happening is one reason; smart religions avoid specific dates for future events for a reason. According to Church Times (UK), individuals can lose faith at any time for a number of reasons, such as when several of the following traits are found in the person:

- If other practitioners are hard to live with
- If the religion is too hard to practice
- If the teachings are too hard to understand
- If they resist submitting to authority
- If they're above average intelligence
- If they crave experience

These can happen to someone even if the gods are real, though it begs the question of whether one gets smitten for leaving the religion.

For a religion to die, we may need nothing more than a sufficient number of people abandoning it. This can happen en masse if major life events cause inner turmoil in enough people, and the religion cannot offer comfort. Rather than having an epiphany of belief, a revelation of perceived false promises occurs instead. If the religion was a state religion, meaning a sovereign power made it official, and the state collapses, the religion can vanish, too. This might be easy for world builders to implement because destroying a sovereign power is simple; see *Creating Places*. One religion can also supplant another.

In "Creating Gods" from *Creating Life (The Art of World Building, #1)*, we discussed creating end-of-world myths. Every religion will have one. That demise may not be inevitable, which could mean that worshippers can prevent this with their conduct. Or the righteous can be saved while everyone else is damned. If we've already created that myth, what we want to decide now is how this end of world scenario makes practitioners act because this can motivate devotion to religious practices, some of which might exist to bring about a positive end for adherents. If the myth comes true, that's the end of the religion, but if a specific date was given and nothing happens, that can also end the religion due to lost credibility.

Are people expected to pray at given intervals specifically for this myth? Do they avoid certain foods or behaviors thought to bring an untimely end to themselves or the world? Religions focus on daily life and its morality much more than the end of the world, so this tends to be a background idea or connotation that is only occasionally mentioned. Or the avoidance or destruction can be part of prayers and, when recited every day or week, become familiar enough that people don't worry about it much as a practical matter.

Since destruction hasn't happened yet, we don't have the advantages that creating a religion offers. There are no artifacts, for example, or holy sites. It is therefore wise to keep the behaviors inspired by the potential end of the world simple. Incorporate them into prayers and expressions. "May Armageddon never be," characters could say, to use a name from Earth.

BELIEFS

Without beliefs, religions don't exist. There's a difference between facts and beliefs. A fact is provable and generally accepted by those who lack a bias for ignoring it. But a belief exists in the absence of proof. If we had proof, it would be a fact, not a belief. Some might debate this, but it's relevant with religions and gods because, on Earth, most of us accept that no gods are real, with the possible exception of the one God. No one believes in Zeus, right? But people once did, and when they stopped, Zeus vanished. We had invented him.

This is relevant because we should answer the question as to whether the religion is centered around a real god or an imagined one. If real, that god likely has directions he has given to the species. Or the religion is acting on its own and may have concerns about doing its deity justice, given the lack of direction. Or it may be a combination of the two. If the god is not real, none of this arises.

Using the history we've created, and the traits of the god (real or imagined), we can invent beliefs within the religion. They are typically centered on spiritual, mythological, and supernatural elements of either the deity or the religion. Here are some fundamental subjects about which to create beliefs (some may be facts if the god is real):

- Where the god originated
- What the god represents
- What the god wants of the world, his followers, and possibly his/their enemies
- How the god wants to be worshipped
- What followers must do to be accepted and remain in his good graces
- How the god rewards or punishes, and for what
- How and under what circumstances the god's power manifests in the world, including interaction with mortals and other beings

These basic ideas can result in several behaviors that come to define this religion. Religions are known for their beliefs and how its followers behave (in service of those beliefs), so this cannot be skipped while inventing one. Invent an answer for each, and much of the principal work to create a religion is done.

NAMES

A religion's name can be based on someone from its origins or a major lesson or attitude. Islam means submission. Christianity is obviously named after Jesus Christ, but the word Christ means chosen one. Buddha from Buddhism means enlightened one. We don't need to deviate from such things and can invent a word that means one of these or anything else; we may never explain it anyway. Create a word we admire and like the ring of, but ensure that a suffix can be added to create additional forms of it, like Buddhism from Buddha. Nicknames might also exist but are optional. A god of fire's religion might also be called "the burning faith." To create these, we'll need this religion well-defined. Chapter nine has many techniques for inventing names.

Followers

Becoming a Follower

Many religions have no requirement for becoming a follower. This is the easiest route for world builders as our work is essentially done. People can believe in a god or religion without ever attending church, praying, or giving outward sign of their faith. Others will do some or all of these things and become part of a community that bolsters itself through shared belief, regularly seeing each other at places of worship. None of this requires much development. But we might want a religion that requires specific acts that are witnessed before someone is allowed to officially join the church. This could include:

• Donations of money, food, or possessions
• Visible adherence to requirements for dress, prayer, food/alcohol, and more
• Missionary work to spread the word
• Sacrifice (of lifestyle or killing of something, or someone)

That list is in order of severity, and the farther down it we go, the more this religion impacts the life of the follower, since killing people can lead to the killer's imprisonment or death. Going so far can cause the individual to feel more heavily invested in their beliefs, and this degree of devotion is one reason a religion might ask such things; not only does the believer demonstrate the strength of their faith, but the extreme act, once committed, makes the belief that much stronger. The god we're creating a religion for can suggest sensible alternatives that make these decisions easier. Consider their attributes, what you'd like to achieve with this religion, and how you will use it.

LEAVING

In religions without formal admission, departure is a choice and nothing more. But in others, one might need permission to leave the church. Members might be questioned (even tortured?) to find out why they want to go. They might be banned from entry into that religion's holy sites thereafter. If a tattoo or other permanent mark was affixed upon joining, this might be altered to make them a pariah. A more benevolent religion is more lenient, naturally, and may allow for return one day, whereas a nefarious one might condemn someone to death for merely being suspected of wanting to leave.

EXPULSION

Only religions that formally accept members are likely to expel them. The obvious reasons are failure to adhere to the teachings and behaviors mandated in that religion. Being seen with those of opposing religions, or conversing with them, or having friends, lovers, or children with them, could even be considered a sin. We can invent whatever heresy makes sense for our deity, based on their attributes. The stricter the religion, the easier for this to befall someone. In the more extreme cases, the person could be put to death simply to sow fear in others, or to hide that this has occurred from outsiders (who might perceive the religion as losing its hold on people – dead men tell no tales), or simply because the deity, like a god of death, demands it.

WORSHIP

We can decide the details on how and when people worship (whether characters follow this or not). If our story doesn't need much, keep this simple. It helps to know when a priest or religious character is unavailable because they must worship somewhere at a given time, with other characters aware of this.

For location, they could use a church/mosque or shrine to worship. The former will have priests who can lead prayers. A small shrine is likely to have fewer priests, if any, and the level of formality may be lower, but shrines can be churches by another name, and their size will reflect this. A god of war might want a large, formidable structure, as a god of greed could want something ornate. We can spin this in different ways so just choose something that seems sensible for the deity.

Followers might also use their home or something in the wilderness, like a sacred grove. The latter is more likely for a nature goddess, for example, while it's a practical matter to worship from home. This can also suggest a time of day, such as morning or night. A more domineering god may be strict while a more benevolent one might not care, but this is also about the religion, and species create these, which means they might be the strict ones. We can decide that people must attend a formal worship at a given interval, such as once a week, with less formal worship expected other times.

When people pray, do they kneel or stand? If on the floor or ground, do they use a mat and what is it made of? Maybe there's a sacred kind of reed or cloth it's spun from, or it must be decorated with a symbol or color. Do people use a talisman in their prayers, like the cross or rosary beads? Things used during worship allow an easy way for enemies to defame the god, by defacing what the worshipers use, which can be as simple as stepping on it, if the bottom of the foot is considered unclean?

Some religions require fasting, which can be an interval of our choosing, such as one day a week or a period of sunrise-to-sunset for several weeks, once a year. The timing will coincide with the most holy of periods in the religion. There are advantages to the body, such as increased metabolism and improved concentration, but the reasons for religions to desire fasting is for purification of the body and, by extension, the mind and soul. The goal is often akin to seeking a god's forgiveness or a similar, humble virtue. Gods that might desire this could be those where purity or devotion seem desirable, and this can extend from food and drink to sex. Specific foods can be forbidden due to a negative association, such as that animal playing a role in a story; if the prophet was searching for his lost flock of some animal when he became a prophet (or when he died), then this can result in not only food from that animal, but fur and other products, being desired or shunned. It's possible that a god or religion could also insist on certain foods and drinks being consumed in great quantities, such as a week-long feast once a year, and smaller feasts being once a week. Sacrifice can include animal life – and that means the humanoid species, too.

Many religions have a holy text, regardless of form (book, scroll, stone tablets, iPad), but some may be oral.

Illiteracy can lead many to depend on priests, which gives them even more power. Religious songs like hymns will exist and if we'd like a character to sing a few lines, we'll need to compose a portion of it. Some songs might be in a language some characters don't understand.

HOLIDAYS

Religions can declare days or entire weeks as holy periods. Whether these are recognized by a settlement or sovereign power is another matter to be indicated in our world building files. These times will correspond to significant historical events, such as the day the prophet became one, died, or was born (or reborn). This is one reason we need history. If sacred texts or artifacts were revealed, created, developed, destroyed, or used memorably, each can be associated with a holiday. We may be developing multiple religions and can end up with a holiday every week if we're not careful. Two opposing religions can clash over a shared holiday.

Events can involve prayers on a given day(s) and at a holy that is mobbed by crowds, which can cause problems, from lack of adequate food and shelter to stampedes and accidental death. A largescale pilgrimage is likely only once a year. A commemorative event like this is based on a historical one. Leverage the history we've invented.

LOCATIONS

Not much is needed to determine the location preferences of religions, as most want to be a central point of life and therefore be present if not dominant in settlements everywhere. We can assume they prefer having a church in each. What we'll need to work out is where they are accepted, adored, despised, banned, and just tolerated. This is not a single decision for our religion template, found in the appendix, but in each settlement and sovereign power file for our world. The reason is that this will change from location to location.

What we *can* decide here is whether they have special sites. These are places where a significant act occurred. Many will have the equivalent of a small shrine or at least statue to note the location, which might be remote and unguarded; they might have supernatural or technological elements to protect these sites from vandalism. Churches can acquire mythic status due to age, rarity, uniqueness, or treasured artifacts or remains there (such as bodies of saints). Such places are easy to invent because we can state, with little justification or explanation, that it's the oldest place, or the only one with something, or lots of saints are buried there.

IDENTIFIERS

COLORS

Color can be used to indicate mood and state of mind, both of which religions hope to influence. Some Earth religions believe that achieving an enlightened state is expressed using a color for wardrobe, buildings, and decorations. This could mean that someone is expected to wear those colors at ceremonies or significant events like marriage or a life milestone. Priests of a lower rank might be denied a color like white, which is the most enlightened state because it represents all colors; a rainbow can carry the same significance.

We can put any plausible spin on a color, making it seem good or bad. For example, red is often associated with passion, sensuality, and blood. Another association would be purity (Hinduism). Most of these are good, but while blood keeps us alive, we tend to ignore this unless it's spilled, which is bad. Yellow can be associated with fire, which is good unless it's out of control, but others associate it with happiness. Blue is considered cool and soothing, but some religions find it brave and manly instead. Make it believable and our decision is taken as truth for our inhabitants.

SYMBOLS

All religions have at least one revered symbol. To create this, use an attribute of the god, a prophet, or a story involving them, their behavior, or the actions of the most prominent followers from the religion's earliest days. The average person, not a skilled artist, should be capable of drawing this symbol, which needs to be simple.

Obvious examples of attributes include a depiction of the sun for the sun goddess, a lightning bolt for a storm god, or a skull for the deity of death. We can be more creative, but expected icons are powerful and easy to remember. Practitioners want strength, clarity, and confidence, not confusion, wondering, and trying to decipher meaning. As world builders, we have other opportunities to be creative. If the god uses an item, like Thor's hammer or Poseidon's trident, these are easy choices, but a god might lead multiple religions, so if one is already using a symbol like

Thor's hammer, another is less likely to do so, or at least with a twist on it.

CLERGY

Some religions accept anyone as potential priests while others might have strict requirements. Prerequisites could include being beautiful, a virgin, or having taken a life. Some professions might be desired, like warriors, while others are forbidden. The ability to read and write is likely mandatory if the religion uses holy texts, but not if they don't exist. Some religions might require an experience like an out-of-body one, or a demonstration of the ability to communicate with the divine. Perhaps a priest must reach out to a god and receive reciprocal contact, implying that the deity has chosen them to serve. Someone might need to heal with their touch. Consider what role you'd like priests to play in the story and don't give them more demanding requirements than is necessary; if they don't need to heal, for example, then don't make that required.

A religion must typically accept a priest into it. Imagine a Catholic person declaring themselves a priest without the blessing of the church. Such a person won't be allowed to do sermons or other behaviors in a holy location and might be shunned or even imprisoned, but very informal religions can exist, with someone declaring themselves a priest. In remote areas, this can happen, and if a sovereign power's people arrive, their formal religion might declare that person a fraud. We don't need to work out how a priest gets accepted unless the detail matters, but a governing body will interview and investigate the person. A candidate may be accepted on probation.

Once accepted, most will undergo training that we don't need to develop unless featuring this in our tale. Much of it will involve administrative functions or theological interpretations that this religion teaches about a holy text, to ensure a consistent message from priests. Most religions are a bureaucracy and people start at the bottom and work their way up, meeting new requirements and gaining approval to advance. Keep it simple:

- Someone died or was transferred, and a position opened up, and they're promoted
- They reached a service requirement, such as two years in a previous role
- They performed a deed (on purpose or not) that warrants recognition/promotion

Are all genders and species treated equally as either clergy or practitioners? Are some not accepted at all, or with a reduced role? A female goddess might turn the tables and insist that males cannot attain higher positions in the priesthood. Adding this detail can cause a reputation among that religion, its followers, and those who dislike it. If a religion condemns us as bad for gender, sexuality, race, or anything else that we feel is not a choice, we're likely to disrespect the faith. Decide if your characters can benefit from the tension this adds.

IMPORTANT MEMBERS

A religion may have saints, prophets, and other religious leaders who impacted the faith, sometimes negatively with a betrayal of an oath or the god and teachings. Perhaps they went too far in pushing an agenda and either

gods or species turned on them. They could also have inspired brutal administration of policies that result in harsh
treatments. On the more positive side are those who inspire people. Create a few names, decide when they lived
and died, and what they did to earn their esteem; just have
them embody what the religion stands for, or part of it,
with a significant deed or years of adherence to the ideals.
They are a symbol. Focus on ones our characters reference
or who will appear in our work.

SECTS

A religion can have sects that disagree about interpretations of texts. Go easy on this if creating a pantheon due to
the volume of work that could result. If we have two or
more thoughts on how something could be done, use both,
assigning ideas to sects. Each will oppose the other(s) and
likely want them eradicated or drawn "into the fold," making this a good source of tension. This is especially helpful
if our world has only one god, because one religion causes
little tension, whereas multiple interpretations and doc-
trines cause conflict. Create a few incidents in the past,
ones that solidify dislike of the other(s) and exemplify and
justify the animosity.

RELATIONSHIPS

This religion, its followers, and its clergy have relationships with settlements, sovereign powers, species, and
other groups, whether that's another religion or the military. This can be a lot to work out, and most of that can be
decided on a case-by-case basis when we need it, not in

advance. Species are different and should be fleshed out in our overview of this religion. One, like humans, might be drawn to this faith while another tends to be repulsed by it. To decide this, we'll need to have a solid understanding of the species and its outlook, which includes areas of turmoil that a religion can calm. This might be one of the last things we decide for this faith because a comprehensive sense is needed to form this association.

Does the religion feel that members of a species are in particular need of their teachings? Are they known for targeting elves, for example? Elves would likely know this and possibly feel irritation or outright hostility if this is considered condescending. Exasperation with a religion is a common feeling, while bonding with those of a different one is another. Decide what's typical of a species, using their outlook, the religion's, and the story needs as a guide.

WORLD VIEW

LANGUAGES

To decide on the religion's official language, we should choose which species the prophet(s) belonged to. The other option would be the god's language, should one exist. It could also be the language of those the god most wishes to reach, which could be a species other than the prophet's. For older religions, the language could be one no longer spoken, such as Latin, which can make it unique, prized, and mysterious. Holy texts are likely written in the official language unless translated.

Choosing where this prophet became one can help determine a likely species, but arguably most religions will want to convert other species, too. If they're not considered worthy, by mortals or a god, this inclusion or exclusion will determine the availability of translations to other languages. Even if the clergy don't create them, others may. The willingness to reach others will also decide which, if any, species languages clergy are expected to know and to what degree.

PLACE IN SOCIETY

It can be difficult to generalize a religion's place in society because this will depend on the society. It might be a state religion in one place and banned in another. What we want to decide is, for places where it is accepted, what role can it play in society and the lives of individuals?

For example, it could be prominent at sporting events if the religion promotes athletics or prowess in battle. Priests could be blessing the games or acting as fair judges. If the religion helps alcoholics and others similarly afflicted, it can provide hostels or treatment for free, perhaps with backing from the settlement or sovereign power (which is paying their bills). Which religion's priests perform marriages, burial rituals, or life's milestone ceremonies? All of this will be based on the god(s) we've created and what they care about.

One reason these matter is that members of a society will think of a religion's reputation when it is mentioned, their buildings are passed, or their priests are encountered. Even the followers, if wearing the religion's symbols, can elicit a reaction, whether subtle (a frown or smile) or excessive (taunting). Arguably, every character we invent should have a religion (and might have switched in their past) or none, but there's typically a reason for the latter, such as trauma or upbringing causing loss of faith. This will, in turn, cause their reaction to their own or other religions and such details are realistic.

CUSTOMS

Invent religious customs based on a deity. A god of war might want a show of strength that results in a firm handshake. The words might be bold and decisive, such as, "Fierce is the heart!" A god of peace might wish blessings and be gentler in touch. A goddess of pain might slap a hand painfully. We can invent these beforehand or while writing. They often don't need explanation because the depiction tells the audience what they need to know. Refer to chapter 1 on creating cultures for what to invent, using the deity as inspiration.

OUTREACH

Some religions may send clergy out as missionaries early in their career; older priests are more established in the community and will be missed if sent far away. They can be inspired to do this or commanded to by clergy or deity. Are they aggressive or passive about proselyting? The same religion might be aggressive in one area and less so elsewhere due to local leadership or situations among those to be "saved" by conversion. Determine if there's a set number of years this work must be done.

COMBAT

Some religious orders forbid the use of force or carrying weapons while others have armed and trained warriors. A decision is easy for a god of war or peace, though the latter could acknowledge that people must defend themselves and that peace can be achieved through might, so we can once again put a spin on our invention. If we go with a less obvious rationale like this, we can state why with exposition or a scene like this one:

> Kier disdainfully glared at the priest, hefting his sword. "Stand aside or be cut down."
>
> The priest patted the blade slung at his waist. "My goddess may treasure peace, but she's not foolish enough to simply turn the other cheek. I know how to use this."
>
> "You had better, or you will meet her soon enough." Kier advanced only to find the priest swiftly raising a blade that clanged against his twice before his fell to the floor.

For each religion we invent, a sense of the god's impact (through clergy) on the world and our story can guide our decisions. Do we want priests to be passive and easily bossed around or do we want more strength of behavior like the one depicted just now? Decide what feels right.

When weapons are forbidden, there's often a rationale, which can be a deep part of a religion's views. With Christianity, Jesus taught about turning the other cheek, and this humility is an inherent part of every religion that is based on his teachings. With our invented religion, do we have a rationale we can use to justify a lack of violence? A god of greed might want followers to fight to gain or keep what they have, or at least see it as a practical necessity. But does a goddess of the forest feel this way? Maybe not for a long time, but if species begins decimating woodland like we've done on Earth, and all manner of non-violence has not inhibited the destruction, perhaps a change of approach is in order. Either way, don't be afraid to challenge perceptions and expectations, which on Earth lead many to assume priests are defenseless wimps.

We should also decide if priests are to accompany warriors, whether this is for war or smaller outings. This may be sanctioned, or the clergy may find themselves in this position against their will, such as trying to save a wounded soldier only to find himself and allies fighting for their own lives. Are priests members of the armed forces and what rank do they have? It is presumably not every religion, so which ones gets this role? They sometimes must also administer last rites to the dead and dying.

If we've decided they use weapons or wear armor, we should specify what they are expected to have...

WEAPONS

We should consider the effect weapons have on victims when deciding what priests are likely to use. A religion might forbid the spilling of blood and therefore suggest blunt weapons like the staff or mace. These still cause bleeding, of course, but it tends toward being internal. Blood is not only a symbol of life but also carries diseases, so whether it's symbolic or a practical matter, this viewpoint can arise. Gods of war or death might prefer its spilling and allow especially destructive weapons like hollow-point bullets. Technology allows for weapons that kill in other ways, such as radiation. Light sabers or similar laser-like weapons cauterize wounds and prevent bleeding.

Consider whether suffering is something they want to minimize or maximize. A faith might promote a swift death if it's to happen at all and prefer bladed weapons (blood loss kills in minutes verses hours or even days). Others might prefer subduing someone and train people in martial arts. Such a tactic might leave the practitioner relatively defenseless against better armed and armored opponents.

ARMOR

Priests are only likely to wear armor when sent into combat on purpose, just like everyone else. For everyday living, local hostility levels will determine the feasibility of wearing light protection. What we want to decide is, *if* they're armored, what is it? If there's a lightweight chainmail, this can be worn under robes. Leather is another option, but even knights only rarely employ plate armor, so this is less likely. In SF, we might have technological armor akin to Kevlar, and we can invent these to be light and slim. These can also absorb or resist magical, godly, or technological power (like radiation).

Decide what sorts of forces they're likely to encounter because this is what will determine the armor choice. Is there an aspect of this religion that informs the choice? For example, if leather is made from an animal that they consider unclean or sacred, then this is ruled out. If metal somehow interferes with communing with a god, so much for chain mail and the like. Armor might even be considered a barrier to being reunited with their god (through death) and therefore be frowned upon. Being creative with a choice makes this more entertaining for us and audiences. Otherwise, keep it simple.

THE AFTERLIFE

Our first decision on the afterlife is whether it's real or imagined. If it's real, then likely a god created it and the rules are incontrovertible. In this case, our religion is probably right about anything going on there or how to arrive, though having them be wrong is one way to make someone lose faith. Being right can add considerable weight to pronouncements about what one's behavior may cause. That, in turn, could inspire devotion. The question is how people learn that the priests are right and then tell people, given that they're dead?

But if the afterlife isn't real, this means a species invented it, if the concept exists. This means they're wrong, and if they're wrong about this, they probably are about other things. One aspect to consider is that, if wrong, the followers have likely tailored the concept to fit the religion and its teachings. But whether they're wrong or not, we'll craft those lessons and world view to create an afterlife that fits. If the good are rewarded and the evil punished, we only need to invent those environments to our muse.

There may be more than one afterlife, depending on how we count it. Heaven and hell can be considered two, each distinct but both arrived at by the same means: your conduct and/or faith. If each religion has more than one and we're creating a number of religions, this could become overwhelming. It might be better to have a few afterlifes that are universal (because the gods created them and they're real) and which are less tied to a religion. Either that, or a religion has a special area in an afterlife, such as Catholics and Protestants both going to heaven but having their own version or area, whether they ever meet or not.

Can people visit the afterlife while still alive? Fantasy tales are full of this trope. This is one way for the truth of it to be confirmed or compromised. Communing with the dead is another way. If an afterlife can be reached by the living, we must decide how, such as a physical or spiritual journey, one often fraught with peril. The challenges faced can have no meaning or be based upon gods or just the story we're telling and its needs for character development or plot coupons. Some of the perils can be real while the species might have invented others that either don't exist or are quite different than imagined. This can cause problems for those journeying there if they've mis-prepared based on a lie. Besides, there's less tension in a journey that goes as expected.

In Earth's history, there have been various overarching ideas on the afterlife over the centuries, the details tweaked for the times, and we can leverage any or all of them. The first three here are considered good while the others are bad:

- Paradise (heaven) – a wonderful place without needs or wants
- Ascension – becoming a higher being, such as a demigod of a trait you exemplified
- Rebirth – another life with or without memory of the previous one(s)
- Oblivion – the soul simply ends upon bodily death and that's it
- Torture (hell) – perpetual horror and pain
- Boredom – monotony unending

Finally, remember to name the afterlife(s) with a word that suggests whether they're menacing or hopeful. A great name can elevate these to being memorable, though what we decide exists in them helps, too.

WHERE TO START

After determining the god this religion follows, world builders should start with history because we can incorporate this in the invention of a religion. Almost every religion pays great attention to its beginnings. This will include historical figures that performed influential deeds, and the symbols that are crucial to it. The world view and place in society is another early subject to flesh out, as are relationships with species and which ones are typically members and/or clergy. How people worship can come next. The details of becoming a priest are an area to save for later unless we need it. Combat is perhaps the last subject to work on unless fighting is a major aspect of the religion, as with a god of war.

CHAPTER FIVE

THE SUPERNATURAL

Some could argue that a fantasy world without the supernatural isn't fantasy, but we can still consider it that if it has all the other trappings, such as fictional species and races. But in SF, we can skip the supernatural altogether and not ruffle any feathers; unexplained phenomena are considered science we don't understand. In either case, the supernatural can significantly impact the world(s) we invent, so we should look at what we can invent. Chapter Six covers magic systems and there is some overlap of subjects covered, so readers may want to peruse both.

SUPERNATURAL ENERGY

The most obvious type of supernatural energy is magic, but divine power also exists. While radiation, dark matter, and similar items that we might find in SF aren't necessarily supernatural, they can be considered this way by both us and inhabitants; this means we can invent fictional types or decide what happens when characters are exposed to those or real ones. Humans have seldom if ever been exposed to many real energies in large doses, or at least, most of us don't think we have. This allows us to do things like invent The Incredible Hulk, Spiderman, or the Fantastic Four due to exposure and audiences will believe it. As usual, plausibility is the bar to get over.

Regardless of the source or what we call it (magic, radiation, etc.), we are inventing details about:

1. Its origins
2. Its properties
3. Where it occurs
4. Whether it can be controlled and how
5. What protection against it exists
6. Past incidents involving it

Origin is an area we can skip if desired because scientists often don't know the source of an energy in the real world; it can take decades to discover this and omitting the source adds mystery. But gods are typically considered the source of their own power, while magic is thought to derive from them if they exist in our setting.

We may want to name the types of energy because inhabitants will, and it eases all references to them. SF authors can invent them or use existing radiation, like gamma rays, while inventing new effects, and fantasy authors may have even greater leeway to start fresh. Try to find a name that sounds cool or intimidating; a nickname can help and can be based on something that once happened when someone was exposed to the energy.

Decide where this energy can be found, such as only in space, in a lab, in areas prone to supernatural phenomenon, or in seemingly random places. Are there conditions that must be met before this energy is detected or surges to life? With this decided, we'll know how often it's encountered and by who. If such a location is near an elven settlement, for example, they'll probably be local experts. This can help when the energy (or something like it) is found elsewhere in our world, with that expert elf present for our story, to explain facts and suspicions to audiences and companions alike.

Inventing the properties of our energy is useful and fun to do. This includes its appearance, with invisibility being one option. Does it remind people of anything? If it looks like blue fire, there's a nickname we can use. Does it give off heat or cold? Maybe it does neither until we touch it. Can people detect it before making contact, and if so, what does it feel like? Electricity, heat, and cold are some options. How close do people need to be before they are affected, or is there a range of effects based on proximity? How intense is it at each distance? If the phenomenon is temporary, we can also decide on duration, such as it happening in a given location but each flare up is only a few minutes and maybe predictable (like "Old Faithful").

Deciding if and how this energy can be controlled is another subject for the imagination. The ability to control it may come and go. Perhaps long ago no one could, now they can, but in a nearby future, technology needed for that control will be destroyed. What if it's been brought into civilized areas and now it's out of control? Or unforeseen circumstances, such as interaction with a nearby and different energy, causing changes to its behaviors or properties? For SF, we'll invent technological devices that include weapons, defenses, and containment fields. In fantasy, this energy may be assumed to be magic unless we offer some explanation that it's different. If people can control magic with spells but not this energy, that helps distinguish the two. We may want some supernatural energy to still exist naturally so that people encounter it either by accident or on purpose.

We can add interest to this energy by inventing past incidents involving it. This can result in monsters, tall tales, myths, legends, and famous characters that may provide a cautionary tale. These can be as short as a few sentences tossed into our narrative, like this:

Nasha blanched at the idea of passing through the Nifling Hills on the way to Illiandor. "Isn't that where Olian the Fool had half his face burned off?"

Kier nodded at the legend. "They say the flames got him, if you believe that story."

"You don't?"

"Blue Fire coming out of the ground without warning? Seems far-fetched."

A template in the appendix can assist with the invention of supernatural energies.

MAGIC PATHS

In some fantasy settings, there's an alternate way of traveling that amounts to magical paths, which may have a corresponding magical doorway for access. Using these paths offers an advantage accompanied by great risk. A common advantage is much faster travel, which can help story issues when we need them to get somewhere faster than possible. The usual dangers are nasty and dangerous things one might encounter, whether living, dead, or inanimate (and possibly supernatural). This adds adventure, as well.

Other people could be walking these paths, posing another risk. Maybe they (or our characters) are lost and have been so long that this place has changed them, whether actual mutation or desperation leading to mind-sets they've never had or acts they wouldn't normally commit. Do they prey on travelers for survival? The normal rules of physics sometimes don't exist in these places, such as time moving differently.

In the real world, a path leads through and around other locations. We can invent these within this supernatural landscape, from buildings like castles, homes, and magical towers, to land features like forests, rivers, and mountains, all with supernatural properties or life within them. If we create enough sufficiently interesting places, they can become another reason people enter this land, to acquire something found within, rather than to travel through it. Perhaps wizards can find rare items to use in their spells, or send someone else to fetch them; this is the basis for my free novella, *The Ever Fiend (Talon Stormbringer, #1)*.

The doorways into this other world can be wholly supernatural or physical with supernatural properties. They may be located in places that are inherently dangerous or which have become that way due to being guarded by something, or that territory being controlled by something nefarious. Consider naming not only this supernatural land but the doorways. Inventing an origin is optional but helps with realism and our invention of additional details. An obvious source for a supernatural land is the gods. Omitting an origin adds to the place's mystery, though we might want to decide in our files and withhold the revelation from an audience.

A template in the appendix can assist with the invention of supernatural lands.

ALTERNATE REALITIES

Most of us have probably seen an alternate reality depicted, especially in SF. There used to be a TV show called *Sliders* where, in every episode, the characters were forced into an alternate reality from Earth. These variations can be easy to create. All we need to do is make some changes that have a significant impact, even if the average person doesn't realize the influence it would have (until reading our story). For example, on Earth, what if the Nazis had won WWII? What if we'd never invented GPS? What if global warming has raised the sea level by ten feet?

These examples are extreme, but we can do variations that impact fewer people, such as just our main characters. One who is married in one reality is not in another, or is a parent, or lost a sibling in a way that affected their outlook. When we've developed backstory for a character (to shape who they are), and then we want an alternate reality for them, we can change the backstory. We're trying to change who they are by presenting them with an alternate view of themselves or their life, one that causes them to question their choices or even their personality in their own reality.

SUPERNATURAL BEINGS

DEMI-GODS

A chapter from *Creating Life (The Art of World Building, #1)* covered the creation of gods and pantheons in detail, but here we'll cover lesser beings: the demi-gods.

The term can mean many things, so for our purposes, we're discussing any supernatural being that has less power than gods but is in some way related to them, and works with them in some capacity. They are often the offspring of gods or a human who has been given divine powers or rank. Some, like Hercules, are the result of a human (or another species, even an animal) mating with a god. The term would include angels and demons on Earth.

In mythology, demi-gods often serve a specific purpose, such as being a messenger of the gods. As world builders, this means we can invent someone when we need them for our story, though we may want a few of them in advance. Such a universally used character, as the messenger, might get more frequent use and mention by us and our world's inhabitants. On the other hand, a figure like Cupid only comes up in love scenarios. For these beings, we need little more than a name and function until we show them in a tale. This means they're easy to create and flesh out later. Decide if any are needed. Here are a few roles they can play:

1. Harbinger of doom
2. Harbinger of love
3. Harbinger of good
4. Messenger

Other figures can be invented when we need them, though it helps to hint at their existence beforehand so that it doesn't seem too convenient that just the right one has popped up when our story needed it.

If we invent half-gods, meaning they have a mortal (i.e., human or other species) parent, too, decide on their abilities, which don't need to come directly from the divine parent. Deriving talent from the divine parent makes it easier to decide who their divine parent was, but there's an idea that talent skips a generation, for example. I have musical talent and so does at least one of my kids, but neither of my parents do, though a grandparent had some. When we invent these half-gods, we are implying that deities have sexual relations with mortals. Does that conform to the view we've developed of their relations?

CREATURES

In *Creating Life*, we discussed both animals and monsters, so these won't be covered here, but we can take any of them and add supernatural elements.

We don't always need to decide where a creature originated, but it helps us determine everything else we need to invent for it. Under circumstances we invent, predetermined sources of energy can give rise to this creature. Having decided where such energy is available helps us establish a physical point of origin. How and even if our creature relocates can also add believability. Does it need a new habitat due to the way its body now functions? Perhaps it can't abide certain temperatures or other environmental issues, or just craves a specific environment now and adapts its habitat accordingly.

The creature's physical properties and capabilities are often linked, though they needn't be. What changes can we make to its appearance based on its supernatural abilities? Perhaps there are marks on the skin that react to external stimuli. That said, it can be advantageous to have this creation externally indistinguishable from the source; that allows for surprises when they prove to be other than they appeared. Decide on whether this subterfuge is helpful. If not, pair the skill to the body, such as ears that can move in odd ways because their hearing is superior, or eyes that look different (color, pupil shape, etc.) because their vision is altered.

FIGURES OF NOTE

Earth mythologies are full of interesting characters that are not gods or humans. This includes Charon, who ferries souls across the rivers Styx and Acheron. There's Cerberus, the three-headed dog in Greek mythology, who prevents the dead from leaving Hades. For ideas, all we need to do is look at other mythologies. We may want to start with a role or job function, which will also give us a location this individual occupies, and its characteristics. If the River Styx has properties we've already invented, and effects on people, then our version of Charon might be able to control or counteract these for at least himself.

The gods are often the source of such figures, who arguably need their approval to perform the function they serve. But these figures can come from any source, such as supernatural accidents before they are put to the use they now serve. A god may be the only one who can control it, possibly using a device that can fall into the wrong hands. Other times, an individual from a species or race might have been transformed into this figure, possibly due to their devotion to an idea that the god agrees with. For example, Charon could believe that everyone must be judged upon death and was so fervent about this in life that Hades assigned him to transporting souls. This gives such a character an attitude that can be revealed while interacting with our characters.

SUPERHEROES

We may not think of cartoon characters like Spiderman or the X-men as supernatural beings, but they're close. Most of us would agree that they have supernatural abilities though not intrinsically supernatural. There are few limits on using these elements to transform them if it's credible. What happened to them, when, why, and how did it affect them physically? Decide how much control they have over their skills at the point of the story that they'll be used. Like any character, they need backstory, just one with extra information.

FAMILIARS

Another supernatural being is the "familiar" of wizardry. They originate in medieval folklore and were though to assist witches, or perhaps in our case, wizards, including protecting them, whether that means physically or scouting and warning. They may also possess specialized knowledge, particularly of a different plane of existence. They are usually in the form of a small animal and appear corporeal rather than ghostly, though we're free to do either. We can make them invisible to others, too. Whether they're considered good or evil depends on who they serve; they might be considered fairies or demons. Familiars are sometimes given as a gift, or appear when someone is alone or in trouble, after which they are bonded from weeks to decades.

PREVALENCE

Throughout this chapter, we've touched on the idea that supernatural elements may only sometimes be available for our characters to encounter. This is true for beings and energies that might exist all the time but only periodically flare up in a given location. However, we also need to decide how prevalent the supernatural is generally in our setting. Do we want a world that is mostly like Earth in the medieval ages with a little bit of magic? This is a default depiction found in fantasy.

Or do we want a setting where the supernatural is as common as electricity is in Earth's modern times? This will have a significantly greater impact on the world and our story. If we want this, we can benefit from reading fantasy works where others have already thought through this impact and given us ideas. Otherwise, we'll have to do a mental deep dive into questioning everything about everyday life. This can be an exhausting exercise due to the sheer number of modifications we'll envision, but it can be well worth it; we'll look more at this in the next section.

The prevalence includes attitudes about the supernatural. People fear the unusual, but even the deadliest phenomena can elicit indifference if it's commonplace. If we are used to harnessing and controlling the supernatural, this can also lead to complacency about its dangers. This correlation is built-in; we just need to be aware of it and make a note in our files about it. If the supernatural is everywhere, only someone traumatized by it is likely to react strongly to its use.

THE IMPACT

The influence that the supernatural has on a setting can be enormous unless the supernatural is rare. In fantasy, places are often presented as if they're medieval-like with a smattering of wizardry thrown in. Theoretically, this only makes sense if magic can only be performed by a small group of people. By contrast, if everyone is capable of performing a degree of magic, this would impact society, depending on the nature of this magic and what people can do with it.

Let's imagine a world where most people can perform simple spells. First, we should define what is meant by "simple." There are many options, but what if we can move small objects? Wouldn't we use this ability to clean our homes? Who wouldn't like the ability to cast a spell or two and have everything put back in its place and wiped down? This could eliminate the entire housekeeping industry, plus the tips we leave after a hotel stay (unless we're too lazy to cast the spells and hire people to do it for us). What if we can cast a spell to prepare food? This might eliminate the restaurant business and the concept of dining out. But maybe some recipes are too complicated and only people with more power can pull them off; restaurants and "chefs" still exist. If I can cast a spell to style and color my hair, then I never need to visit a barber, eliminating another industry, unless, once again, some choices are too advanced for me. If we can cast a spell to dress ourselves, perhaps we have no wardrobe, or closets in our house, and there's no such thing as department stores. In a world where all of this is possible, does anyone even have a job?

If we can make food for ourselves, do we have it have it appear on a plate or right into our mouth? Why not go one step further and have it in our stomach? Imagine how easy it would be to lose weight if we could transport the food into our stomach and bypass the tyranny of the tongue that tempts us to each too much due to loving the taste. We could use magic to brush or repair/replace our teeth, eliminating the dentistry profession.

A more advanced spell might be teleporting between locations, which would eliminate the need for vehicles and parking, not to mention fuel. But it might cause other problems, such as someone appearing in our bathroom when we're not wearing anything. Perhaps there's a law against such a thing, or spells to prevent that by protecting a certain room. We would have no need of roads either. This would suggest that the path between one home and another is grass or whatever naturally grows there, if anything. This also makes it possible to have a house in unusual locations, assuming one can be built there, because getting to it isn't an issue. Magic can be used to construct one and there's no issue with builders needing to reach our chosen spot. Maybe magic can be used to alter the shape of a home, or simply move the entire house from one location to another. That might make finding someone difficult unless there is something in the house that acts like a location beacon, which can be turned on and off for privacy so that no one can find us if we don't want them to.

This thought exercise can get us thinking about how just magic, not to mention other supernatural issues, can influence life. What if supernatural creatures can appear at any time? How would this change us and our environments? If the gods can appear and smite us, then would anyone swear with a god's name? If there are magic paths available and a doorway near us, do we purposely live farther away so that nothing nasty comes out and wreaks havoc on us? How do people compensate for the existence of each supernatural element in our world, and are these issues positive, negative, or a little of both? We must decide the prevalence of each element and where it occurs.

We should also consider the limits on each, including the toll that performing magic takes on people. Are there restrictions, and are they natural or imposed by laws or preventive measures that others have taken? For example, if I can teleport myself, then, in theory, I can send you somewhere as well. Presumably, this is frowned upon when done without your permission. But if there were no witnesses, how can someone prove that I sent you somewhere? Is there a class of police investigators who can determine what happened? If not, then what's to stop me from teleporting myself somewhere and claiming that you did it, getting you arrested (if that's a crime)?

Unless we want to invent an entire system of laws and methods to investigate crimes of magic, we may decide that teleporting another person is not possible, for example, or go one step further and decide that magic has limitations to prevent this from happening. This seems to be the default approach for many world builders, and it works when those limits exist. The problem is when everyone can do some magic and we haven't considered how this would realistically change a setting.

We can't cover every scenario here, but these examples should get us thinking about how much impact the supernatural has on our world and what elements can be eliminated, altered, or replaced by it.

WHERE TO START

When we start inventing the supernatural, we should determine how large an impact we'd like this to have on the setting and stories. This determines the prevalence and character reactions or ability to manipulate. Elements can be developed independently of one another, so that there's no particular order to follow. Don't be afraid to revisit ideas to see how they hold up, and try connecting them to other elements we've invented in the meantime.

CHAPTER SIX

MAGIC SYSTEMS

Some may assume that only fantasy settings involve magic, but SF can have it, too. There's a tendency to assume worlds have one or the other, which begs the question of what happens when planet-hopping SF characters land on one without technology, but magic instead? Regardless, world builders will know if they need or want magic for a world. If so, read on. But before we invent spells or systems of magic, we should understand our options and some theories.

PRINCIPLES OF GOOD MAGIC SYSTEMS

Before creating a magic system, we should consider some guiding principles.

SANDERSON'S THREE LAWS

Author Brandon Sanderson once proposed three laws of magic that we'll examine for perspective. Any quotes in this section are directly from his website, brandonsanderson.com, unless otherwise stated, with the rest paraphrased.

Sanderson's first law is "an author's ability to solve conflict with magic is *directly proportional* to how well the reader understands said magic." Try not to give characters abilities unless we've already shown they possess them. Determine how problems can be solved without magic or within the system, before altering it. And if we do change it, don't give them abilities that perfectly solve their problem. Breaking this law can make magic too convenient.

Sanderson's second law is: "limitations are greater than powers." What characters can't do forces them to stretch and forces our story in other directions. This adds dimension, depth, and tension, so we gain more with limits than we do by granting powers that just resolve everything.

Sanderson's third law is: "expand what you already have before you add something new." We can make our system too complicated if we're adding new elements rather than refining what we have. We also run the risk of contradiction when the goal for our characters might be achievable with an expansion of our current system.

SOFT MAGIC VS HARD MAGIC

Sanderson also discussed what he calls soft vs. hard magic. In his view, soft magic is not rigidly defined (if defined at all), allowing for authors to "preserve the sense of wonder in their books." By not explaining how magic works, we feel a sense of amazement because we don't understand how it works or what is possible. It is mysterious and exciting, but also dangerous and unpredictable. It adds tension. Authors who use such systems don't let magic solve problems for their characters, who seem like a small part of a vast world that can overwhelm them with its power.

By contrast, in hard magic, "the author explicitly describes the rules of magic." We identify what it can do and what it can't. Therefore, when a character needs to do something, we aren't surprised by their ability (or lack thereof). Though it's a comic book character, his example of Spiderman is a good one: we already know his abilities and simply accept it when he uses one of them, but he doesn't acquire new abilities on the spur of the moment. He has to use the tools we've already defined.

Sanderson also talks about a middle ground, where some things are defined but others aren't, allowing for flexibility and that feeling of mystery that soft magic allows, while also providing the structure and understanding that hard magic gives.

What's a Law?

Sanderson's use of the word "law" led me on an interesting thought exercise that adds clarity to creating magic systems. According to Merriam-Webster's The Third New International Dictionary, "Law is a binding custom or practice of a community; a rule or mode of conduct or action that is prescribed or formally recognized as binding by a supreme controlling authority or is made obligatory by a sanction (as an edict, decree, rescript, order, ordinance, statute, resolution, rule, judicial decision, or usage) made,

recognized, or enforced by the controlling authority."
Laws are authoritative, definitive, to the point, and arguably avoid explanation to minimize public arguments when accused of breaking one.

By calling his principles "laws" and asserting that there are three of them, Sanderson invokes comparison to Isaac Asimov's famous Three Laws of Robotics. However, Asimov's laws were invented for specific stories and societies described in those stories, meaning they are actual laws there. By contrast, Sanderson has proposed three laws for building magic systems. But no world builder is beholden to another's ideas on this (and he admits he does not intend that). His laws do not apply to any society, invented physics/limitations, world builders, or even stories. He cannot enforce them except on himself, which applies to us: we can choose what to enforce on ourselves.

Sanderson's laws are restated here as a single sentence for comparison. None are declarative and each leaves room for interpretation:

1. "An author's ability to solve conflict with magic is *directly proportional* to how well the reader understands said magic."
2. Limitations are greater than powers.
3. "Expand what you already have before you add something new."

LOCAL LAWS

Compare those to the following laws I invented for this section. These are laws that might exist in a city or sovereign power, both of which have authority to impose and enforce laws. They are designed to instruct people on what's permitted and when. We might craft something similar for localities.

1. Magic shall not be performed within the city limits except within designated areas or by those holding a valid permit.
2. Magic shall not be used to inflict physical harm or death on a living being except in defense of one's own life or that of another.
3. Magic shall not be performed on the Holy Day.

LAWS OF MAGIC

What about laws of magic? These would delineate what is possible and what isn't, due to the equivalent of physics for magic, like nature's "laws," such as the law of gravity. These would be *discovered* and defined by the species through experience and observation of what [usually] works and what doesn't. Here are some examples:

1. Black Magic and White Magic cannot be performed by the same wizard.
2. Magic cannot be performed by virgins.
3. Magic can only be performed by spells, or by items imbued with spells.
4. Wizards of the Moon must be exposed to two hours of moonlight each night to perform Moon Magic between then and the next moonrise.

WORLD BUILDING LAWS

What about laws that world builders should follow when creating a magic system? This is what Sanderson intended. These are ones that will impact the storytelling we do and what local laws and laws of magic we design; as such, they should come first in our work. The next section has my thoughts on this.

ELLEFSON'S SEVEN LAWS

World builders can choose to enforce any, all, or none of my laws for creating magic systems for themselves. These laws are not about how to use a magic system once created, but how to create those systems. Most are self-explanatory with a single sentence, but a few words follow each. Some include examples, which are not meant to build upon each, but rather offer possibilities and world building prompts. Use these ideas as guidance for what we should do to craft a magic system.

FIRST LAW

World builders shall decide what the laws of magic are.
The universe (or another authority such as gods) has determined what works and what doesn't, and under what conditions. This should be defined for all magic types.
Examples:

1. Spells are required.
2. Magic can be performed at-will like a god.

3. There is a finite amount of magic energy and once consumed, it is gone.
4. Naturally occurring places exist where magic doesn't work.
5. With rare exceptions, a wizard can only perform one type of magic and they do not get to choose.
6. Elves cannot perform elemental magic.

SECOND LAW

World builders shall define what makes someone capable of performing each magic type, and how common practitioners are.

Examples:

1. Anyone born with the talent can perform magic. These people are rare.
2. The gods decide who can do magic and can grant or revoke ability at will.
3. Anyone who consumes a specific item with a specific frequency acquires the ability as long as said item continues to be consumed.
4. Witchcraft requires a deal with Satan. Witches are common.
5. A near-death experience is required to become a shaman. Shamans are rare.
6. Consumption of alcohol eliminates the ability to perform magic for several days.

THIRD LAW

If multiple types of magic exist, world builders shall define what is possible in each, the differences between them, and whether practitioners can perform more than one type (and under what circumstances).

Short examples (yours should be much more in depth):

1. There are two types of magic, with most practitioners relegated to one type:
   a. Low magic: only simple spells to assist daily living (like cantrips)
   b. High magic: all higher level, more powerful spells
2. There are several magic types:
   a. Alchemists: can only work with materials to affect personal change
   b. High wizardry: can draw on magic energy in the environment
   c. : must work with spirits or demons for power

FOURTH LAW

World builders shall determine what happens when an attempt to use magic fails.

Examples:

1. A spell either works within its parameters or fails. There are no accidental results.
2. A failed spell will visibly/invisibly release gathered energy chaotically/safely.

3. A failed spell traps gathered energy within the caster's body until released

4. A failed spell produces an unexpected result of a different nature but not extremely so.

5. Magic (done without spells) energy is safely released back to its source when the casting fails.

FIFTH LAW

World builders shall decide what local laws exist in each location where a story takes place.

Examples:

1. Alchemists must register with the local guild.
2. Wizards must surrender their staves upon entering the city limits.
3. Only valend wizards may create magic items.
4. Only those with a valid permit may use magic items within city limits.
5. Wizards will be killed on sight.
6. Necromancy is forbidden except within 48 hours of the deceased's burial.
7. Wizards are not allowed on the city council.
8. Those accused of witchcraft must identify another witch to avoid execution.
9. Unlicensed mindreading, without written permission from the subject, is illegal.
10. Public sources (such as the water well, torches, etc.) are not to be used for elemental magic.
11. Elemental wizards who do not participate in resolving a public crises (like a flood or fire) are to be sentenced to one year's hard labor.

SIXTH LAW

World builders shall follow the rules they set forth.

This rule applies to all world building, not just magic systems. Fantasy and SF audiences are adept at noticing our mistakes, so keep a list of all rules and abide by them. It can be best to narrate a rule with some flexibility. For example, "*most* wizards cannot do so-and-so." One trick is to narrate the law this way: "people said wizards couldn't do so-and-so." That makes it popular opinion, not a statement of fact. Another trick is to have a character, not the narrator, state a law. Characters don't always get things right, so when our story proves them wrong, it's not the author breaking our rule. However, do this on purpose. Why would we want to? Because we might want to suggest something to the reader, and then surprise them later, but it must be a good surprise. It is effective when a character finding out the truth protests that another character told them so; this also channels the audience's potential upset into acceptance.

SEVENTH LAW

For each location, world builders shall decide if magical training is available, what form it takes, what is involved, limitations imposed before graduation, testing criteria, and what restrictions if any exist on those who graduate.

This one is more of a suggestion; not doing so is unlikely to cause problems, while doing it will almost certainly benefit us. Examples:

1. Training is only available via an apprenticeship where sanctioned by the sovereign power

2. Wizards must pass the Kierdyn Test by the third attempt or have magic ability suppressed for life
3. Prior to graduation, only low magic spells can be performed outside the guild
4. Wizards are tested for the ability to release magic energy safely

DO WE NEED A MAGIC SYSTEM?

Creating a magic system is about organization; without it, we don't have a "system." The problems with an on-the-fly approach are numerous, one of the biggest being inconsistency. Readers are astute. If rules prohibit a character from doing something at one point, and we have them do it (or something similar) later, in defiance of that rule, readers will notice. This can happen due to forgetfulness and not writing down any spontaneously invented rules. We also sometimes imply a rule without realizing we've done so, only to break it later. And breaking our own rules makes it apparent we don't know what we're doing.

Another problem is giving people the ability to solve something with magic right when they need it. Deus ex machina is considered poor storytelling. If we want to do this, we shouldn't make the magical solution perfect. If they need to go fifty miles, make the spell only transport them forty miles, depositing them somewhere that presents new issues. Perfect solutions eliminate conflict, which is the heart of any story. Having a system helps us create limits. Without a system, it's harder to contrast multiple styles or types of magic. Each should have its rules, limits, benefits, and problems. The point of a system is to decide who can do what and under which circumstances, bringing order to the potential chaos of magic being everywhere and there being no limits.

But we don't always need a system. If we're writing a short story, we're less likely to break rules, for example, because our tale will end before we can. The longer a work is, or the more times we'll use the setting, the more we need a system. And if magic is very prevalent, we'll need a system to impose limits and be realistic; without one, we're at greater risk of inconsistency and mistakes. But if magic is rare or a minor part of a story, we may do well enough without one.

TYPES OF MAGIC

When most of us think of magic, we mean wizardry unless indicating a subtype as described in this section. Wizardry is broadly defined as the harnessing of magical energy, using any combination of words, gestures, and components (aka ingredients), with practitioners in a robe, wielding a staff, and being of advanced age; all of these clichés are best avoided.

Once we define types of magic, we begin breaking them into groups that people can perform or not. What follows is a high-level discussion of several types, but more can be found with an internet search. There are specialized forms of magic that other world builders have imagined, which are public domain, and which we might want to include in a setting in addition to anything we devise.

When deciding on our needs, we should consider how many people can perform each type of magic and why that is. Rarity means more valuable and feared. The specialists in this section are just that and can be treated as less available unless setting and story requires a lot of them. The next chart lists reasons for magic being rare or common.

Reasons for Rarity	Reasons for Commonplace
It's dangerous	It's safe
It's feared	It's accepted
Practitioners are feared	Practitioners are admired
Training is unavailable, limited, hard, or costly	Training is available, easy, and inexpensive
Materials needed to perform it are hard to acquire	Materials are plentiful
Spell books are rare or poor	Spell books are common and good
Talent is rare	Talent is common
There's no money in it	It's lucrative
Family and friends shun you	Family and friends are not impacted

Figure 10 Magic Rarity Chart

For each magic type in our setting, we can mix and match commonplace and rarity, such as making the talent or spell books common, the magic dangerous, and the materials rare. Such variations make our worlds more believable and help distinguish types from each other.

WHITE AND BLACK MAGIC

Magic can either be beneficial or harmful to others and the environment. These are referred to as white and black magic, respectively. We can also think of them as good and evil, possibly associating them with good and evil beings (gods, demons, etc.) as the provider of each. This can mean that a wizard aligns himself with a deity, who might have requirements for behavior and their mental or spiritual state. A white wizard might need to be noble, benevolent, and kind, for example, and perform mostly for the benefit of others (rather than the self) or access to the power fails.

Black magic may include voodoo with its hexes, curses, poisons, and association with zombies. What must a black magic wizard be like or do regularly? Sacrifice animals or people? Sow discord? Black magic is considered bad due to being used for selfish or evil purposes. In popular culture, practitioners are feared and shunned not only for their practices, but what those practices say about them as people. This is a convenient way to characterize someone.

Those with a poor understanding of either may confuse someone doing white magic with one doing black magic; this trope has been used with witches, where all are branded evil due to ignorance and fear of their practices, reputation, or appearance. Other types of magic in this section can be considered black, such as necromancy or shamanism, but this often results from ignorance about the practices. People fear what they don't understand, and we can cause conflict by including magic practitioners that act, dress, or talk strangely or secretively (even if for good reasons). For all magic types, consider dividing them along this good vs. evil axis. Another option is "grey magic" that lies between these extremes.

ALCHEMY

Alchemy is the practice of turning one material into another, usually an ordinary item to a valuable one, such as lead into gold. While this is not possible on Earth, it might be in a world we invent. The practice held other goals of interest, such as creating healing potions, an elixir of immortality, or a universal solvent that can dissolve anything (called an alkahest). If you've ever wondered why the British edition of the first Harry Potter book is titled *Harry Potter and the Philosopher's Stone*, this refers to a legendary item that combines all of these powers and which was the ultimate goal of an alchemist.

The morphing of material is thought to be an analogy for personal transformation into a better, purer state, meaning alchemy is considered a spiritual matter, not just physical. We could see alchemists as a cross between the wizards and priests of our world. The transmutation of specific materials can be thought to cause specific changes within a person, and we have leeway to invent these. For example, if I turn a piece of lead in your hand to gold, perhaps I've made your spirit more noble and high-minded, too. Maybe this can reform a criminal, and the opposite can be done to someone pompous, like an absolute dictator. Or maybe the impact is to make you more knowledgeable, or change your desire or aptitude for learning rather than outright granting knowledge.

Due to the power inherent in these changes, alchemists guarded their knowledge so that any written information was done in a language only they understood or which had a cypher to obscure understanding. Their books and scrolls could be quite cryptic. Most were trying to create the aforementioned stone, a project known as the "magnum opus," which in ancient times had four stages, each associated with a color, the final state being the goal of personal development via alchemy. In later times, these were expanded, but the original four stages, each with a spiritual or psychological aspect achieved through the listed physical transformation, were:

1. Nigreo (blackening): facing one's internal demons, through a cleansing and decomposition/putrefaction of the base material.
2. Aledo (whitening): achieving an awakened, receptive soul, caused by purification.
3. Citrinitas (yellowing): achieving wisdom (in one's soul), by the transmutation of moonlight to sunlight (silver to gold).
4. Rubedo (reddening): discovering and attaining one's true nature in body, mind, and soul.

Alchemy has an advantage over magic for writers; magic is often thought to be only physical manipulation to achieve a physical result. By contrast, alchemy achieves change within the self or others by transmutation of physical objects that represent something. As authors and audiences enjoy symbolism, this makes alchemy useful in adding meaning to an alchemist's behaviors. It's a missed opportunity to portray one as solely wanting to become rich by changing lead to gold, for example.

Adopt symbols to represent these stages. On Earth, birds have often been used to represent the progression. This includes the phoenix, already known for its transformation. The colors are sometimes emblazoned on the clothing of those interested in achieving a higher state. We can add both symbols and colors to anything, including government buildings, homes, or institutions that consider themselves to be in pursuit of enlightenment.

WITCHCRAFT

While we all know what's typically meant by witchcraft, also known as witchery, the term is a broad one.

Both white and black magic interpretations exist on Earth. It can mean using the supernatural to cause harm or be more beneficial such as divination. Using spirits for these practices is assumed to be dangerous and possibly evil; there is an assumption that spirits who have not gone to the afterlife, or are willing to be contacted by the living, must be nefarious. This rises from fear, ignorance, and lack of comfort with all of it, with people assuming the worst about what these spirits and those contacting them are capable of.

Pagans have often been considered witches, which has led to many associations, such as full or partial nudity, being barefoot, wearing loose and flowing clothing, chanting, singing, and dancing in the woods to conjure spirits, typically at night and during specific moon phases. The celebration of basic natural elements can be seen as championing base human needs and instincts like sex. This combination, along with fear, leads to the assumption of copulation with the devil or similar figures as a means of gaining supernatural powers.

One practice common to witchcraft is the use of archaic runes or symbols inscribed on a target, such a person, building, or item that is the spell's focus. Another is a poppet, a figure made of wax or clay to represent another person, with the spell cast on this. Incantations differ slightly from speech in other magic types in that they are often chanted or sung rather than simply spoken, sometimes specific actions being taken at moments within the incantation, rather than there being no coordination. Witchcraft that involves scrying often makes use of reflective materials such as a mirror, blade, or scrying ball. This reliance on a material, the existing properties of which offer some aid, helps distinguish witchery from other magic types.

As with necromancy, we should understand the afterlife in our world if any interaction with the dead is to take place. And if beings like demons are to be communed with, we'll benefit from having worked out places like Hell, where they dwell. The rules we've devised for such places can impact the rules we craft for witches and others to interact with the beings there.

NECROMANCY

Magic that involves the dead is called necromancy, which can be its own type of magic in our world. Communication with the dead means understanding how the afterlife works. After all, if spirits are simply obliterated, bringing one back or interacting with it is impossible. The nature of an afterlife might also aid or inhibit the recruitment with or contacting of the dead. Would a Satan-like figure make that contact easier so that more hell is loosed upon the Earth? Would a God-like figure inhibit it? Or would God allow interaction because it might be benevolent? Having a justification and multiple barriers can make scenarios more plausible.

Communication can mean the equivalent of a long-distance phone call; the spirit never leaves where it resides. This seems easier than summoning the spirit to cross boundaries; this is where inventing afterlife barriers figures more. A third option is raising a body from the dead and restoring the soul into it, a more intense experience for both necromancer and victim. This is especially true if the target does not become undead but a living person once again. By dividing these concerns this way, we can begin creating a system of magic for necromancy.

We should also understand what death has been like, as this impacts the mind or emotions of anyone thus contacted. That, in turn, will affect behavior, including how cooperative they are, though perhaps our necromancer can force obedience – at least until he's incapacitated and the undead either get free and go their own way, return to the land of the undead, or take revenge upon the necromancer who awoke them into servitude.

We can decide that the undead have acquired unlimited knowledge, increasing their value, or only have firsthand knowledge as in life. The Roman poet Ovid speculated that an underworld marketplace exists where undead exchange news and gossip, which not only expands what undead know, but creates a place where the living can travel. Perhaps knowledge isn't the only item traded.

THEIR PRACTICES

Necromancer rituals can last for hours, days, or even weeks, and sometimes use moon phases or the placement/configuration of other heavenly bodies. These often take place in or near graveyards, tombs, and mausoleums, though the churches of evil deities are an option. While words, gestures, or materials might be involved, these rituals often involve a circle drawn in blood, holy water or an equivalent, salt, or writing. These serve to protect the practitioner from possession, assault, death, kidnapping, and more, from the very forces they seek to control, which are a threat to their lives and soul. These circles can also concentrate magic power where the target dead will be imprisoned after summoning; bringing a potentially malignant being to this realm is inherently dangerous and unpredictable, making this precaution wise.

Sacred talismans, relics of the dead, and body parts such as bones may be involved, whether worn, laid on circles or altars, or used during gestures. They could be mutilated, incinerated, or otherwise destroyed, which naturally means they can't be reused, which places emphasis on success the first time. Placing a limit adds urgency that benefits stories. The practitioner may be wearing the deceased's clothes or an item that held importance to them.

Foods that symbolize death, and fluids like blood, are often present. These are consumed by either the necromancer or enthralled spirits. We can invent a reason for this, such as giving a spirit more substance and therefore power over a world of which they are no longer a part. Perhaps consuming it binds them to the world, to the necromancer, or to do the deed for which they're now recalled. Can the necromancer force them to consume it?

A more extreme practice involves sacrifice, which could be an item, animal or human (or other species). This might mean a life or the soul, too. The victim could be the infamous virgin, but an excuse for this might help alleviate this cliché to something more palatable. If we state that innocence, more than virginity, can counter the evil forces involved in necromancy, or fool a guardian of the underworld into letting our necromancer access a spirit by suggesting we have pure intentions, this concept makes more sense. Youth also seems plausible for younger people's strength, but a baby has little, so a teenager might be ideal.

Shamanism

In shamanism, the shaman communicates with spirits or other beings believed to be in another plane of existence, one that intersects with ours. It often involves an altered state of consciousness achieved through meditation, trace, or hallucinogenic drugs. In SF, we might choose to inject something or more advanced technology such as

direct brain stimulation or implants, but in less technological settings, we're likely using liquids (drinks), solids
(food), gas (to be inhaled), meditation and ritual, or a
combination. Shamans experience dreams or visions that
have messages, but they can also physically, or more commonly, spiritually enter a spiritual realm. A shaman may
also try to bring energies from the spirit world into his
own. That there can be benevolent and malevolent spirits
adds danger and unpredictability to shamanism.

Within a culture or village, different shamans can exist,
specializing in specific functions. We can divide these as
we wish. Some functions include healing, communicating,
fortune-telling, leading souls to their rightful afterlife
place, or keeping traditions alive by knowing and relating
stories that teach, instruct, and bring the community together. Reasons for such divisions can include the difficulty or danger inherent in certain tasks. Perhaps a younger
and physically stronger shaman should do certain things,
or if a shaman dies performing a function, only some of
their knowledge dies with them because other shamans
perform other duties. Another shaman can always contact
them in the afterlife for that information, assuming another can do it.

To become a shaman, someone is expected to become
so sick as to risk death, and possibly die, before returning
to life. This will assist their ability to access the after-
life/underworld. The thought is that, to understand sickness and heal others from ailments, they must have
experienced something as severe first. It should come as
no surprise that some would-be shamans don't survive.
Others might be scarred physically or another way from
the ordeal, though being of sound-mind and not having "a
demon" would be required; if they haven't healed their
mind/soul from the ordeal, how can they do so for others?

A spirit guide may help a shaman, who can acquire more than one. These acts as guides, messengers, or protectors. As world builders, we can choose the form and power a guide may take, including animals of our invention. These spirit guides can lend strength to the shaman on his journey and even provide the power needed to enter the spirit realm. The guide's form, such as a duck, is sometimes chosen as one that is comfortable both below and above water (including flying), which symbolizes the ability to navigate both the normal world and underworld.

GOALS

The goals of shamanism vary but include:

- Communication
- Divination
- Bringing otherworldly forces into ours
- Healing

Communication with the undead allows access to what ancestors knew when alive or knowledge that they gained in the afterlife. This trope gives our characters another way to learn something about the world or current situations (in other places or the earthly one). Whether that intel, or the person providing it, can be trusted is another matter, and this creates another storytelling dynamic.

Divination, the practice of gaining knowledge of the future, can come through visions or direct interaction with spirits who may know, or claim to know, what is to come. When ancestors are contacted, a presumption of truth telling and well-wishing toward the living may give confidence in the answer. This will still depend on the ancestor contacted, for as we all know, not everyone gets along.

Bringing forces from another realm into ours requires more power, experience, possibly training, and maybe a stronger connection to the ancestors, possibly through increased interaction as a shaman; this is unlikely to be a task for a novice. A willing force is much different from an unwilling one. Either may require compensation.

Healing via shamanism is an alternative to supernatural healing by priests. Perhaps the latter invokes the [consistent] power of gods while shamans invoke the unpredictable, potentially evil power of spirits, who might exact a price from healer or healed. Moreover, if an ailment is considered to arise from one's soul, that's the kind of illness that shamanism is thought to heal, as opposed to a physical matter. In a world where wandering spirits (or something else like a weapon) can cause supernatural damage, perhaps such a wound is on one's spirit in a literal sense, not just the figurative.

The latter means someone has "a demon" that causes bad behavior. For example, a trauma in childhood could create a demon that leads to alcoholism. The demon is a metaphor, not something literal, though in SF and fantasy, we often make it so. Similarly, we may say their spirit is wounded. Thus, on Earth, a shaman attempts to heal this figurative wound. Or in our invented world, it's literal, maybe one that doesn't respond to other means of healing.

This conjures a philosophical debate for figurative wounds of the spirit. Is it better for an external source, like a shaman, to fix us, or should we self-heal, possibly by forming a better understanding of ourselves and our psychology, growing as a person and overcoming our demon without such outside assistance? The former offers a quick and easy fix for the wounded. Where would modern psychology be today if shamans could wave their metaphorical magic wand and my demons, and yours, could be vanquished so that I'm just a happy, productive member of society instead of argumentative, boozing, and generally screwing up my life because a demon haunts me? Am I stronger because I grew as a person, the hard way? Yes. Am I stronger because a shaman "fixed" me the easy way? Not really. I only lost a problem that made me weaker.

PSIONICS

Psionics is the ability to communicate or perceive beyond the five physical senses. This fits our definition of magic. While fictional, these are considered innate talents people are either born with or develop. They're usually depicted as natural, meaning they don't require spells, but we've also seen them portrayed as needing an external element. The crystal ball is the most famous of these. We can add anything we desire to make these unique in our setting, while also making them easier or harder to accomplish. Multiple subtypes exist and are briefly summarized next. Any combination of these can exist in the setting. We can treat all of them like magic, meaning we decide their prevalence, training needed, the distance restrictions, and other elements discussed in this chapter.

Ability	Description
Clairvoyance	This is the ability to see events or people beyond the range of normal sight. This can be broken down into precognition (the future), retrocognition (the past), and remote viewing (the present). It can also imply clairaudience (hearing) or be mutually exclusive,

Ability	Description
	meaning some people only have one talent. A theme of this chapter is imposing limits, so don't be afraid to restrict them.
Empathy	An "empath" can read or sense another person's emotions and may even be able to control or influence them.
Mind control	One person impacts another's mind, including removing, suppressing, or replacing memories, or causing the victim to sense phantom pain.
Psychometry	The talent for gaining foresight by touching objects.
Telekinesis	Telekinesis is the ability to move objects with the mind.
Telepathy	Reading another person's thoughts or communicating directly with their mind.

Figure 11 Psionics Chart

ELEMENTAL MAGIC

Using the elements is one way to organize our magic. In addition to the four elements of water, air, earth, and fire, people sometimes decide that spirit is a fifth. We can also invent other elements, especially on non-Earth like worlds. Whatever we decide, this is a convenient way to divide spells because many spells will only use a given element. If we want our wizard to be able to do something with fire but he is a water wizard, this restriction is built in. We can also have rare individuals who are able to do one or all of them. But we don't need to decide that people can only do one element. Perhaps everyone can do all four but there's a "high" and "low" magic that distinguishes them. Or some are just better suited to one and, while they can do all, struggle with some.

We can decide that practitioners need the element to manipulate and cannot conjure it from "thin air." For example, in a desert, a water wizard would have nothing to work with. Or we can decide they're able to sense and draw it from wherever it is within a given range; while there may appear to be no water in a desert, it's still there somewhere. Water and fire are the only two that might be unavailable, generally, but even water is usually around. It's fire that's less naturally occurring, putting such wizards at a disadvantage.

Element	Possible Uses
Air	The ability to fly, manipulate weather, suffocate others, breathe underwater, cause fog
Fire	Starting/extinguishing fires, fireball spells, wall of flames
Earth	Causing earthquakes/sinkholes, softening or hardening of earth (to create mud or stone), creating or commanding stone golems
Water	Dehydrating someone, hydrating them, creating drinking water, parting the sea, walking on water, causing rain, and possibly controlling sea life
Spirit	Control, communicate, or summon/banish ghosts

Figure 12 Elemental Magic

MAGIC PREVALENCE

Just like with technology, we need to determine how common magic and the ability to control it is. Rarity makes it more special, valuable, and feared, while it being common tends to get it taken for granted. We don't need to explain the prevalence unless it has changed in the setting, such as hardly anyone having the ability and suddenly almost everyone does. We can just state it's one way or another, but how do we decide what we want? By understanding the impact on setting and stories.

The more common magic is, the more it affects life (and stories), just like Earth technologies today. Do we want it everywhere? Magic will dominate. If we skip thinking this through, we risk a mistake: magic can resolve plot problems when we didn't want it to. Let's say we plot a story where the characters need to get somewhere in two days by horse, and along the way, someone joins their group, and they acquire both important information and an item. Then we decide magic is pervasive and there are magic gates they can use to traverse this distance in ten seconds. Now it doesn't make sense that they'll go by horse. They won't learn the information and don't have the item or companion. Now we must fix our plot. Avoid this by working out the magic prevalence first.

If magic is rare, we get the usual fantasy setting of a few people being able to do it. Most life happens without magic, which is used by individuals mostly for their own benefit. If magic is common, it's likely been commercialized so that society benefits from it. Just as we have engineers who work for a settlement/government, we might have wizards whose jobs involve using magic for the benefit of all. We must decide the degree of this. An easy way is to think about modern technology and its advantages, and then determine a magical equivalent. It helps to divide life into categories, such as farming, manufacturing, government, communications, and daily life. What can they do with it?

Magic items are a primary result of this. Think of appliances in your life and whether something comparable exists, but don't do a one-for-one switch where the only difference is whether there's a plug for electricity or not. A magic toaster likely works and looks differently than an electric one. We're not just replacing the energy source, but reimagining how the end result can be achieved via an item with the same purpose. Combining purposes is one way to achieve this. We may have a toaster, microwave, stove top, bread maker, panini press, and oven in our house, plus a grill out back. Do they just have one thing and the spells are the difference?

Instead of items, we can have wizards who use their skills "in real time." An example would be that there are no magic gateways to travel between locations, but there are wizards who excel at transporting others and they work for the government doing this, stationed at specific locations, just like a train depot, for example. They'd likely have insurance via their employer for accidents. Do they have an 8-hour workday? Imagine the fatigue. They may work in teams for that reason. We could have different spell types for this, each named, with some being preferred and more expensive. We can do this exercise with any aspect of modern Earth life.

WHERE DOES MAGIC COME FROM?

Even a physicist might say that magic must come from somewhere. There's a fine distinction between the origins of magic and its sources.

ORIGINS

The origins of magic in our world is the answer to the question, "Where does magic come from?" And the answer can be the universe (nature) or the gods (or a being with god-like abilities). There aren't many more options, though we can get more specific than the "nature" option, such as saying it's radiation, or a lifeforce, or some other energy. We don't need to explain it to an audience. Magic is accepted. Its origins are a philosophical question and therefore ignored if we choose to, whereas the source of a wizard's power is a practical matter to which we should pay some attention.

SOURCES

To perform magic, a wizard must draw power from a source regardless of the origins of that source's existence. Inventing sources is an easy way to create multiple types of magic, one per source, if desired. What follows an inexhaustive list of possible sources:

- The planet
    - Elements
    - Gravity
    - Magnetics
- The solar system
    - The sun
    - The moon(s)
    - Ring system (like Saturn)
    - Comets
- Other realities
    - Other planes (like the Astral plane)

- o   Parallel dimensions
- Beings
  - o   God(s)
  - o   Demons/angels, etc.
  - o   Aliens
  - o   Plants, animals, humanoids, etc.
  - o   Souls (possibly from the living) or "lifeforce"
- The "force" from *Star Wars*

The latter option is an implied one in many stories, though only *Star Wars* calls it that. The energy just exists all around us and those with the talent can sense and manipulate it. A large source, such as the universe, has an advantage. When a wizard draws energy from a source, it seems reasonable that the source is temporarily drained. An analogy would be blood drawn from us. It replenishes in time, but of course someone can take it all, killing us. A truly powerful source like the sun or the universe is unlikely to be noticeably drained.

But if magic draws energy from living beings, it seems clear we could kill them by taking too much at once, or too often. Wizards could draw from multiple sources to mitigate this. We should determine the source of our magic and within what radius from the wizard that source must be. This is irrelevant with some sources that permeate everything or are seemingly always the same distance; while a planet gets farther or nearer to the sun, this is imperceptible to the naked eye, but what if wizards are always weaker in winter because their source, the sun, is dimmer? But then perhaps it doesn't matter that the radiation and other elements the sun expels in our direction change distance. It's up to us to decide. But we're always looking for ways to limit what sorcerers can do and this is one way.

If a wizard draws from the living, it's an obvious way to kill people, intentionally or not. But perhaps only some species can be so drained. Either way, imagine this person leaving a trail of corpses or people who've suddenly got a type of "sickness" with symptoms indicating a wizard used them as a source, likely in violation of the law. Consequences make for conflict, which makes for story. If we don't have a need of this source being impacted, then we can decide the source is everywhere, in which case, we can also avoid mentioning it at all.

THE COST OF MAGIC

Everything requires energy, and magic is expending it, or at least redirecting it elsewhere. We can say the same amount of energy exists before as after, and we've repurposed it, but this is a philosophical subject. We care more about the cost to the practitioner here. Those who suffer few or no effects of performing magic are almost gods, but mortals aren't so lucky. Adding a cost to wizardry is an easy way to limit their powers.

The obvious and default answer, which no one will feel is a cliché, is that it's physically draining to perform wizardry. Everything else is, so why wouldn't it be? We also can decide that using it is like alcohol, which is a depressant but, in the short term, acts as a stimulant instead; people can feel energized during a magical battle but "crash" when it's over, needing a deep sleep if they expended a lot of energy; use an analogy of your choice with different side effects to invent something original. We can decide that magic ages the practitioner prematurely, or reduces their ability to have children due to exposure to the energy, as does radiation. An old idea is that a spell needs to be memorized and, once cast, the wizard forgets it and must re-learn it; what if casting it affects the mind in other ways? Maybe the spell isn't the only thing they forget. Or perhaps magic makes them have nightmares or slowly go crazy. Just be sure to invent a price.

SOCIAL ASPECTS

Whether magic is rare or not, there may be laws that vary by location about its usage. We can create an entire area of law, crime, and punishments. These often originate from problems that have already occurred, so think about wizards doing bad things, especially in public, and how society has tried to deter this. We can invent some history and infamous incidents and characters (including victims), after whom a law may be named.

How can they inhibit wizards? The purposeful use of anti-magic zones is one way, or a device that can be placed on someone to cut them off from magic. Maybe they've figured out how to permanently remove the ability. Perhaps hey can only limit access, such as making someone weaker so that only minor spells can be done. If they don't have a supernatural way to inhibit, they could just drug someone so that they're too weak to do it and regularly administer this. We can invent plants that have this effect once prepared. Where there's a will, there's a way.

The more common magic usage is, the more social customs will arise from it. Casting a spell on our date without their permission is probably frowned on! But is casting a spell on ourselves prior to it okay? That likely depends on the result. If it's considered dishonest, like making us appear 100 lbs. lighter, this is probably bad, but if we only changed our hair color, maybe not. It depends on whether we're up front about these things. To create these, think about how life would be and what you'd want to do if you had magic and how others would react to you doing it.

There's a power disparity between wizards and muggles, to use a Harry Potter term. Do people consider it rude for a wizard to use magic with non-magical people? How concerned are people about this? Imagine being one of the few who can't do magic and how intimidating that might be, and how we might try to hide it or compensate. What if we're the lone person who's unaffected by magic? What sort of bullying is done due to magic or via it? Be prepared to think about these elements if magic is prevalent.

Some communities might reject magic while others take advantage of it. Religious beliefs or conservative values (that resist change) can affect this. So can fear and significant historical acts. It's an oversight to not have such places, or even zealots who denounce wizards or are on a crusade to capture, kill, or render them magicless. By contrast, some will worship the powerful or seek to be an apprentice, resulting in fierce competition. Sorcerers might be viewed like athletes are here. Give serious thought to what social elements are impacted.

WHAT'S IN A NAME?

The words for magic users can be generic or imply meanings. The phrase "magic user" is a catchall that includes everything: wizards, mages, sorcerers, magicians, necromancers, witches/warlocks, and more. Many of these are virtual synonyms that carry no specific meaning unless we decide to differentiate them.

"Magician" sometimes implies a trickster or a charlatan. If we have true magic users and charlatans, "magician" might be for the latter and seen as an insult. On Earth, a magician is an "illusionist," who appears to be doing magic. Such people can exist on a world with actual magic, so it's likely there's a word for them, and real wizards hate being considered one. This adds a dynamic. If we use "magician" for real magic users, we need another term, such as "trickster," or "illusionist," for these other guys.

"Mage" is familiar to fantasy audiences as a synonym for magician, but some haven't heard this term. A simple reference will educate them, like this example: "Kier was a mage, or magician, of great renown." This is slightly better than, "Kier was a mage, or wizard," because the first ties "mage" and "magician" together better than "mage" and "wizard." The word itself is archaic and fell out of usage until fantasy games like as *Dungeons & Dragons* revived it.

If we've invented types of magic, each needs a name. The inhabitants will have named them even if we try to skirt this issue. We can append other words to it, such as "high magic" and "low magic," or create new words altogether, like my "valendry" from Llurien. We can also use the words in this section to refer to different practitioners.

ARE SPELLS NEEDED?

It may seem obvious that spells are needed to perform magic, but that depends on our definition of "spell" and "magic." Magic is considered powers that don't exist on Earth. But in our fictional world, magic is real, so does this definition fail? On that world, yes, but our audience is on Earth, so it still holds. But any physical changes that can be done without manually manipulating something, or using tech, can be considered magic. As for spells, this typically means words, gestures, physical materials, or some combination of these, to perform said magic. If all of this seems obvious, there's a reason the distinction is being made.

Gods are considered real in fantasy worlds especially. And gods make things happen that don't occur in the real world of Earth. Does that mean they're doing magic? Unless we have a pressing reason for using a different word, yes. Perhaps gods and mortals are tapping into the same well of supernatural power, but one difference is that people are weakened by this and gods either aren't, or to a lesser degree, but we can safely say gods (usually all of them) are capable of magic.

But are gods using spells? Or are they doing magic by force of will? I'm inclined to say it's will power for several reasons. One is that we should distinguish between gods and mortals. It seems clear that gods can innately do magic (will power), but mortals must struggle to learn and master it, even if they have the talent. Gods may have imposed limits, via spells, on what mortals can do. We can find other ways to impose limits, but it still raises the point: either beings can do magic by force of will or they need spells.

We've seen depictions of gods making gestures or speaking words to achieve their result, which suggests they're using a spell, but perhaps they're just controlling the force better this way. In visual media, people are typically shown doing these as visual/audible cues as to who is causing something to happen. This is sometimes omitted when it's already been established who in the scene has the ability, such as Darth Vader in *Star Wars*, or when ambiguity is desired (either by characters or storytellers). Since will power is innate, gods may not need spells. Non-gods are typically portrayed as needing to learn how magic works; they study various things like the language of magic (an innate skill for gods), and then read spell books to learn how each spell is done. Then they practice. What little power they start with grows with that practice. We assume gods aren't doing any of this because we show them as strong. Whether gods are using spells or not is semantics, except that if we have a choice between gods and mortals using willpower, the least sensible option is gods needing spells and mortals using willpower, because the latter suggests fewer restrictions and more power, both of which apply to gods.

What about mortals? Can they do magic via will power or are spells the only way? We may want to have both and use a name for each, like wizard vs. sorcerer.

SPELLS ARE NEEDED

Let's say spells are needed to perform magic. The spells would harness magical energy, but if the spell is performed wrong, we have two options: nothing happens, or magic still happens but in unintended ways. Both are plausible. Failure can mean that the energy wasn't harnessed at all, which seems the safest poor result. Failure can also mean the energy was harnessed but discharged improperly, resulting in an alternate outcome, whether that's a deadly explosion or a minor variation in the intended result. It's up to us to decide which we want.

Comic results are sometimes desired, particularly in children's books like Harry Potter. But we can also show the dangers of magic with perilous failure. Imagine how few people would want to do this if it's so dangerous. By contrast, if nothing happens, an attempt is less fraught with worry. We might badly need the spell to succeed and feel pressure for that reason, but if we can't do it right, we and others aren't dead or worse. Decide how dangerous magic should be in the setting. It's easy to imagine wizards who are a nervous wreck when doing something powerful if disaster could result. This can also cause strong restrictions by governments and others. It also ramps up the apprehension people feel when someone tries a spell. If you're a wizard and about to do something, I might run for my life even if you're my friend and I trust you. All of this can be significant reason for training facilities. But if nothing happens when failure occurs, everyone would be far more casual about it. What do they have to lose?

We can also invent solutions per situation or spell type (or even magic type). What if I'm a spell author and I know how to make my spell recipes safely dissipate energy when done wrong? But another guy had no idea and his spells are therefore more dangerous? My spell recipes are more desired. Why would anyone use the other guy's spells? Because those are the only ones they've found.

Breaking a spell down into parts helps with this. Maybe the energy must be harnessed first, then manipulated before being expended. Can a wizard sense the harnessing? If so and it's not working, he might stop right there. This failure will not expel energy and therefore nothing will happen. But if the energy is harnessed, and then the expulsion part of the spell is where failure occurs, an accidental result seems more plausible. For this reason, maybe some wizards craft their spells in reverse: the part to control the energy comes first, followed by the gathering of energy. This way, if failure happens during the first part, the harnessing also fails and nothing happens. Regardless of the order, some spell authors might've put in a failsafe that causes energy to be quietly released back to where it came from or safely dispersed elsewhere.

It seems plausible that all of these options would exist in the same world. We can have individual spell creators with a reputation for one thing or another. There can be entire schools of magic that only teach one kind of spell, whereas rogue wizards are willing to do the more dangerous spells. Perhaps the latter are only created by rogue authors trying to achieve an end result that sanctioned places, like a school of wizardry, forbid. Or maybe truly powerful spells require so much of the wizard's energy to perform that some spell authors dispensed with the safeguards because it made the spell that much more taxing or complicated. Short cuts happen in all parts of life, even when unwise.

Spells Are Not Needed

Let's decide spells are not needed. Mortals can do magic without them. All those safeguards we just discussed will be absent. There's no recipe, path, or guideline to follow. There's no "if I do this, I will get this result." We may will something to be and have unconscious thoughts intrude and be willed into reality. Or maybe we weren't thinking of one aspect of our intention and it's omitted as a result. We may be able to fix these mistakes at once, but it might also be too late, such as willing an arrow fired at us to veer to one side, causing it to strike our best friend and killing him instantly. If we're not powerful enough to bring someone back or reverse time and opt for a redo, we're out of luck.

This willpower business is inherently more dangerous and uncontrolled – and one reason to reserve it for gods. The odds of a mortal wizard doing something wrong but still achieving an accidental result are probably far higher. And this might be why *optional* spells still exist, to achieve and control a specific result (within a defined range of possibilities). Spells would therefore place limits on magic, not make magic possible.

Given this, does it make sense to cast a spell and have it go wrong but still do something? If we wanted that to happen, we wouldn't be using the spell. It should be a pass/fail scenario – either we do it right and it works (within parameters) or we do it wrong and nothing happens. This is a viable option to consider for our world.

There can be more to this. Willpower wizards can draw energy without help from a spell. This suggests that the point of spells is to control the energy's release, which they can also do, but that this will aid them in doing so. There might also be issues with controlling the drawing of energy (such as taking too much or from poor sources), and therefore spells *do* include this. And authors of spells can include or omit safety features or be better or worse at inventing them, as we discussed in the previous section.

So where does that leave us? Whether using spells or not, we can have magic go wrong and still produce a result, even when the whole point of spells is to do it right. But we should generally opt for a pass/fail scenario if spells aren't required. If spells are likely to be of little help, then many people wouldn't bother with them. Perhaps they're viewed like training wheels on bikes and few people use them after a certain experience level.

THE LIFE OF MAGIC-USERS

We won't look at how a wizard, shaman, or other type of practitioner spends his day so much as the phases of his career, from how the ability is gained and lost, their training, what life is like at the height of power and then if they begin to lose strength with age.

How the Ability is Gained and Lost

Even if everyone in a setting can perform magic, we must decide how the ability is gained (or lost). Our default is that it's like talent; you've either got it or you don't. However, even among those who do, they sometimes don't know it, feel it, or have it until they reach a given milestone. This can be an age or event, such as losing virginity, a first period for a female, or the first time we draw blood or kill someone. Maybe we even need to die and be reborn. Perhaps the ability can be given like a gift under certain conditions. We might have to consume something once or regularly, like a potion, pill, plant, or animal.

What about losing the ability? This seldom gets a mention but is worth focusing on. If magic is a talent, then it theoretically never goes away. But maybe it depends on how the magic works. Songwriters always have the talent to write music, but as we all know, some are better than others and there are times when a band seems unable to write great music anymore. If performing magic requires some originality or inspiration, then maybe some wizards have fallen from grace, their "heyday" behind them. They can still do it, but they're out of ideas for new actions. They're the equivalent of a "has been" band still touring and playing their greatest hits.

If an event causes magic ability, can another make it stop? Maybe a potion, pill, plant, or animal takes it away. Perhaps someone must be celibate like a priest; this raises the unfortunate prospect of rape being used to render a wizard non-magical. What if killing someone, drawing blood, or another act causes the ability to weaken or fade? The gods can make this a reality to punish people, particularly if magic was used to perform the act. A benevolent god might do this, but perhaps a nefarious one grants the talent for causing mayhem.

If the ability is gained or lost, decide if this is permanent or not. Maybe having it was never forever anyway. Maybe the sun gives the ability, but the sun is too far away in winter and wizards cease to be one for part of the year. Do magic items stop working at that time, too? What if an item was holding up a building?

TRAINING

Even wizards who can do magic with will power, not spells, can benefit from training. One element that distinguishes mankind (at least on Earth) is the ability to learn from predecessors. And wizards are likely the elite, having more specialized knowledge that can be passed down. While some of that can be done via books or scrolls, personal interaction tends to be superior to written material. To determine how much training is available and what form it likely takes, we should determine the prevalence of magic as previously discussed.

At its rarest, magic will only be taught by individual wizards in a master/apprentice scenario. At its most common, there are wizardry schools, possibly many of them held in differing esteem, and with practices. Aside from prevalence, the other major factor determining this is public and government attitudes toward magic. Naturally, where it's forbidden, the secret apprenticeship is more likely, but where it is openly accepted and plenty of wizards are around, a school may exist.

We can use this to develop character backstory. If they have little to no training, that will explain some mishaps and inconsistency. They may even be able to do some spells without all of the words, gestures, or ingredients, somehow compensating for it. Someone who goes to a prestigious wizardry school will be known for that. Those who had a secret internship, possibly with someone disreputable, may keep quiet about it and refuse to admit to their master's whereabouts. Every wizard is likely to have an accident of some kind in their past, and training certainly influences the number and severity of these, plus the emotional and even physical scars that result. A wizard without fear is a fool.

To create a school of magic and its curriculum, we can leverage subjects from our own schooling. What typically exists? Potions, summoning, communication, creating and using items, material usage (plants, animals, etc.), history, school of magic, types of magic, general spell casting 101, and more. Unless we're planning to have a character in a Harry Potter-like setting, we don't need too many details, but it's worth inventing this once and having it in mind for most of our fantasy worlds because much of it would exist on all of them, even if the class or book titles change. Inventing a magic curriculum can be fun.

Determine how long school lasts in hours per day, months, and years and if there are ranks that people achieve at various stages. This can help break "wizards" from one organized mass into smaller groups distinguished from each other. An obvious decision is for multiple years, and with this chosen, we can choose ranks. For example, if it's seven years, we can use the seven colors in the spectrum to denote those at each stage of completion, and maybe they wear robes of a given color to show it. If it's four, maybe we use seasons or elements.

Are there tests that must be passed to advance? It seems obvious. We don't have to decide what they are, but it can add interest, particularly if each year has one test that is more feared than the predecessors. It's a chance to invent stories about what happened to one person or an-other when failing. We shouldn't go too far with this sort of thing unless our story is to heavily feature it.

At what point do graduates become eligible to teach others, whether at school or in an apprenticeship? Why would someone want my teaching instead of yours? Expertise and prestige are two reasons. We can gain the latter due to pedigree, training, accomplishments, and fame. Or even having past students of a given instructor go on to achieve greatness. Invent a famous instructor in the setting and determine why this is so.

We should also determine what happens if someone fails training or is expelled. Are they literally marked in some way, like a thief with a notch in their ear? Or perhaps their abilities have been removed. These people will be around and it makes our setting more believable that one should be encountered, particularly in longer tales. Their fate should be a warning to those in training.

HEIGHT OF POWER

When wizards are in their prime, we should determine their options in society. Deciding on magic prevalence once against helps us decide their prospects. For example, if magic is common and accepted, they might begin to instruct others, possibly at schools. They can live openly, make people feel safe, be honored (with statues or presiding at ceremonies), and enjoy good relations with leaders, military, and anyone else. When magic is rare and wizards are feared, they may teach in secret, maybe far from others, hide their location or nature, be shunned, and have an attitude about all of it. All of this would be on someone's mind when entering into wizardry just as we envision our prospects in any career. Don't overlook this. Use the techniques in chapter one to invent a culture for them, and be sure to vary it by sovereign power and, to a lesser extent, within regions and settlements.

Wizards are often thought to amass powerful items and wealth, whether it's true or not. When magic is common, there may be special vaults and banks like what we see in Harry Potter, but without this, keeping their hoard close (such as at home) is more likely. This can lead them to become a target, one who has various kinds of protection (magical or otherwise) to conceal and protect their homes, whether there's anything valuable there or not. We need to think about where they might choose to live, based on how magic and its practitioners are viewed. They'll want to feel safe, whether that means living openly or in secret, and with physical or supernatural protection or not, and even though they might be very powerful and inspire fear, the terrified often attack in the name of preemptively defending themselves.

All of this affects a wizard's family life, too. They're so often shown to be loners that we can easily overlook this. Don't they have friends, lovers, children? Are some of them magical? Or strong in other ways, like knights? Many will be just as respectable or disrespectable. It's tempting to see a wizard as all-powerful, but even they get sick, injured, or tired. Fantasy is prone to sorting people as good or evil, but many supposedly "evil" people just have a different viewpoint, one shared by many others, around whom they'd feel safer in weak moments.

The Waning Years

Powerful wizards have powerful enemies, but sooner or later they are going to start aging and become increasingly vulnerable. Who is going to protect them? Maybe this is a scenario where the wizard's apprentices protect their former master, or do they prey upon him? This is part of the magical culture. This could also be one reason that there are magic guilds, with one of the benefits of joining being this protection as we age and become weaker and vulnerable to our enemies. Might not a wayward wizard in youth curb his worse tendencies as he ages so that he'll be accepted – and protected?

Just as we imagine our prospects for a career, we might think of our retirement. How is a feared wizard going to live peacefully? Move away so people don't realize? Who wants to end their life in hiding, away from anyone they care about? It seems reasonable to find another way. Might not a wizard cultivate good relations for just this very issue? Even an evil wizard, if smart, would find at least one kingdom where they're see as good and retire *there*.

Attire

The default attire many audiences have in mind is the robe, with the color or something else denoting the type of magic or skill level the practitioner has attained. There's no real reason for the robe other than cliché, but they do offer the chance to have an unknown quantity of pockets within, each holding ingredients for spells. However, other clothing can achieve the same; cargo pants come to mind, though the pockets are visible. Do we really need a wizard to hide how much stuff they're carrying? Quick access to pockets during fights is wise, but a belt or bandoleer (used for bullets) can do the same.

Question how practitioners are dressed and why. A robe could be considered formal and mostly worn while at official functions. Perhaps a shorter version is for travel, worn with trousers to cover the lower legs when it's cold. A robe might be tradition or enforced on wizards in societies that insist on immediate identification (in this case, via clothing) of practitioners. Some wizards might wish to hide their abilities for any number of reasons.

Another old cliché is that wizards can't wear armor. This may have been conceived to make such powerful characters more vulnerable, but we have other ways to do this. Armor interfering with gestures doesn't make sense as a justification, given that sword fighting, for example, requires far more mobility. But another explanation is that metal somehow interferes with the wizardry; we can make such a factor true of one magic but not another to create distinctions, but it also seems that an enterprising person would fashion armor that doesn't cause this, with such armor being hard to acquire.

Consider that the audience only benefits from a visual cue in visual mediums, so print authors have greater leeway to completely abandon all stereotypical garb. In other mediums, we may want an immediately recognizable style in our story world. Then we just need to establish it, which takes no more than a line of dialogue when someone comments on the outfit. In *Star Wars*, we know who's a Jedi knight at once due to inference.

CREATING LIMITS

A system is all about limits. Whether we're doing hard or soft magic, we must still decide on limits unless we genuinely want an all-powerful being. There are arguably two kinds of limits: those imposed by the universe/gods and those caused by mortals. For the latter, this means that someone has devised a system of magic on our world.

For example, the arch wizard Kier discovered and developed a series of spells now known as Kierzadry. Another wizard called Taria invented Tariandry. Both had their talents, knowledge, inventiveness, research ability, and access to materials with which to experiment. They also ran into problems, solving some and not others, and deciding they'd found a limit (whether true or not) to one thing or another. And they built on their work over possibly decades, crafting spells that considered their learning. The result is two different schools of magic (or types), each with their own rules.

Let's say Kier lived with varied landscapes nearby, with unique wildlife and plants, like the Amazon on Earth. It's likely his spells use exotic materials, and maybe gestures or magic words are lesser parts of his spells. But Taria lived in a desert city when none of that was available, so her spells rely much more on words and gestures. Maybe she even contacted spirits, demons, or the like, and these supernatural forces are part of what she developed. Do we need to explain any of this to the audience? No, but imagining the origin of a magic type helps us develop it and use the natural limits of the physical world to define it.

Maybe those who practice Kierzardy are good at the manipulation of materials but struggle to perform Tariandry due to the complex gestures and words, and lack skill in contacting spirits, who might be unfamiliar with them and reluctant to answer. A Kierzardist might subsequently imagine this is another limit and wrongly tell others Tariandry can't be done by them. A Tariandist might decide that it's difficult to get the materials needed to perform Kierzardry, even at stores, and that even once acquired, processing them in the correct way is too much like cooking with rare materials that they don't understand. It's also possible that these are rival schools of magic and practitioners generally refuse to teach each other. The last thing they want is someone who's adept at both.

GET ORGANIZED

Creating limits has much to do with organization. An example is elemental magic. Given that there are four elements, this is structured for us. We can also create high and low magic, black and white (and grey), moon and sun, light and dark, good and evil, and color magic. We can also decide a specific requirement is a type, such as blood or sex magic requiring an item (blood) or act (intercourse).

Explanations are optional. They can significantly impede our ability to create and define magic types because we're trying to justify many fictional things. It's time to act like the world building gods that we are; things are this or that way because we said so. End of story. If we think of an explanation for any decision, that's great, but avoid getting bogged down in this. Besides, we can say Tariandry and Kierzardy are incompatible without saying why because our world's inhabitants may not know either (some mystery is good). A simple explanation could be that Kier and Taria are not mortals, but gods who hate each other and don't want their wizards crossing over like that, so they included limits.

PROS AND CONS

Even magic systems have pros and cons, which is one way to further define our system(s). Some pros have little to do with the type but rather the society. For example, if training or materials are widely available or cheap, that's a plus and may result in easier refinement of the talent. On the other hand, this could also result in numerous practitioners so that it's harder to gain employment as one or distinguish oneself, for example. There may be pros and cons that are specific to the type, rather than general benefits of wizardry. For example, many practitioners can help their community, or make a difference in life, finding meaning and purpose in their powers, but this is true across magic types. We're looking to define what's beneficial about a type.

CREATE BENEFITS

Why does anyone want to perform this type of magic? If they don't get to choose between types, this matters less, as they only have one option: develop their talent/ability or not. Reasons to forge ahead can include the obvious ones, like power, prestige, wealth, personal safety, and gaining advantage for ourselves or others, but even if none of these appeal to someone, there's a default reason: they have an innate ability and may sometimes cause things to happen by accident, so they need to learn control.

Regardless, we should craft some benefits of each magic type. A built-in benefit might be that a necromancer can communicate with the dead and possibility comfort the living by fostering interaction. If the dead have advance knowledge of the future, this can also be advantageous.

Alchemy is thought to cause noble changes within a person, whether the practitioner or the target, and doing so may align with a person's outlook to make the world a better place; it's the similar set of reasons for why people become priests. For an elemental wizard, bringing rain to a barren land is an example. Psionics can help us understand each other or avoid problems. To craft these, consider what uses practitioners have for this magic. What are their goals? What can be done with it?

Our intended story, if we have one, can also assist. What problems will the characters face and how might this magic type assist them? If a trap lies in their future, perhaps they can see it in advance. If they can't find an item physically, maybe this wizardry can locate it. Reading minds helps overcome an enemy, or creates allies. How can they resolve conflict? Be careful not to perfectly solve the plot or character issues with magic!

While pros don't help us craft limits to define a magic type, they can help us envision cons that do by way of contrast. And these benefits are only possibilities, not guarantees. The cons can prevent realization of these benefits.

CREATE PROBLEMS

What problems does this magic type pose? All types can be dangerous, so we're once again trying to decide on specifics for a type. Reasons to not develop the talent can be economic, lack of education, lack of materials, social problems caused by being a practitioner, personality traits (lack of desire, follow through, and more), or other problems inherent to the type.

Necromancy can revive the dead, who may have ideas about obeying commands or what to do now that they're animated. They may now have supernatural traits that can harm the necromancer or expose the practitioner to knowledge that haunts them. Some types like witchcraft may require a bargain with an evil entity like a demon, who eventually comes to collect. Either of these could result in prolonged contact with other conscious forces (demons, ghosts) that increase the risk of being compromised by them. We could become enthralled by them, enslaved. We might die and our spirit enter their world. To avoid such fates, a spell may have a time-limit on it.

Practitioners aren't the only ones for whom problems can be caused. Do I want a clairvoyant in my head? Is society okay with necromancy? A government or high-minded individuals can place limits, not simply by creating laws, but by incorporating limits in the spell. Imagine that our wizard Kier, who invented Kierzardy, tried to protect himself, devotees, or people in general by adding the limits. Or maybe he didn't and later, a government hires a disciple to alter the spells and does so, with older versions being confiscated. This thinking allows us to imagine catastrophes and then what people did to imbue spells with limits.

Our intended story can help us determine problems. What sort of issue might the character face because they have this talent or ability? Breaking laws is not what we're after, but magic going wrong and causing problems, which might have resulted in limits being imposed on the magic system by practitioners, or the spells' creators, or those who control the source of the energy (such as gods).

HOW TO INVENT SPELLS

As we all know, spells are a combination of words, gestures, and ingredients. One way to invent spells is to decide that each of these serves a different role in each magic system. If we can't make up our mind, we can have one type of magic use gestures, for example, in one way, and another type use them for another. It's the divide and conquer approach to not only inventing spells but magic systems. One choice to make is whether gestures, words, or ingredients are the difference between two spells; we might have a single spell to make a pie, with ingredients determining whether it's apple or blueberry. Or maybe ingredients don't include the fruit at all and there are indeed two spells, one for each type of pie.

GESTURES

While gestures could mean anything, it seems sensible that they're used for assisting with the width of spell for the area affected and the distance from the caster. If I only want people before me to fall asleep via my spell, I would control my gesture to indicate them but omit people to their left and right. If I want to affect people who stand within 20 feet of me, perhaps my arm is a given distance from my body but not too far, so that those more than 20 feet away are unaffected. If I want them to fall asleep instantly, perhaps my gesture is quick, whereas a slower motion might cause a less sudden effect and a gentler fall into sleep (and to the floor).

A spell that targets individuals more precisely can be imagined in a similar way. If three magic missiles will depart my fingers, perhaps I point them at the chosen targets. This could be done in succession with three pointing motions or all at once with one or two hands; we can imagine some inaccuracy with this, plus people being tipped off as to what's coming. Some variants on spells might require contact with the target, such as wanting to make a single person be the victim. Generally, the more people or wider impact area, the more difficult and tasking we can imagine the spell to be for the caster.

Gestures might also indicate the power level due to the force with which they're made. Imagine that we're casting a wind spell and merely flick our finger, versus a strong sweeping motion with one or both arms. The first might blow out a candle's flame leaving the candlestick standing while the other might knock over everything in its path. This is not a rule, but it's another way to decide what is required of the wizard. Viewed this way, a gesture might indicate passion and determination, which might please the source of that power if a god is the origin and they approve of the result; this could, in turn, convince that source to grant greater power to the wizard.

We can also decide that the wizard has harnessed energy and that, to disperse it away from themselves, these gestures are necessary, or the spell goes off in their face. With that in mind, if others know this, they might try to inhibit such a gesture, so the wizard hurts themselves. A bound wizard might be unable or unwilling to cast various spells. Imposing this limit lets us understand when they can and can't do something.

INGREDIENTS

Whether creating spells, potions, or magic items, viewing ingredients as like those for a recipe is a useful analogy. Everything has its purpose, or it isn't there. The combination of water and flour make dough, which is needed for anything requiring bread or a crust. Yeast is to make dough rise. Spices are optional flavoring. Fruits, meats, and vegetables are for flavor and nutrition. For cooking, the heat can melt items together, bake some ingredients, or convert separate items into a whole. The type of pot matters. Some things can be fudged ("add spices to taste") while others will botch the result if not exact.

We can use all these cooking techniques to determine spell ingredients. Just as yeast is used to make dough rise, we can decide a common plant is used to bind elements together. A spell that has words, gestures, and only one ingredient doesn't need this plant, but one with two or more ingredients does. Similarly, maybe there's a spell type that results in a glass object and we therefore need a bit of sand, warm water (for its heat), or actual glass to achieve this. Whether someone is creating a crystal ball or an orb for light, these same ingredients would be needed even though the spells differ in other respects. Quantity would depend on the object's size.

The point of a spell is to achieve a specific result, just like cooking recipes. If we're following the recipe for apple pie, but don't get the preparation or quantities and/or ingredients right, we don't end up with a blueberry pie. Or an apple. Or a plant. We also don't melt the countertop, destroy the baking dish, or grant life to the apple slices. That said, it is possible to substitute ingredients, which is a good way to allow a wizard not fully prepared to cast a spell produce something similar with the ingredients available. Decide how flexible the spells are. If they need two oz of white sand but only have two ounces of black sand, what happens? If they have the white sand but only 1.5 oz, does the spell still work but results are smaller than it would have been? Less range? Less powerful? To answer these questions, know what each element of a spell is causing. We can start with our cooking analogy, the purpose of various items, and then imagine substitutes.

Element and Purpose	Substitute
Warm water and flour (wheat, bread, whole, etc.) to create dough	A liquid and a grounded plant. The liquid could be ordinary or unusual/magical
Dough to form a container, base, or new whole, and which can be shaped many ways (pie, pretzel, muffin)	"Dough" to act as containers, projectiles
Yeast (makes dough rise)	Grounded plant to alter/accentuate ingredients
Water to cook (noodles, rice), sanitize, break down or congeal ingredients	Any liquid to boil, purify, breakdown or congeal ingredients
Spices for variations in taste	Small materials for variation in power/other details
Meats, fruits, and vegetables for nutrition	Meats (for strength), plants, and other elements for shaping results
Pots, pans, containers of metal, glass	Same, possibly of unique materials
Tongs, spatula, etc., to handle hot items	Same

Figure 13 Spell Ingredients

WORDS

The mystery of magic is often the viewers' inability to understand what a wizard is doing, or how, and finding out that the words mean something unimpressive ruins this. So we may not want to decide them for every (or any) spell. But we should still decide what they're for.

The words might be bringing everything together. Without the words, do we just have gestures and materials? Words can be what makes magic work, from the gathering of energies, to the merging of this with any gestures and ingredients, to the channeling of those elements. Seen this way, words serve as the control, with gestures assisting in any stage of this. They're a kind of "on" and "off" function for spell casting, words at least beginning if not ending the casting. Some spells could still be manipulated with gestures once the speaker goes silent, though there's likely a time limit on that. Does a wizard have five seconds or thirty to manipulate the energies he's collected?

If we invent a magic language, this implies that those words grant access to magic so that the same words spoken in another tongue have no effect. Whether we show this magic language or not, working out what must be said can distinguish one spell from another. A generic pie spell might only have a single word different (rhubarb vs. blueberry) in a placeholder sort of way, or the entire spoken lines could be different. If we have an invented language, it will be less effort (and cheaper if someone must do it for us) to just replace a word than the entire contents.

Let's say these are the words:

"Oh god of plenty, hear my prayer,
Make this joy of many layers,
A scrumptious treat of apple pie,
Without which I shall surely die."

This generic spell is specific only once, the word "apple," and can be swapped with blueberry, cherry, pumpkin, or whatever. This is not only easier for us, but for the wizards in our world. If we have two types of magic, we can decide that one type uses this simple word substitution, allowing for wizards to quickly learn a range of only fractionally different spells. Contrast that with another magic type where the spells are so different that it is more difficult to learn. What if this is what was required just to switch to a blueberry pie?

> *"In the land of Kingshire grows,*
> *A fruit that cures all hunger woes,*
> *Blue and berry it rightly be,*
> *Till baked as pie and had with tea."*

The length of the lines should be kept short for simple spells and lengthened for more complex. We want to avoid similar phrasing, unlike those examples. We can use names of places and individuals as appropriate, making some almost like prayers. We can decide the lines are a bit like recipe instructions, where we tell the magic what to do with the ingredients, how, in what order, and what the result should be. This can take the place of gestures, and if we'd like spells that don't feature a motion, then perhaps the spell's words are what impact this. For example, a spoken "strike down those behind me" would take the place of needing to turn around and wave an arm.

WHERE TO START

Early decisions to make in creating a magic system include what types of magic we want to include in the setting, how prevalent each is, what the source is, and whether mortals need spells to do it. These choices will guide everything that follows. Then we can consider the cost of magic to a practitioner and other limits. We should also decide if we're inventing more than one type of magic for the setting and the limits of each, adding a name. With this in mind, we can then decide on training. We can invent specific spells, being careful not to craft many, if any, that solve a plot problem in a story we're planning. Finally, we can invent local laws.

CHAPTER SEVEN

ITEMS

There are three main categories of items we can create: magical, technological, and ones that are neither. In this chapter, "technology" means SF items that don't exist on Earth, as we don't need to invent things that *do* exist. Such items are in their own section, "Regular Items."

OWNERSHIP

Regardless of type, the question of ownership matters for world builders. We need to know who's got the object now and whether they're considered the real owner or not. Lost items add intrigue, especially if someone's got it and doesn't know what it really is or who owns it – and how much peril this may place them in. Even an item created for someone may never have found its way to that person. Decide if the current possessor is the rightful owner; if not, invent another character and a story about how it transferred. It's likely that the owner, if still alive, wants it back and may appear in our tale. Or the item might be famous, and others covet it.

Games like *Dungeons and Dragons* are full of items our characters acquire and little is done with origins, but storytellers should pay attention to where they found it. If characters are in a ruin, long abandoned, this suggests any claimants are long gone. But if they find something lying in the middle of an alley in a thriving town, that means someone (who is still around) owns it. An ancient item covered in rust is likely the discoverer's to keep, but a freshly oiled blade may provide conflict.

REGULAR ITEMS

Our world can benefit from important items that are neither supernatural nor technological. In the former case, people can attribute supernatural properties to objects that don't necessarily have them, as is the case on Earth. Religious ones come to mind. Something associated with a prophet can be considered holy. These include the Shroud of Turin, the Holy Grail, and even John the Baptist's head. But we also have items that were present at an important moment or which were memorably used, such as a weapon that killed a famous villain, or a possession of that villain or a hero.

Our regular items won't have unique properties quite like those of magical or technological ones, so we don't need much more than its description. A unique appearance makes it more identifiable in visual mediums, even if that was achieved not by design, but by usage. An example would be a sword that had no special properties but was used to kill a powerful villain and is now revered.

The origins are likely as mundane as the item itself, but needn't be. Sometimes people like the idea that a seemingly ordinary item was special all along, but it only revealed itself to be when someone did something with it. This is mythological thinking. People may later decide that a sword which slew a victim had a property incorporated by the forging blacksmith. We can even have such characters build a reputation on this. Maybe our current hero wants a sword forged by that blacksmith, thinking it has an advantage that it doesn't. This adds realism.

When creating a regular item, the form may matter if our characters will use it. A coveted decorative wall hanging may be anything, but if we need them to wield it as a weapon, then it needs to be a blade. If our characters won't use it, consider making the item a less expected form, like a tea pot. If poison was in that, or it was the last one from which a ruler was served before death, this can make some think it's special.

MAGIC ITEMS

Any item can be turned into a magic one by assigning it supernatural properties. We have some standards to choose from, such as rings, bracelets, and other jewelry, and the stereotypical wizard's staff. By contrast, a wand is something no one has unless they're a wizard (or a classical music conductor). Every item we see around us can be given magical properties, but we shouldn't make everything magical unless it dominates our setting (even then, moderation is best). How do we decide on a limit?

PROPERTIES

One way to create limits is to invent problematic items. For example, a cloak that always makes us invisible is an issue because we must securely store it somewhere when not in use. Make an item difficult to control and people will avoid using it. Study how real-world tools you use malfunction, then imagine how the invented item does this. Is the item defective? We can have fun with this, such as that cloak making our body disappear but not our shadow and the character not realizing the cloak doesn't take care of both. Does it sometimes go on by itself? Is it expected to deteriorate? Does it have the coveted "on/off" property?

Not all items are created equal and we can have different versions of anything. Poorer characters might get by without features while wealthier ones expect them. The existence of some features might not be apparent to some users, or they could assume one exists and be disappointed that it doesn't. Maybe they even counted on it and found out at the worst time that their assumption was wrong. We can use such things to aid story, as tales where everything goes as planned offer less tension.

Limit an item's unique powers through quantity and quality or our characters have too much power. Most magic items have one or two related uses, which is sensible, but a wand or wizard's staff are exceptions because it's seemingly their nature to provide assistance on a wide array of matters; they're also controlled by those with talent, skill, training and more, which may be untrue with other items. For everyone else, dividing up abilities helps us focus and not create the equivalent of a Swiss army knife.

Some items are sentient, but the infamous talking sword has become a symbol of unimaginative writing; some magazines immediately reject a story with one. Getting away with such things has much to do with originality and whether it's downplayed or in the audience's face. We may have better luck with SF where an AI can be the source of that speech.

ORIGINS

The more commonplace an item is, the less we need to decide its origins, but the more unique it is, the more audiences will wonder. Are there people who specialize in creating magic items? If so, these are presumably for sale. Their items are likely higher quality as they are more experienced. They and their store likely have good protection, physical and supernatural. How common is this? Depends on the prevalence of magic; if magic's rare, these would be correspondingly unusual, probably located in the populous and wealthiest cities. The profession for these people can be named for ease of reference, possibly by the type of magic. By doing this, we can create more highly prized items that characters are thrilled to find or possess.

Some items may originate with the gods, whether for their use, for use by demi-gods (like Cupid's bow), or for mortals. If it's for the gods or demi-gods but a mortal possesses it, it's likely been misplaced or stolen. Why would deities create items for mortals? The mischievous or villainous ones might want to give their followers an edge. Benevolent gods might subsequently try to counter that by granting special items to their own, but they may just wish to reward someone. Or perhaps use of the item benefits the god, such as attracting followers eager for it to be used on them. The recipient is likely a member of their religious order, but needn't be. Consider the god's aims.

FORM

The item's physical form has implications that render inventing them easier, but form often has little to do with function. A magic broom may be used as transportation, which has nothing to do with its form and function (to sweep). Rings and wands have little to no impact on how they're used, but a weapon or tool does. Consider our use and if it makes sense to marry function to form.

Wearable items have the advantage of seldom being left behind by accident. They're also with us when we suddenly need them. This is why jewelry is so commonly used it's become a cliché. Jewelry often serves no real purpose, making it ideal for magic properties that have little to do with form. A ring that makes the wearer invisible is more plausible than one which bakes cookies, as the spell applies directly to the wearer. Worn items typically affect a person for as long as activated. Whether magic or not, some weapons can be worn but might not be allowed in certain places, which can pose a problem if characters must leave behind a crucial item. They might just skip going in.

Some items are not expected to travel much if at all, like a tea pot or genie's "lamp" unless an existing one elsewhere won't do. Smaller magic items lend themselves to being carried in hand, bags, or pockets; transporting others might not be feasible. This is truer with freestanding items, such as furniture, transportation, or magical doorways. Such items tend to be guarded. What sort of protection does it have?

USERS

We should decide who can use each magic item. Knowing the item's purpose and our story's need for it guides this decision. If the item accentuates a wizard's power, like a staff or wand, then it may not work at all for others or only provide simple functions, like casting a light. Generally, a wizard wouldn't want a non-wizard gaining much ability from their items.

Can someone without magic talent use it? Without a "magic word" to control some, even they might fail. Some items could be activated or deactivated only by wizards but be functional for others. If there are different types of magic in our world, are people able to use all of them, or only the types for which they have affinity, talent, training, or skill? When inventing a magic system, we will decide on such rules and can apply them to items. Worn items can be lost and used by someone else, while anyone can come across a freestanding item, depending on where it's located. Consider the likelihood of someone else using it and whether the inventor would've inhibited this.

TECHNOLOGICAL ITEMS

Unlike with magic items, technological ones are unique, rather than repurposing an everyday item, like a ring, to have technological significance. Both can be done. A smart watch is more than just a watch but was created to have those extra features, rather than being repurposed. With all tech objects, we'll want to balance the good with the bad so that few items are without their issues. How to do this is covered throughout this section but amounts to altering properties, forms, and origins to produce pros and cons. Characters complaining or praising these details adds believability, as does their avoidance of some things and pursuit of others.

Technological Prevalence

How common is technology in the setting? This will have an impact on how it's perceived and the likelihood of our characters having technological problems. Many objects will be taken for granted, but how often does technology fail or get in the way? We notice a failure more than expected results. The frequency of technology ruining plans may be on par with how often they help. This can be a story issue, but the more technology that exists, the more likely things are to fail and affect lives.

Properties

Aside from what purpose this item serves, we should determine considerations such as battery life (and if its rechargeable), reliability, durability, usability, its interface, and data connectivity abilities. Technological items almost always have an "on/off" switch, and possibly a battery that will eventually die. Decide that most can be switched on and then we only need to decide which ones miss this feature – or have a flaky one.

Reliability doesn't need an explanation because we all understand that some items are great and others aren't. Just decide some manufacturers produce items at one extreme or another, based on what we know about the species/race, sovereign power, or company involved. Battery life may be an issue at the item, product line, manufacturer, or species level. It's less common that everything by a race, for example, has poor battery life.

For durability, higher priced items are typically better, but manufacturers know that if an item lasts forever, we'll never buy another from them, so the conspiracy theory that some are designed to break down after a given time—right after the warranty expires, say—is quite believable.

Usability and the interface are major areas for us to characterize. Who hasn't complained about how something is designed? Give every manufacturer a reputation and our characters will have an attitude about their other products. The interface can mean how intuitive or cumbersome it is and is a way to give a good item a flaw. Maybe it's powerful but hard to use.

For connectivity, our default should be that a technology does not play well with technologies from other planets unless someone has purposely built that in, which requires previous interaction with species from that world, or at least acquisition of and familiarity with their technology and language. This is a believable limitation. Even on Earth today, if we travel from Europe to the U.S. or vice versa, we need an adapter for something as simple as electricity. The tech for advanced systems is interdependent and simply hooking up to something shouldn't be as easy as it's often shown in SF.

ORIGINS

In SF, the origins of an item are often overlooked, which is fine if it's commonplace, or assumed to be from the military if the character is a soldier. Many items are likely for sale. Characters care who made their items just as we do about our smartphone, vehicle, computer, and appliances. This will be truer if species/races on other planets created them. Everything should have distinct traits, such as the difficulty of use or reliability. Even the look and feel or its reputation will affect response to one. Someone might wish for the power of a Nissen plasma gun with the reliability of an Muirdo one and the accuracy of a Raita one, these being races or corporations. One character might be pleased to find one of the Nissen guns only to have another say it's unreliable.

To improve the impact of origins, we can decide different species or races are capable of different qualities (and even quantities) of production. Both cause value. Maybe only the Nissen can create that plasma rifle, or they're the only rifles that are worth having. Spend a little time dividing up item types and deciding which race (or even sovereign power of that race) is good, bad, or mediocre at creating each. As with magic items, we can have individuals who excel at creating them, rather than companies or kingdoms. As long as we juxtapose origins with properties or values, we're creating believability – and finding ways to give characters something they need but which doesn't perfectly do the job. If they really need a plasma rifle but it's not the Muirdo kind, then maybe it's going to fail in a crisis. This is how we use origins.

It's worthwhile to create several manufacturers for any SF setting, their names emblazoned on products and ads. Each will elicit a response from people, that opinion differing according to the individual and company. We can characterize both and make the world and people more relatable. And when their items show up in faraway places, people can be surprised, even comforted by something from home. They may be amused if another species thinks it's great.

FORM

Form and function may go together with technological items, but not always. Some devices like a smart phone offer far more functions than a person unfamiliar with one might guess, such as GPS or motion sensing tech. Since we're inventing tech, we can decide whether form and function have anything to do with each other. Items that scan or transmit signals can be in any shape; the days of needing an antenna are long over on Earth, but maybe not on our invented world. Anything computer related can be divorced from its form. This is also true of wearable items, though not those designed to augment the form, such as a cloak that makes any covered part of us invisible.

Weapons would appear to be those where shape matters, but this depends on the type. If we're swinging it like a sword, for example, and the technology in it has something to do with this, such as increasing the force or accuracy, then the form still matters. Weapons that fire physical projectiles also need a barrel, so a gun that shoots a smart bullet likely still looks like a gun. But what about weapons that fire lasers or the beams of light we see in *Star Wars*, for example? They're always shaped like a gun, but is that necessary? If the laser requires manual targeting, then it is possible characters are used to using guns with physical projectiles, and the accuracy is improved this way. By contrast, it might be hard to aim a weapon that's a round disk held in the palm, with the beam emitting from the center. And of course, audiences are used to the gun shape and won't question it. Should we?

If the laser is not manually targeted by the hand, then yes. We can manually target a large gun like the cannons seen on space craft, but in those cases, the gun itself isn't held. It's attached to the ship. The character might be using a computer to fire. Think of any game controller, ones with multiple buttons for each hand and little levers controlled with thumbs, that you've used while watching the action on a TV via the gaming console. Even though we're manually controlling the aiming, the actual weapon needn't have a barrel. These are virtual guns. When this is the case, consider changing the form to something with fewer limitations, like an orb that can fire in any direction without requiring turning.

When manual targeting isn't involved at all, and no physical projectile is fired, why would we have a gun barrel shape? Think of a good reason or opt for something more unique. The missile fired may begin dispersing once shot and a barrel delays how soon this happens. Or perhaps the energy needs to be collected before it can be fired in a given direction and the barrel aids this. Maybe the weapon's engineers just aren't smart (or original) enough to go without this. Any weapon designed to affect a wide area is also a candidate for avoiding a gun shape.

USERS

Technology tends to be user-agnostic, but a species might want to put biological controls into their items so that only they can use them. This is especially true of weapons and informational items, depending on what sort of data the latter typically holds. Many items require specific knowledge for how to control them, so we must decide if the device is intuitive or not. In TV and film, we often see people facing no obstacles at all with this and it's not realistic. Plan for them to need an item that they can control and make them work to find it, instead of just being able to use whatever is on hand. If a species uses biological controls, a human won't bother trying to steal their ship, for example. Instead, they may opt for stowing away, or an alternative, to flee their present situation.

Which functions are necessary to an item we're inventing determines how technical it must be. The complexity will affect the degree to which users unfamiliar with it can figure it out. Consider having simple functions more obvious but more elaborate features less intuitive and beyond the characters. Even experts in that field may have difficulty figuring out something designed by another culture. We need things to go wrong and not understanding how to use an item is a believable way to achieve this. We can also have them achieve the opposite result they wanted or even cause problems with this unfamiliar device.

The gun is infamous for being a way to "level the playing field." Before that, physical prowess mattered more during conflicts, but now even a toddler can kill an adult. This is why the "safety" exists, so does the item we're inventing include such a thing? SF often features particularly deadly items, so the obvious answer seems affirmative, but include known hacks to get around that equivalent (known to a select few, like our wiliest character, of course). Weapons aren't the only leveler. Think of disadvantages the protagonists have compared to their nemesis and figure out what possession of the latter can fall into the hands of the former and even the fight. Then avoid making it too easy for our heroes to use it.

CREATING AN A.I.

An Artificial Intelligence (A.I.) has become a staple of SF, particularly in the form of a ship that can be controlled via the A.I., which typically gets a name for ease of reference. Let's call ours Surance, which sounds female, and that is a decision to make. Is the gender fixed or can users change it? This arguably matters more in TV/film because every change of voice or appearance means another actor, plus a brief explanation, which can be as short as someone answering raised eyebrows from crewmates with a shrug and saying, "I changed her." This change matters less in books because the reader won't notice, which begs the question of why we'd do it.

And the answer is that Surance may have the ability to impersonate others, both visually and vocally, because it can be useful for the crew (and us). We live in a world where genders are not viewed and treated equally despite attempts to change this. What if our crew welcomes aboard a race, hostile to females, which takes offense at Surance? It's both a storytelling decision and a character one for whether the crew changes the A.I. gender to be sensitive, takes a "too bad for you" attitude and leaves it as is, or splits the difference (leaving gender unchanged and explaining to and "educating" the visitors on their own cultural views). We can think of other scenarios for gender changing, with the caveat being that gender is theoretically irrelevant with a non-living being, but we all know that most of us look male or female. We can choose a neutral one to bypass the whole question.

We must also decide where the A.I. "lives." These are often shown as part of a vessel or structure like a house, but there's no reason Surance can't be portable and as small as a pendant. Think of how we use Siri or Alexa devices and the possibility of having it everywhere. Surance can manifest as a full body projection standing near a character (decide on the range of this), or maybe she's a floating head, or just a voice, one that maybe only the wearer can hear (via a matching earpiece). If Surance appears, is it apparent that she's an A.I. or can she seem real? Can she appear as more than one person at once? Imagine needing to give the impression you have more fighters by your side so that someone pursuing you backs off.

We should decide if there's the equivalent of an internet or if all of the A.I.'s data store is local to them. How much info can they take with them? With the advances in memory storage on Earth, we can give them everything but the latest changes. But this may not be true in a universe unconnected to us. Then again, a society capable of producing some A.I.s must surely be able to create portable memory storage? They can likely connect to other systems unless we decide to restrict them.

PERSONALITY

Personality is another major area to invent, but we'll do so much like with any other character. While we can make them human-like, we can also assign the A.I. another race and culture, which makes sense if an alien species designed the ship. This can make them less cooperative unless hacked and altered (with one degree of success or another). Unless Surance has been programmed to respect something like modesty or secrets, this can result in awkward situations, including being watched or listened to without permission. Decide how much of a conscience has been included.

An A.I.'s personality can be used as a counterpoint to those on the crew. Being more serious is likely, even a default. Think about it from a manufacturer's point of view. You might like a sarcastic A.I., but plenty of people don't. If I'm in the market for a ship and you're a spaceship dealer, you could lose a sale over an obnoxious A.I. This certainly suggests that Surance is modifiable, possibly with aftermarket parts or programming. Consider this and the age of an item (a ship for example), not to mention its origin, to determine the status of the A.I.

LIMITS

An all-powerful A.I. is as problematic as anything else, maybe even more so. They're designed to control an entire ship, house, or wherever they reside, deeply impacting living beings, even sustaining or killing them via environmental controls. It's important to determine a way they can be turned off while leaving the item (let's say a ship) still controllable, albeit with minimal systems? This has been done before but it's an obvious plot device to have someone hack the A.I. or for it to suffer other problems. This is as realistic as a computer bug or car maintenance problems, so don't avoid it. Just use it when it permits a new spin on the story. In our modern world, virus attacks are constant; they will be in a world with A.I.s, too.

Decide what tasks the A.I. is designed to do and to what degree. What can't it do? What does it need living beings (or at least physical machines) to do for it? How many backups are there and how robust? A spaceship would likely have more than one, given its importance, but of course doing so is less fun for storytellers because restoration can happen quickly enough to ruin the tension introduced. An A.I. with less important functions is more likely to have one or even no backup.

Can Surance's abilities be augmented? It's a program after all. Maybe there's a crew member tasked with maintenance and enhancements. As a professional software developer, I see tons of poor work and processes resulting in bugs. Cocky coders make mistakes, and the geniuses often shown in SF are likely worse. Prudent design requires teams of people, with a project manager and others in oversight roles, involved in any such effort. This would likely be true on a large vessel, so keep this in mind. Imagine living in a ship where everything about our life is on the line if someone codes a mistake into the A.I. The idea of a single coder is not believable in many situations.

WHERE TO START

We can start in one of several places with inventing items, including how we intend them to be used and how we want characters to think of them. Is it a plot coupon they need to acquire to accomplish goals? If so, decide why they can't reach those goals without it and how they'll use it to be successful; it helps to think of what can go wrong, too, because tasks that go as planned offer less drama. Its function determines properties, which can then help with form. Origin is optional but adds a good detail that can also determine where this item is now and why, a little history adding depth. A final decision can then be which one of our characters has the skills or attributes to use it. But all of these can be done in whatever order works, and starting with an idea is always best, wherever it leads.

CHAPTER EIGHT

LANGUAGES

Constructed languages, known as conlangs, are a staple of fantasy and science fiction stories and gaming. Creating a language is one of the most optional subjects in world building. It has a limited positive return, given the difficulty of the task, the learning curve, and the time-consuming nature. And no one will be able to understand it; we need to translate everything anyway. For authors, this relegates the words to a visual display, one that's generally incomprehensible. For those in film, TV, and gaming, a constructed language can at least be spoken and go a long way to characterizing the speakers, but in those situations, it's likely that the studio has hired an expert to do it.

If an author has an audiobook made, they will have to speak the language well enough to narrate personally or teach a narrator. Some narrators may be unwilling to do this or charge extra for it.

This chapter will not teach you how to create a language. There are books on the subject, written by experts, and it is recommended that interested readers consider them. What this chapter *will* do is look at what is involved at a high level, what we might be getting ourselves into, and the cost to world builders of skipping it.

As of 2020, the following books about the art of inventing languages are available and are recommended resources to start your journey. I have read the first two – and they convinced me not to do this.

1. *The Art of Language Invention*, by David J. Petersen, inventor for *Game of Thrones, Star Trek*, and more.
2. *The Language Construction Kit*, by Mark Rosenfelder
3. *Advanced Language Construction*, by Mark Rosenfelder

SHOULD WE CREATE ONE?

We often benefit from questioning what goal we hope to achieve with our world building. This is true of inventing languages. Clarifying our motivation will help determine the degree to which we do this, if at all.

One reason to invent a language is vanity—we have a language all our own. This is arguably a poor excuse. Having a successful writing career or writing a bestseller will impress more people, if we care about such things. Time spent on our writing/gaming craft (or how to promote our work) is probably wiser.

Creating a naming language, discussed in this chapter, is among the better reasons to craft one as, at a minimum, it prevents every location or character in our world from having similar names. But if we look at a map of Earth, many names are similar across countries. One reason is the influence of Greek and Latin, which influenced not only English, but French and Spanish. We can therefore use a similar naming style in different sovereign powers.

A good reason to invent languages is that we may have different species in our setting and they sometimes greet others in their own language before switching to a common tongue. They might mutter under their breath in their language, or talk openly to members of their own species, thinking bystanders won't understand. It can be good, and natural, to *show* these words. The other option is to *tell*, such as narrating, "They exchanged words in their own tongue right in front of the humans, not realizing that some of them knew enough to understand." However, storytellers tend to not show greetings, etc., after initially showing some because they don't advance a story; people who are often together may not bother greeting each other at all anyway; when was the last time you really greeted your friends or family in more than the most cursory fashion?

Creating the feel of another world is another reason to create a language, which lends credibility to the idea that this place is real. After all, it's even got its own language (or several). This also makes us seem serious about our work. However, there are many other ways to do both, with a better return on our time investment.

We may feel that a language is expected, but that depends on medium. Book audiences don't expect one whereas gaming, TV, and film probably do; a studio is likely to hire an expert for this. People may understand that this is a significant time investment for an author, but a studio has tons of people working on a project and money, too. Many authors just throw in phrases invented on the fly and which do not originate from a working language. This can give the impression that we've made a language when we haven't. For some of us, this is enough.

But if our work is ever turned into a film, etc., much more language will be needed. Are we prepared to supply all of the phrases and train actors? Can we even do so? Because if we invented the language, no one can do it for us.

And if we just made up junk phrases that don't work, it can cost us respect among real conlangers. Most of us don't have the luxury of worrying about this (our stories are unlikely to be optioned for film, etc.), but it's something to consider. If a conlanger is hired to take over what we've done, they may have a hard time creating a complete language because our work is unusable.

We should also think about how often we'll use the world. If it's for one book, we could spend more time inventing the language than writing the book. By contrast, if this is the only or most in-depth world we're going to create, one that we intend to use for decades, then the time or money investment is much more worth it.

The Medium

Conlangs are arguably best suited to being spoken because we can hear inflection and tone despite not understanding it. Gestures and expressions help us infer meaning. Sometimes a character translates for other characters and us. Subtitles render these a moot point but can be tedious for the audience if it goes on for too long; this is one why some scenes start with actors speaking a conlang before switching to English, as if a universal translator has been switched on via the camera. That device helps characters *and* audiences bypass the impractical nature of invented languages. And of course, if we're working in TV or film, someone else may be tasked with this project, another reason we don't have to worry about it as much.

Readers have none of these to help them. Authors must repeat the sentences, doubling the word count of the sample, though it's doubtful we'd do this enough to significantly impact manuscript length. Sometimes we'll have a character sum up what's been said. If the audience is like me, they just skip over the conlang rather than trying to sound it out or understand it, since they're unlikely to succeed. This makes our effort a waste of time. Something else to consider is that pausing to examine the conlang will pull readers out of our story. We should avoid this. The main takeaway a reader will get is a sense of the tone, such as guttural versus elegant. A conlang allows us to show this rather than tell. This can be an important way to characterize a race/species or society, more than just the speaker.

OUR OPTIONS

We have several options for inventing a language.

First, we can ignore the subject altogether. This means that a book written in English has every last word in English. At best, we allude to other languages by narrating something like, "He said hello in his language before switching to Common." For authors, a minority of readers will object, but many won't even notice. For other industries, especially in SF, the universal translator idea spares us complaints.

A second option is to not invent a language but just make up words and phrases as we go along. This is what many world builders do. The only real downside is that any linguist or conlanger can tell we're doing this, but this minority understands how complicated inventing languages is and, while disappointed, likely understands our avoidance. How important is their opinion to you? Will you feel ashamed when they call you out, assuming they do (they won't)?

A third option is to create a language to one degree or another, such as a naming language. If we do this, it's recommended that we read more than one book on the art and invest ourselves in it. If we don't do it well, we're only pretending to do better than options one and two. This is only for those who:

• Are not intimidated by the books noted at this chapter's start
• Really want to do this
• Have the time, and
• Possibly intend to use the setting and therefore the language for a long time

The fourth option is to hire someone. Those with money to spare, or who are already profiting from their career, should seriously consider this, especially as a first foray into constructed languages. After all, we will have one of our own that we can learn how to use, and this may help us if we later invent one ourselves.

How to Hire Someone

We can hire a conlanger via the Language Creation Society's (LCS) site at https://conlang.org/. Simply fill out an application that includes details of what is needed and by when, and potential conlangers will contact us about fulfilling the job; LCS recommends providing 2-3 months lead time. As they note, clients (that's us) always want to know how quickly we can receive a translation for our needs; patience and planning are helpful.

Even when hiring someone, they're likely to use terms we don't understand if we haven't read any of the books mentioned in this chapter. For example, do we know what phonology is? Our conlanger may use terms like this and it behooves us to know what they're talking about and what we're buying, not to mention how to use it.

LCS suggests four order options, based on how much material we receive from the conlanger, who retains the right to suggest their own pricing. What follows are quotes, as of 2020, from their website: https://jobs.conlang.org/pricing

OPTION 1

- "Naming Language"
- Phonology (the sounds of the language)
- No grammar at all
- 2 dozen names
- $100 United States dollars (USD)

OPTION 2

- "Conlang Sketch"
- Phonology (the sounds of the language)
- A few basic forms of grammar
- 50 lexical items (vocabulary words, including names)
- $200 USD

OPTION 3

- Phonology (the sounds of the language)
- Basic grammar
- 150 lexical items (vocabulary words, including names)
- 5 sample sentences

- $400 USD

Option 4

- Phonology (the sounds of the language)
- Detailed grammar
- 500 lexical items (vocabulary words, including names)
- 20 sample sentences
- $800 USD

Where to Start

The first decision is whether we want to *use* an invented language, for what, and how often. This will determine whether the time or money invested is worth it. We should also decide if we're comfortable with inventing phrases as we go along without worrying whether they make sense to linguists, a small portion of the audience. If we think we will frequently use extensive passages, or the world is one we intend to use for decades, inventing (or hiring) may be worth it. Time spent on this world building task is time away from another task; do we have the time? For those who are already making money with their work or can afford it, this is one of the few world building tasks we can hire someone else to do for us. It's worth considering. The next recommended step is to buy one of the listed resource books, because even hiring someone requires knowledge – unless we've decided to ignore the subject altogether.

CHAPTER NINE

Names

Creating names for people, places, and things can be a challenging but necessary part of world building. This chapter will discuss techniques for inventing names, how language invention can inform our choices, and options regarding the different parts of names.

People Names

In order to explore naming, we should first understand which parts of one we're discussing. Differing terms are used for the parts, such as given name, surname, first name, last name, and more.

How Many Names?

Up until about the 12th century on Earth, not everyone had a first and last name, known as "given name" and "surname," which means having both is optional for our invented world. People in some countries have two or more surnames (and which can come before the given name). Hereditary last names are also not universal. Knowing the reasons for these variations will help us decide where on our world we could do similar things. We have flexibility.

The order of these names can vary, but in Western countries, the given name is typically the first name and the surname is the last. In Eastern countries, this order is often reversed. In Spanish-speaking countries, the given name is followed by the father's surname and then the mother's. This mostly matters to us if we're presenting both names to our audience. It's a simple way to distinguish one culture from another.

On Earth, some religions have saints, and those names have sometimes been adopted by others. One result is many people with the first name John, for example, resulting in a need for surnames to distinguish between them. One point here is that if we have famous knights or wizards in our world, their name can be highly sought.

GIVEN NAMES

The "given name" is bestowed (hence the term) upon the person, usually by their parents, but it can be decided by other relatives, particularly if the parents are absent or incapacitated. Or the cultural choice can be different, like grandparents doing it. Or an older sibling. We might decide that the state does it, especially in an authoritarian regime or a futuristic one where people are given a number instead. Consider the government type that this person was born into for whether people have freedom to name a child or not.

The name is typically given at birth but could be changed later if an important event or religious ceremony occurs. This could be as simple as the child's first, eighteenth, or twenty-first birthday. We can decide a boy becomes a man on losing his virginity and then he gets another given name; the same can be done with a girl, or when she bears a first child. They'll be known by something else in the meantime, or perhaps their initial name is replaced by another in a coming-of-age milestone of our choosing. If a character obtains magical power at puberty, for example, perhaps they get a wizarding name then, whether they or their instructor choose it. Names are sometimes changed when immigrating to another country, possibly to fit in. Ethnicity might be downplayed this way if the character has reason to fear hostility.

How might world builders use such information? Explaining via narration is the least attractive option. Dialogue might be better, such as one character noticing another's ethnicity but that their name doesn't quite match and then remarking on this, possibly snidely: "Your name won't hide what you are!"

On Earth, the given name distinguishes one person from another in a family or clan (because they'll all have the same surname/last name). Sometimes there is more than one given name, which means that one of them, referred to as the forename, is spoken first if both are used. Either one could have more prominence and be the main name for this person, but it's often the first one.

As for why a name is chosen, the reasons vary and are often combined. The simplest reason is that parents like the name. This may not apply to world builders, but wanting a name that's clear of negative associations can also rule out some choices; a relative of mine gave his daughter the name of a despised woman I once knew and for years, I thought of this every time I heard the girl's name. Names can be chosen in hopes that the child will have the character trait, such as Hope or Faith. On our invented world, we could decide a word like Kier means "heroic" in an old language and give this name to a character. We're only likely to mention such things on occasion.

Occupations can be another source of names, which is especially true of surnames, such as Smith. Objects can be chosen, as can places, the time of birth, or physical characteristics. Sometimes a surname becomes a given name, like Harrison.

Many names have a meaning that we may be unaware of because the name is based on old disused words. One issue is that names based on something can come across as literal unless we explain them, and it seems less like a name. For example, few of us know that David means beloved, so we'd have to explain that or call the character "Beloved," which might seem odd. As a result, this information is interesting but potentially not useful. If you're like most people, you may not know your own name's meaning. Your parents might not have either. Or they looked it up out of curiosity and then forgot what it means a month later.

It is possible to voluntarily choose a new name, in which case the phrase "given name" makes less sense unless we think of this as giving ourselves a new name.

SURNAMES

In contrast to the given name, the surname is inherited from either the family or a clan, but not all surnames are inherited. They are often chosen or changed, either by the individual or someone else, such as a servant's lord, or even government officials. Many who immigrated to the United States were simply given new surnames upon arrival. Sometimes those new names had something to do with their original name, such as a misspelling or Americaniza-tion of it, while other previous surnames were simply ditched by officials.

The original meaning of a surname is often lost in time. This is especially true if the spelling has been altered. In our work, we're more interested in giving characters names that mean something to not only them and other characters, but to the audience.

Any of our characters might have earned a name or simply inherited it.

USING PLACES

Surnames are often used to distinguish between two people in the same settlement who have the same given name. This means that in a small town or village, surnames might not be used. Galen is simply Galen. If he travels, he might be asked where he's from, resulting in others calling him Galen of Norin, which in time might become Galen Norin. This could become his surname if he's moved into a culture where others have one and there might be more than one Galen. One's place of birth need not be the sur-name, as later residences can apply instead.

If there's a prominent land feature, this can also be used, as can names of castles or other prominent buildings. The name of an actual hill can be used, so that Galen, who lives near Ardo Hill, becomes Galen Ardo, or the generic word for the feature can be used, resulting in Galen Hill. Regions such as counties, states, kingdoms (including long forgotten ones) and more can be used.

A knight might wish to suggest he comes from a re-spectable city instead of the less-favored one from where he actually originated. Said knight need have never even visited, much less lived, in that city. Few if any are likely to contest such a claim unless advanced technology, the kind found in SF, allows them to easily verify his origin. That said, a character doing this might have an accent that betrays him, for example, and be unaware his ruse is known or suspected.

In some countries or regions, an article is placed before the surname, such as "de" in France, resulting in Galen de Borun, and this is sometimes later altered to d'Borun or Deborun. When using an apostrophe in names, remember that the punctuation is replacing something. We can make a list of articles used in a given country; remember that not every name should have them as that looks too consistent and planned.

USING OCCUPATIONS

Surnames were often derived from an occupation, such as a blacksmith or ironsmith. This latter point raises an issue for fantasy authors. There are almost certainly blacksmiths in your world. If you call someone Galen Smith, that surname looks too much like a name from our world, which interferes with our attempts to create a world that appears different from Earth. The way to avoid this is, well, to avoid this. Choose occupational surnames that are likely for your world but don't exist in ours. Another option is to leave that example as Galen Blacksmith, because that's less familiar. This also allows us to introduce a character and state their profession simultaneously (unless it's different, in which case this can be a problem).

In some countries, servants took the first or last name of their employer as a surname, adding an "s" to the end. Galen's maid, Sori, becomes Sori Galens, or maybe Sori Isa-

Boruns. An actor who always plays the role of a king in plays becomes Galen King.

USING FIRST NAME

A surname is sometimes created from a first name. Using Galen again, his son could be Rogin Galenson or Rogin Galen. This first makes sense but also looks a too little Earth-like. His daughter might be Galendaughter, a common naming convention in some European countries. A shorter suffix might be simpler. In Russia, girls inherit their father's last name just like boys do, with one distinction: the letter "a" is added to a girl's last name. For example, Galen's son would be Rogin Ori Isa-Borun and his daughter would be Suri Pia Isa-Boruna. Simply adding "a" works for some names but not for others, so we'd need more than one version.

USING NICKNAMES

While we sometimes associate nicknames with being unflattering, not all of them are, and in either case, these can become a surname. Those who've refused to choose a surname are sometimes given an unflattering one. In our world, Trollman could be someone who has specialized in dealing with trolls or who resembled a troll. Any physical or even personal/mental characteristic can be used. If someone acts haughty like a hated nobleman, they could end up with that nobleman's surname, which is the reason some people on Earth have Caesar for a last name. To be more precise, a relative may have been given that surname derisively and then passed it down. In some cases, families remove unflattering names in later generations.

Another variant is using something unrelated to the individual, sometimes as an affectation. Someone can be named after the morning sun, a beautiful (or even deadly) flower, or an animal known for its strength.

COMPOUND SURNAMES

Where an individual has two last names, this is called a compound surname. Several varieties exist on Earth and can be leveraged for our world. Each of the two names is typically derived from one parent. Let's take the name Galen Sori Isa Borun and break it down:

First Given Name	Second Given Name	Paternal Last Name	Maternal Last Name
Galen	Sori	Isa	Borun

Figure 14 Compound Names

Galen Sori is his first and second given name. Isa is his paternal last name (i.e., his father's surname was Isa), and Borun is his maternal last name (his mother's surname was Borun).

If Galen has children, they can either inherit just Isa or both Isa Borun, but in Hispanic cultures, seldom if ever is only the maternal name (Borun) inherited alone. There's no reason we have to follow that, of course, but it shows some variations are available even here.

If Galen has children who inherit Isa Borun as a surname, and then they have children, it can become more complicated. For example, let's say Galen's son Rogin Ori Isa Borun marries a woman whose last name is also a compound name, Sine Tiona. They have a son, whose name could be Uron Dain Isa Borun Sine Tiona. Those wanting to shorten his name can call leave off his middle name "Dain," but they can also use only his father's surname, calling him Uron Isa Borun. Since it's not okay to use only the mother's surname, Sine Tiona, we can't call him Uron Sine Tiona. Variants on all of this exist.

Similarly, his father's surname being Isa Borun means it would be wrong to call Uron by just one of those: Uron Isa or Uron Borun are both wrong. This is again assuming we're following the Hispanic convention. We can invent our own rules.

To help avoid confusion, we can use punctuation: Galen Sori Isa-Borun has a son Rogin Ori Isa-Borun, who marries a woman with the last name Sine-Tiona. Their son is called Uron Dain Isa-Borun Sine-Tiona. In our work, we're seldom going to want to use all of these names, as audiences expect to be on a "first-name basis" as the expression goes in the United States, with our characters. This is considered more personal, and audiences want personal connections with characters.

PLACE NAMES

Naming places has a few unique considerations.

In our modern world, at least in the United States, few of us have any idea why any location bears its name. This may be true in our invented setting as well, and likely depends on how old places are. Since many places are named for someone, the person for whom they are named also has an impact if that association is remembered. Being named for someone that a culture has forgotten relegates the connection between person and place to the unknown. This is also affected by how long ago that person lived.

For example, we assume anywhere named Washington is named after the first president, but Dallas is just Dallas. In reality, the latter is named after George M. Dallas, but few know that, care, or have any idea why they should. In a world where travel is easy, such ignorance is more likely due to the sheer number of distant places (over a hundred miles) we can visit. But in a fantasy-like setting with restricted travel and far less information about the wider world, it's more likely that people know why each location within a certain distance bears its name. This is partly due to a lack of information overload that comes with technology. Consider this before spending too much time inventing justifications for names; your characters may be unlikely to know or discover this and we therefore have little reason to worry about it ourselves.

In a single work, we should avoid explaining the reason every place bears its name. It can start to sound like we're educating the audience or doing exposition housekeeping. Strategically pick the one or two places that are worth this, and briefly sneak in any such exposition. We decide based on whether the place's name and its origin can characterize the setting or not.

We can have our characters see a statue, painting, or carving, at city gates, on flags, on awnings, or on prominent buildings, possibly with a plaque that commemorates the namesake. Something that depicts the person is a little better because their appearance can give an idea who they were without explanation.

For example, "As he entered the gates of Kierdon, Antar smirked at the statue of Kier looming overhead, sword aloft, plate armor emblazoned with the knighthood's symbol, cloak swirling around him, for if Kier had still lived, he would've been mortified at the squalor and seediness that scurried around the town." We would then go on to paint more details about what Antar experiences as he goes about his business, hopefully making this relevant, too, such as someone stealing from him along the way. We could alternatively have him being chased through town by ruffians before finding himself cornered beneath that statue, which adds commentary to what's occurring.

We can invent place names using several rationales and techniques discussed next.

USING EVENTS

Names of places sometimes change, which can happen for several reasons. We don't have to worry about what the place was called before unless desired.

One of these is an event that creates the current name. If a shipwreck happened there, the ship's name might have renamed the place. A named weapon fired from that location could be the source. A nearby land feature can be the source of a disease name; Ebola was named after the Ebola River near one of the initial breakout sites.

Being conquered often results in a new name connected to the conquerors. An obvious example from Earth is the litany of cities named Alexandria after Alexander the Great conquered them. He could've named them after a god or hero, too. This is one way to create a name in a region, where that name is unlike those already there; sometimes these new names stay long after the conquerors are gone, though this seems more likely if occupation lasted a number of years; otherwise the conquered might just switch back to the old name.

The opposite is also true – the name of a place is given to an event, like a battle named after it. In SF, we might have an item being built here, like a well-known ship, weapon, or device named for the town of origin.

Another type of event is weather or other natural phenomena. A well-known example would be Winterfell from *Game of Thrones* . On Earth, places have been named Hurricane, Rainbow Springs, Frostproof, Waterproof, Cyclone, Snow, Tornado, Summer Lake, and Winter. The more literal names are less artful than Rainbow Springs and can suggest we didn't put much effort into them.

USING PEOPLE

One option is to name a place after a character or a surname. We see this on Earth all the time with names like Jacksonville or Harrisonburg. Other examples include the Cook Islands (named after Captain James Cook), Dominican Republic (Saint Dominic), and Seychelles (Jean Moreau de Seychelles). This can be done from villages all the way up to countries. We can add requirements, such as the person needing to be royalty before a place can be named after them. For more ideas, look at this very long list at Wikipedia: http://bit.ly/PlaceNamesPeople

The main issue with naming places after people is that it means inventing another character; we probably aren't naming a location after someone who's in the story we're telling. They'd have to be pretty old, for one, but it also makes things a little odd. However, if we've invented gods or other legendary figures (as discussed in *Creating Life, The Art of World Building, #1)*, we can leverage those names here. This is one area where building a world used for our entire career, rather than only the story currently on our minds, has an advantage, because we're more likely to have invented people we can repurpose. We might want to do an alternate version of their name to avoid confusion between the place and the person; using prefixes and suffixes (see the next section) makes this easy.

If we've already invented place names, we can retroactively decide these were people. We don't need to spend much time developing them as characters, as a line or two in our notes can suffice. For example, "Kierdon is named after the knight Kier Moonbright of Illiandor, who exemplified honor and valor at the time of the town's founding, for his heroic sacrifice at the Battle of Hestia, where he saved the crown prince at the cost of his own life."

For what reasons do we name places after people? In addition to heroes, legendary figures, and important discoverers and political figures, we often use religious saints. If people embody a positive character trait, such a person may be chosen in a show of optimism about the quality and character of the location's citizens. This trait needs no basis in fact. Those with both good and bad characteristics will exist in every location, so this is a technique we can use to quickly invent past priests or wizards in our world.

ADDING SUFFIXES AND PREFIXES

Some names are based on a surname, which can be more obvious when we're familiar with that surname, such as Washington or Jackson. This familiarity doesn't exist on invented worlds. While we can certainly use such names without alteration, we can also alter them with either a familiar suffix or prefix from Earth or one of our invention.

The examples below can spark imagination:

- Ville (Jacksonville)
- Burg (Harrisonburg)
- Sted (Christiansted)
- Caster (Lancaster)

- Chester (Manchester)
- Avon (Avonmouth)
- Burn (Blackburn)
- Don (Abingdon)
- Den (Willesden)
- Ford (Stafford)
- Gate (Helmsgate)
- Ing (Reading)
- Mere (Windemere)
- Ton (Hamilton)

Doing this in fantasy or SF might result in places names like the following:

- Flamecaster
- Magedon
- Fluxton
- Stafford
- Spellburn
- Orbdon
- Laserton
- Droidsted
- Spellcaster
- Beamdon
- Blasterville
- Cryoton
- Cyberburg
- Rayburn
- Hivemere
- Moonford
- Aeongate
- Unimere

COMPOUND NAMES

We can also combine words, whether we leave a space between them or not. For example, East Haven and Easthaven both work well. This lets us take two somewhat ordinary words and fashion something unique from them. More examples include Black Hollow, Broken Shield, Hero's March, Goldleaf, Ironforge, Oakheart, Raven's Nest, and Silverhelm. A partial list of source words is here (and don't forget to use colors, directions, and plants and animals, either of our invention or not):

- End
- Keep
- Break
- Dale

- Spring
- Streams
- Horn
- Vale
- Ridge
- Falls

- Pass
- Den
- Heart
- Crest
- Field
- Moor

UNIQUENESS

Inventing a name that no one else is using appeals to both world builders and our audience. But it's possible to invent a name that's already in use without realizing it, and we can always claim this excuse, partly because it's unrealistic for us to know every name ever used by every creative person in history. The odds of any author coming up with a name no one has ever done before, or ever will again, are slim. Even so, we should try, because uniqueness prevents confusion and a reader associating the name with something that's already familiar. We often hope that a character, place, or thing we've invented becomes famous; a distinctive and cool name helps this. It's worth noting that combining familiar words helps audiences absorb them quickly. The examples in the previous "Compound Names" section demonstrate this.

Sometimes people who have multiple names become known by just one, like Cher, Bono, and Sting. They are said to be mononymous. But it's far easier to create a unique name by combining words (for places) or given and surnames (for people). There are far more Lukes than there are Luke Skywalkers. There's only one Han Solo. Only one Princess Leia, who could almost be considered mononymous in that she's got a title and one name; it's not clear in the films whether Leia is her given or surname (it's her given; her surname is Organa even though her family name could also be Skywalker were it not for adoption).

When inventing a name, don't worry if you invent a word that, as it turns out, already exists, even if you're naming a plant, animal, or species instead of a character. It's not ideal but also not a big deal. There are countless words in English that have two meanings and there's no reason yours can't become meaning number two. On the other hand, if you find that the word exists and is objectionable in some way, or easily confused with what you're doing, you might change it in one of the ways mentioned in this chapter.

As a case in point, I used "drek" long ago only to later learn that it means "shit" in German. Go ahead and laugh. I did. And then I stopped using that. It pays to Google any word you invent. Ignorance can be bliss until someone in the know sends you an email and you cringe. As "drek" illustrates, a word that doesn't exist in English may exist in another language.

It can become an exercise in futility trying to avoid every last word, so don't worry too much. I once invented "kryll" for one of my Llurien species only to discover many years later that "krill" are a type of marine life. I decided I don't care partly because I spell it differently and few people are going to know that word. And if they do, they know krill are a small crustacean whereas my kryll live on land, meaning there's little reason to confuse one with the other. Nonetheless, a beta-reader once pointed it out with "LOL! Why are you naming this after tiny fish!?!"

A more recent incident brings up another problem: someone far more prominent than you can invent a similar name long after you did. In this case, Seth MacFarlane's show, *The Orville*, also has humanoids called krill. I still frown every time I hear it, but I'm not changing a name

I've been using since 1991 because Seth used a similar one starting in 2017. I know some people will ask why I stole Seth's name instead of using one of my own, criticizing my lack of originality and even claiming I'm a Seth fanboy. On the plus side, I published *The Ever Fiend* in 2016 featuring a kryll, so I have proof I used it first. Still, I wonder why Seth named his humanoids after tiny fish!

LEVERAGING EXISTING NAMES

If there's a name we really like, we can sometimes use it without consequence, but this depends on the name and how much of it we use without alteration. A famous name like Luke Skywalker is one to avoid. Even the surname can't be used due to its heavy association with him. A variation like Airwalker might work, but the similarity in subject matter between air and sky is also more problematic/reminiscent of him. On the other hand, Nightwalker doesn't immediately call him to mind, unless his full name is Luke Nightwalker. Even Lucas Nightwalker might tip off people as to what we're doing. As usual with an analogue, follow my Rule of Three: at least three significant changes. In the case of a name, just two changes may suffice, such as Kier Nightwalker.

There are other names that might not be household ones, but which are still too well known in the genres to use, even in an altered state, without raising some eyebrows. This includes Legolas from *The Lord of the Rings*, Raistlin Majere from *Dragonlance*, or Voldemort (*Harry Potter*). Be careful leveraging such names. It's arguably better to borrow a minor character's name or use one from a lesser known work or author.

General Tips

Making any aspect of our work challenging for the audience can kill enthusiasm and conversation about it, and this includes names. This issue can manifest in several ways, each with its own solution.

Keep it Short

Long names tend to be harder to read, remember, spell, and pronounce than shorter ones. This includes too many names, or syllables within a name.

More than three names may be excessive. In English speaking countries, we typically use just the first name, the surname only when being formal, or both when introducing someone. The middle name is almost never used unless it is part of a stage name or someone goes by that *instead of* the first name. We can invent something different, and other cultures have already done so, but the point is that we seldom use more than this. We can invent a long name like Liminera Solto Ariso Nubien Arta Astol Munir, but few people want to see that more than once.

Names with too many syllables are hard, too. Four syllables is considered long but not unwieldy. Exceed this infrequently (once a story). Strive for between one and three syllables much of the time.

With long names, such as Limineraslyvarisnia, people tend to skip much of it rather than working it out as we did when inventing it. In actual usage, such names get shortened anyway, such as to Limi or maybe Nera. It can still be advantageous to invent such a lengthy one to create a sense of cultural differences, but we'll want to use the long version once or twice, such as when introducing the character in narration, or at a formal ceremony.

In addition, sometimes parents or other authority figures will use the long version when expressing disapproval or affection. By contrast, the short version can be a show of familiarity, whether that's appropriate or not. If we want to use this device in a story, maybe we should still use the short version in narration (implying this is how the character thinks of themselves) and only put the full name in another character's mouth.

When writing content such as a summary or book blurb, use the version that's easiest to absorb. The long version could give the impression we'll be doing that all the time and possibly turn off a potential reader. However, using first and last name can be good if the combination sounds very cool and gives a hint about their character or type, such as Talon Stormbringer, the name of my all-purpose fantasy action hero.

KEEP IT SIMPLE
(APOSTROPHES AND HYPHENS)

People are drawn to simpler things, and that includes names. World builders can easily create a sense of somewhere different from Earth (or another culture in our invented world) with unusual naming conventions, but some approaches can be overused or otherwise annoy readers. This includes too many consonants, hyphens, or apostrophes. One of these per name is better than several, even if spread across a character's given and surnames.

One problem with too many consonants, like Ghlnalenkm, is the difficulty in pronouncing it. Some readers may find this easier than others due to similar occurrences in their language, but others won't and something as simple as a name shouldn't be a point of consternation for our audience. In the case of Ghlnalenkm, the "h" adds no value. We could also surmise that there's a vowel somewhere in the start, such as "Gal" or "Glen," producing Ghalnalenkm or Ghlenalenkm. Why not just write them that way ? Or get rid of the "h" and get Galnalenkm or Glenalenkm.

Hyphens are used to connect two words, like Smith-Davies when a married woman wants to keep her surname when taking her husband's surname, too. While the culture might use hyphens, that doesn't mean we need to show it to our reader all the time. In the above case, maybe mention Smith-Davies and then reduce it to Smith for the rest of the work. We can write something like, "She went by Smith instead of her legal name, Smith-Davies, out of laziness, but never in the presence of her husband, who'd been known to arch an eyebrow when she didn't add his Davies." This smoothly gets in some characterization and tension while doing some housekeeping exposition.

Why is an apostrophe used? It takes the place of an omitted letter, or potentially several of them. This justification reveals how truly optional this is – and therefore how easy it is to avoid. Do we really need to replace a letter? What's wrong with it?

Before doing this, decide what letter is being omitted and whether it seems better that way. Fantasy writers have been using (abusing?) apostrophes for a long time, and this is precisely why many people loathe it. A quick Google search will reveal a heaping of scornful posts about this. Do we want our audience rolling their eyes? That's contempt for us, so probably not.

To avoid that reaction, we should have a justification for it, though the obvious problem with this is the need to explain it. However, a single sentence can do. What justification do we need? Making a long name shorter by replacing letters with an apostrophe is a good one. We can replace Smith-Davies with S'Davies; that's an awkward example because it sounds bad, but you get the idea. We can explain, "Recruits were called Marmillionor partly to haze them with the unwieldly mouthful that had produced widespread derision for eons, and which shortened to M'ionor upon graduation."

An apostrophe is also used for a contraction, such as "can't" instead of "cannot." The main issue we face is that people won't understand what we're contracting unless we explain it, so it looks random. We can get around this with some characterization: "He'd been a wizard of the Marmili Order before becoming one of the famed knights of Ionor, and while the combination was rare, the title of M'Ionor struck awe into everyone but the surly guard barring his way." Note how in this case the "I" is capitalized due this resulting from two titles being combined, unlike the previous example, where letters within a single word were omitted. This could be written Mionor, but the significance of two merged titles is then lost, though many won't realize this detail.

We may want to use the apostrophe to suggest pronunciation. This often happens when several adjacent vowels should be sounded apart rather than as one. For example, the word "Tourten" is likely read as two syllables ("TOR-ten"), but writing it as "To'Urten" makes it three ("tow-UR-ten"). We could further decide that the first two letters are short for "Torni," for example; this means "To'Urten" is short for "Torni Urten."

The one thing we don't want to do with apostrophes is have no reason for using one (or giving the appearance of this). Making a name sound like a fantasy one by including a senseless apostrophe is not a reason. It is the most loathed justification and considered shallow. Even when we have a good reason, we should use them sparingly. "All things in moderation."

The Issue of Similarities

There's an idea that an author should avoid having two characters whose names start with the same letter, such as Adam and Aiden, in the same story. The reason is that people often don't read very carefully and mostly notice the first letter, especially if the names are also roughly the same length. In misreading it, they can think a different character is saying or doing something, causing confusion.

The same principle can be extended to naming places or things in a given work. Don't name one place Newall and another one Norall; in this case I've also made the ending the same to illustrate this point. A variety is easier to accomplish if we're world building to tell a story, because we can invent the names just for that story, but if creating a world for general and repeated use, we do run the risk of inventing two places that appear in the same tale sooner or later. While not a guideline to obsess over, the trick here is to not name adjacent places too similarly, as they're the one most likely to be visited within a single story.

Sound

A name's sound matters more in mediums where people will say it, but authors should still think about the impression it creates and how easy it is to say. Be sure to say your invented words aloud. This tells us much about how feasible it is and whether other characters are likely to use the full term or shorten it. If we're struggling to pronounce it, that's a bad sign. Don't worry if your audience doesn't say it right, as it's bound to happen for even mono-syllable words. If accuracy really matters to you, we have the option of providing a pronunciation guide on the book's website. This can take the form of a short audio file of ourselves saying the name. Modern technology makes it very easy to produce such recordings.

Appearance

Books aren't really considered a visual medium, but the look of a word matters for style. While we can't read elvish, Tolkien's flowing script creates a smooth impression, while many hard consonants can suggest brutality and coarseness. Adding silent letters can change appearance while not interfering with pronunciation. We may want to use certain letters within one culture, such as always using a k instead of a c, or replacing i with y. For example, Lonnieri vs. Lonnyery. Letter combinations can also be frequently repeated, such as "ier" as in the names Kier, Lonnieri, and Raediera.

Techniques for Inventing Names

We can use several techniques while inventing names, which can be more fun than using a name generator. It's more creative and gives a feeling of ownership and pride. These techniques are presented in no order and can be combined.

SILENT OR REPEATED LETTERS

Taking a simple or known word and adding silent or repeated letters is simple. H is great for this. Galen becomes Ghalen. Add an extra l to create Gallen. An extra n makes it Galenn. This can change the pronunciation but that's fine as long as we like it. Other good choices for silent letters are s and m, while many letters can be repeated depending on their position in the word.

VOWEL SUBSTITUTION, ADDITION, OR SUBTRACTION

Vowels can be changed, added, or subtracted to and from existing and invented words. An extra vowel gets us Gaalen or Galeen (with a possible pronunciation change). Maybe Gaelen is better. Or Galan. Swapping y for an i or e gets us Galyn or Galin.

CAPITALIZE ANOTHER LETTER

We can capitalize additional letters, but only two is likely best. This works better in longer words, like GaLendria, but this might work better with an apostrophe, such as Ga'Lendria. We typically capitalize the first letter, but there's no reason a culture can't choose another, resulting in gaLendria or ga'Lendria. We might want an explanation for this, such as humility being prized so that less importance is placed on the self; therefore, the initial letter isn't so tall. That viewpoint could result in the entire name not being capitalized, like some modern performers such as k.d. lang, but it may cause audience confusion and should be used wisely. It might also look like a regular word, not a title. Capitalizing a different letter might also benefit from an explanation, such as galenDria, where galen is the given name and Dria is the surname; the surname takes prominence so that family members have a "family first" attitude.

SWITCHING FIRST LETTERS

We can switch the first letters of known words. Woman becomes Soman, Doman, Roman (maybe not that one), or Loman; I could go on. The computer manufacturer Dell becomes Kell or Xell. Look at your keyboard's letters while doing this. It helps.

ADD SUFFIXES OR PREFIXES

Adding a one syllable suffix to the end of a word helps add style if we use it with some consistency. It can help characterize a region or culture, too. Galen now becomes Galenor or Galendor, though the latter sounds like a place. Instead, maybe Galenda. A prefix could create Dagalen, though that no longer looks like a prefix, partly because it's so short. We could change the capitalization to daGalen. If we used a hyphen or apostrophe, we get Da-Galen, Da'Galen, or da'Galen.

BREAKING KNOWN WORDS UP

A challenging but fun approach is to look at products around us and steal a syllable or two, and maybe change some letter. This often produces very good names. As I wrote this, "Galen" was on a nearby product, which is how that got chosen. So is "solutions," which I can turn into "Lucion" by dropping the first syllable and replacing a letter. More examples: "Plantronics" becomes Ronik, "Contigo" becomes Tigo, and "moisturizer" becomes Irizor and Sturin. If you don't like the result, play with it until you do. Maybe Kirizor and Asturin are better?

Foreign Languages

We can take names from languages foreign to our own, either wholesale or as a basis for modification. This is particularly useful if we want to create a sense of shared names in a culture; if we need many words, inventing them from scratch can be difficult. This is known as an analogue, and while my Rule of Three doesn't apply as much, it's still good to make at least one change, instead of three, to prevent people from recognizing the name. From Asia we can take the names Amida, Bae, and Kaede and convert them to something of ours using techniques in this section, resulting in Amidar, Baedin, or Kaedi, for example.

Be Consistent, Just Not Too Much

When inventing names of people or places within a region, some consistency helps create the impression of unification. To adopt a naming style, use certain elements repeatedly. Which elements will depend on our preference. Any aspect of a name can do. For example, the suffix "or" can be added for Galenor and Ravenor, or the "ae" combo to cause Laeryn and Novinae. Then create a place with both: Daelinor. It's also okay to have names that don't meet these conventions because too much consistency looks too planned.

NAME GENERATORS

Free name generators exist on the internet. Most focus on character names, but we can leverage the results for places or things, too. Some of them allow us to choose what sort of name we'd like, such as Elvish or Klingon. We can also choose the gender. The resulting names will fit the style we've chosen, though this feature won't help us much if we've invented our own species.

The generators can make naming much faster and easier. With a button click, we get dozens of potential names. If we don't like them, another click generates another batch. A side-effect of so many shown to us is that we can become picky and quickly dismissive. This may be why I personally have found most of the results to be poor and unusable, but your luck or standards may differ. We can also use such a name as a starting point, altering it using the techniques in this chapter.

One negative to this is that it lacks creativity. A program is doing the work for us. This reduces or eliminates a personal connection to the result; having less investment in the world we've invented can make us care less about it, which might show in our work and impact the audience's connection for the worse, too. Our personality is also missing. If there's an impression we're hoping to create with names, the name generators are less likely than our minds to produce what we seek.

A few name generators are listed here, the first having over a thousand styles from which to choose and includes places, objects, and more:

- http://fantasynamegenerators.com/
- https://www.name-generator.org.uk/
- http://www.seventhsanctum.com/index-name.php
- http://www.fantasynamegen.com/
- http://www.rinkworks.com/namegen/
- https://www.behindthename.com/

WHERE TO START

We should start inventing names of people before places because we can name those locations after some of our characters. Objects should come later because these are sometimes named after places where they originated or were used dramatically. For people, choose a sovereign power where you wish to create names and think about the culture you've envisioned for them. Do they place importance on family names? Do they wish to honor both mother and father so that both surnames are taken by a child? If so, considering hyphenating that for clarity. This may also suggest names tend to be longer. Choose a rationale for the number and order of names. Decide if an initial given name is replaced by another at an important milestone in life. While inventing names using the techniques in this chapter, choose a few letter combinations, such as prefixes and suffixes, that are common, to begin creating a style of names within that sovereign power.

We'll likely be creating names for multiple powers in our career, so we can just practice with this and improve as we go. I'm much better at this now than twenty years ago and you soon will be, too. Our story or world might also have multiple sovereign powers for which we intend to invent names, so try to vary the style of one place from another, but don't worry over this too much. Countries that speak the same language will have some similarities.

For naming places and objects, the techniques in this chapter can get us started, and we can leverage some of those people names. Using a little ingenuity and some techniques, name generation can be fun. Sometimes we might have momentum doing this and it can be wise to just invent many names at once and save them for later. Lastly, we might also get started with those name generators and modify the results if they're close to our desire.

CHAPTER TEN

OTHER SYSTEMS

This chapter covers other systems that will exist in our world, including educational, health, legal, commerce, and information systems.

EDUCATION SYSTEMS

Educational systems aren't the most glamorous subject but should be given a thought because every character has either gone through one (to one degree of success or another), skipped it, or one didn't exist during their coming of age. Unless every character had the same experience, the differences between them will impact interactions, opportunities, and more. Developing character backstory is incomplete without this.

A system can be easier to devise if we omit explaining it. Few of us know why the system that raised us exists as is, which is one reason we'll accept a different one if presented authoritatively. This is also a subject few are curious about, including audiences. Unless we intend to set a story in a school, we can skimp on inventing details.

Systems are often public, meaning that the government pays for them, likely through taxes, but a church can be the provider as well (paid for with donations?). This means students do not have to pay to attend, but they may need to purchase supplies, including textbooks, and we can change such a detail. The schools that require students to pay are known as private schools that, in theory, provide a superior experience. It is likely that if public education exists, some private instruction might, too. We can decide when we want a character to have attended one, at which point we need a name, specialties, and reputation for the school and students.

Systems can be broken down into basic and special.

BASIC EDUCATION

Basics are the subjects that most of us take for granted: reading, writing, and arithmetic. History, sports, music, art, culture, and more are typically included in earlier years and more specialized extensions are taught to teenagers. That would also mean biology, chemistry, different versions of math (algebra, geometry, trigonometry, etc.), and increasingly advanced uses of language, including foreign ones. The latter is especially important in fantasy and SF that includes multiple species, each with their own verbal and possibly written language. In a world like ours or a more advanced one (SF), we and our audience can assume these subjects exist and characters can learn them. This allows us to largely skip inventing details if desired.

But in a less developed world, less of this will be taught formally if at all. This impacts fantasy authors with a setting like a medieval one. Education may not have gone beyond the equivalent of fifth or sixth grade if it was required at all. One reason is that children must often work in the family business because earning money or performing labor is more important than book learning. The invention of machines to automate or improve the speed of tasks, or increase the yield of something like farming, helps create more resources and "free time" that becomes available for education. Consider whether basic needs are being met in the society without great physical labor. If they're not, it's likely that education is a lower priority.

When this is the case, only a few people will achieve more advanced education, meaning what we might learn in our teenage years (in middle, junior, or high school, or whatever we call them). We can consider this a kind of second tier of basic education, rather than specialized education, which we'll examine next. There will be a criterion for those who are chosen for this extra instruction, such as being wealthy or unusually smart, and special permission may be required. Certainly, nobles are not assigned mundane tasks and therefore have the time for this. It's one way they can easily distinguish themselves from peasants.

Decide how education works based on the story needs for characters who know more than others. Given that basic education may not be forced, this creates ample room for ignorant characters, who only know what they hear and may get by with streets smarts and people skills far more than learning. This seems likely in fantasy settings. Larger settlements provide for people with more specialized skills and this also suggests training for them and better education. It is believable to decide bigger settlements means better (or simply more) education opportunities and therefore that our most educated characters come from cities rather than rural areas.

Our setting might include magic or advanced technology, and if their prevalence is high, basic instruction in them may also be provided. This won't turn someone into a wizard or engineer, but just as grade school teaches students high-level concepts about music or art, the population might know basics about magic or warp drive, for example. Those who become engineers need subsequent advanced education (i.e., college or technical school). Here's what we might write in a society's file for basic education:

For SF: "At age 6, students are legally required to enroll at a public Kierdyn School (named for the famous scientist, Kier), which they attend until age 16. After this, each student must enroll in a technical school for 2 years, learning space sciences. Advanced education beyond this is available in three-year stints, each resulting in a degree."

For fantasy: "At age 6, students may enroll in a private Kierdyn School (named for the god of knowledge, Kier) if their parents can spare the child's work hours and afford the modest price; students may work at the school in lieu of paying in gold. Enrollment is not required. School ends at age 12, though students can leave prior to this. Advanced schooling beyond this is only for nobility or those considered unique or special, and who must pay with not less than ten years of service in their profession after graduation (refusal results in lifelong servitude)."

SPECIAL EDUCATION

Any education that takes a deep dive into a subject can be considered specialized training that not everyone receives. For example, musicians might take specialized lessons as teens or earn one or more college degrees later, becoming an expert. Without basic education, advanced education is unlikely to exist, though we can decide by subject; focus on skills characters need. Someone can become an expert without this education, but there are typically gaps in their understanding or knowledge.

If schooling ends before the teens, this type of education is unlikely except for nobility and rare individuals. In fantasy settings, we typically see less formal schooling. This suggests special education is rare and therefore private, via an apprenticeship or guild. With its advanced technology, SF suggests that specialized education is widespread, but it depends on the setting. A dystopia may feature a destroyed or depleted infrastructure. Many tools are so easy to use that people need only training in how to design and repair them; we don't need to work out the education system to determine this.

So what do we need to decide? Mostly how common different kinds of educated learning is, per subject, if they matter to our story. We can make anything rare by limiting the number of resources available to teach it, whether instructors, actual schools, or textbooks. For anything common, colleges or technical schools will teach it. If we need details, determine prerequisites, training duration, subjects taught, the awarded degree, and professions. Unless it's art, like music, few people get an advanced degree for personal enrichment, but for employment opportunities thus raised. Characters can bond with each other by discussing how much they both hated a subject you decided was disliked.

THE APPRENTICESHIP

With both knights and wizards, we see squires and apprentices respectively; other versions of this can exist in both fantasy and SF. But this is sometimes not part of a system if it's private instruction. Being a knight's squire might have defined expectations and a wizard's apprentice may not, unless that wizard belongs to a guild that sets forth rules; we have leeway here. These understudies typically live with their master for years, doing menial work and otherwise attending to their master's professional and even household needs, in addition to receiving instruction. Decide if this makes sense in the setting for any profession. It is more likely when public education is lacking or when someone is an especially sought-after master. It can also be true when the master or subject is evil, for lack of a better word, because it's unlikely that public education teaches their methods.

Since this is less formal, we may not need to decide at what age apprenticeship can begin, and what duties are expected, what life is like for both master and understudy, and how it ends unless these are standardized. It could be a privileged life of fine dining with powerful people or a miserable one of squalor, suffering, and fear. If the profession is dangerous, this apprenticeship likely is as well. What sort of protection does the master provide, whether physically present or not? What are the benefits beyond the chance to acquire knowledge and skills? Forging personal connections could be a significant attraction, but then it depends on how much respect the apprentice is given. Someone may have had more than one apprenticeship in their past, with wildly different experiences. This is as much a character building as world building issue, other than deciding whether it's available and for what professions, typically, and whether something like a guild or knighthood establishes guidelines.

Other Concerns

For all systems, we should decide how many years of school are typical and at what age it begins and ends. Some governments mandate this so that it's against the law to skip it; the parents are typically the ones responsible for ensuring it happens and the ones punished for refusing, not the child, but we don't have to do that. The child could be punished instead. The problem with doing so is that children understand consequences less than adults, but if you had to complete your homework to get any food, you'd learn the lesson pretty quickly. We can be inventive with this. While that seems cruel, maybe an invented species of ours values self-reliance and isn't above teaching hard lessons.

Are students expected to be separated from parents at any point in their education, living at a school or with a teacher (a boarding school)? This may be only on school days, through a semester or school year, or until graduation. Does segregation exist, such as by gender, species, race, ethnicity, social class, blood line, delinquency, or other elements? Does the school have facilities, such as dorms, gyms, libraries, labs, and other specialty rooms mingled with classrooms, in a separate building, or away from school altogether? These details mostly matter if we're setting a story at school or a character has been impacted, such as not seeing their family for years. But we can also drop little details into stories, such as a wizard's lab being crowded with students after school hours because it's off campus, and now our wizard character must contend with people being in the way.

HEALTH SYSTEMS

MEDICAL

Medical care varies widely between fantasy and SF worlds, though sometimes the latter has systems just as poor. Regardless of genre, it's too convenient for wounded or sick characters to be instantly healed, without needing convalescence. It's like when death loses meaning because dead people are easily revived without consequence; why fear for a character who can return? A recent vampire show featured them snapping each other's necks during disputes. This would kill a mortal, but all it did to them was render them unconscious for an hour or two. Despite this, even other vampire characters would react as if someone they loved had just been murdered and they'd never see them again. Wouldn't they be blasé about it? The neck snapping thing was little more than an inconvenience, so why react with horror? Similarly, if an audience knows characters can return from the dead or be instantly healed without issues, there's no drama in health problems. For this reason, fights in superhero movies have no tension because everyone's going to be fine! Removing tension is the opposite of a smart storytelling device.

It can be hard to generalize about average life expectancy before 1900 on Earth, due to it rising and falling, but it was seldom above thirty. However, if someone made it to age twenty, they could often expect to live another thirty years, especially among the wealthy, who had better access to health care. Children are more susceptible to sickness; the percentage of those reaching adulthood could be as low as 60%. In our fantasy settings, few characters will have living grandparents, or may not have both parents still alive. Most in their twenties are probably long married (even widowed, sometimes more than once) and with a few kids, and yet we seldom see this, perhaps because it gets in the way of adventuring and our escapism. When lifespans lengthened, the marriage age naturally rose, too. We can decide how long people are living, and the effects of this, based on story needs and general understanding of population health and resources.

Magical healing, or "laying on hands," usually means channeling a god's power through one's body as a vessel, to heal the wounded. This often means that a holy person communes with that god, first establishing a relationship through prayer so that he's not a stranger when calling on the god for this favor. Whether we call them a priest or another name doesn't matter. This can exist in either SF or fantasy but is more common in the latter; SF typically has either medicine equivalent to Earth's today or technology far in advance of us. In settings with supernatural power, we may have supernatural wounds that require supernatural healing techniques, as they may not respond to other methods. This is one justification, not that we need one, for magical healing.

Until recently on Earth, the understanding of germs was also poor, resulting in behaviors that spread illness more easily, such as people not washing their hands well or at all. The idea of invisible germs making people sick can be met with skepticism. In the early 1900s in New York, Mary Mallon, better known as Typhoid Mary, was an example of someone being a carrier, which means she showed no symptoms but can transmit that disease. She didn't believe she had it due to the lack of symptoms; she refused to change her habits and infected others continuously until health officials imprisoned her for life to stop her. While some of that is specific to her, we can apply such concepts to inventing pandemics. A fantasy setting without multiple plagues (or lesser outbreaks) in the past may be unrealistic. That a parent (or earlier generation) perished this way is useful character backstory.

Many of us have heard of bloodletting, which has an interesting theory we can incorporate. Ancient physicians believed the body had four "humors" and that an excess or deficiency in any, or a poor mixture of them, resulted in illness. The four humors were blood, yellow bile, phlegm, and black bile, which is thought to be clotted blood (it appears black). Each humor was believed to have origins in specific body parts, and properties that resulted in certain illnesses. For example, yellow bile caused warm illnesses, and so on. Bloodletting attempted to cure someone by removing an excess humor to restore them to normal. People were sometimes made to consume a food or drink to counter a perceived imbalance in humors. These doctors were wrong, of course, but the practices lasted for over two thousand years, had no healing effects (unless coincidentally), and were sometimes harmful to patients. Not only can our invented world have such theories, but maybe we have species that actually work this way.

When medical ignorance abounds, quacks proliferate. Using wild claims of perfect cures, these disreputable people try to sell or otherwise profit from questionable and unproven medical remedies, then flee before the truth is discovered. Sometimes by luck, they actually helped, and not all quacks had malicious intent. They often claimed that exotic materials added to something like oil or a balm would help their foolish or desperate victims; if we've invented unique lifeforms, we can create an alternative to the "snake oil salesman" idea. These could be harmful, addictive, benign, or ease symptoms but not cure as claimed. A new, similar counterpart exists today, when conspiracy theorists claim that something proven to be beneficial, like immunization shots, are making people sick instead, in defiance of evidence to the contrary.

In SF, the exploration of new worlds can result in a flow of new discoveries, including both medical problems and solutions, and therefore, more quacks. There can also be devices, like the polygraph (lie-detector) that do not measure what they claim to. Based on the education system we've imagined, we should form an idea of the likelihood of such scams to succeed, but even today, many believe the polygraph works.

Fantasy worlds are usually akin to our past, meaning poorer health care and shorter lives, which pushes other milestones earlier. Today we consider it scandalous that a girl in her early teens might be expected to marry and give birth (especially when married off against her will), but it was practical because she might've been dead before twenty. There may also be the equivalent of medical devices to supposedly measure some aspect of a person; we have discretion to decide if they actually work or not.

SF offers a wider variety of health care quality due to lack of uniformity across the genre as to technological levels. This is especially true in planet-hopping stories, as every society on a new planet will have developed skills at different rates. Even spacecraft must get their organic medical supplies from somewhere else unless these are being synthesized. Given this wide range, how do we decide who can do what? One answer is story needs. Determine what kind of armed conflict will result, what sort of weapons exist and their damage severity and type, and then how many characters must be killed, maimed, bedridden, or healed (and to what degree) to impact our story for tension.

MENTAL

On Earth, mental health services are a recent development; they hardly existed before two hundred years ago. Before that, people were often thought to be touched by the devil, possessed, or some other nonsense. Many were either killed or confined, whether in more official places like an asylum or in the basement of a village resident assigned to care for these prisoners, who might be shackled day and night. Sometimes sane people were dealt with this way when they went against powerful people or social movements, calling for change.

We can do the same in a fantasy setting or inject our modern compassion and understanding into the world. In SF, it's reasonable that advances in health care parallel those in other areas of technology, but it's not a rule. We've all seen seemingly dystopian SF where ships, space stations, and characters are all filthy and lawlessness seems to predominate; both physical and mental health needs may suffer, too, as the latter can almost be considered a luxury. The case can be made that the development of machinery helps provide for basics like food and shelter more easily and that "free time" is subsequently available for professions like psychology, but when people are struggling to get food, no one wants to spend time helping a disturbed person.

One reason all of this impacts characters is that people hear psychological terms, should they exist, and use them just as we do. But that depends on information flow. It's better in SF, in theory, than in fantasy, as is education. Even a dystopian society where that education system has disintegrated might still be aware of the terms, if they entered common usage before the collapse. Do we want our characters using such terms? They're optional. The term "ego" hadn't been invented in medieval times, but people were aware of it, anyway, using other words like pride.

LEGAL SYSTEMS

Most of our settings will have a legal system, even if it's as simple as "an eye for an eye." This section takes a high level and simplified view of these systems because most world builders will not be writing a legal drama, which is the only scenario where more detail is likely needed. Some places have a mix of the systems we'll cover, and we can do the same, though we may struggle for a reason to. In our setting, the publication of legal decisions, so that everyone can access them, is required; without this, laws are not enforced equally.

With all systems, our usage is primarily to cause trouble for our characters, who run afoul of a law, either by breaking it, encouraging others to do so, or even just speaking out against it. Any of these are more likely when traveling, due to ignorance of local laws, but there are other factors. Characters are usually on a mission and only passing through, and are therefore trying to avoid trouble, but we can have one member who tends to cause problems and another who knows the local laws and tells them what not to do. Use this as a guide. This helps us add an issue that either develops character(s) or plot.

TYPES

There are several types of legal systems. The source of laws is one of their primary differences. The system type arguably matters less than specific laws that impact our story, but they are briefly summarized next.

CIVIL LAW

One of the most widespread systems (along with common law), civil law means that a legislature creates and modifies an authoritative source that formalizes laws. That source is either a constitution (at the sovereign power or federal level) or a statute (at a lower level, such as states in the United States). Constitutional law tends to be broad and interpreted more at the statutory level, which is one reason variations can exist between states within a union. For example, as of this writing, marijuana is illegal at the federal level in the U.S. but legal in some states. To do this in our fictional world, we mostly need to know there's a sovereign power and self-governing bodies (like states or provinces) within it. A character can get themselves into trouble outside their home territory because they didn't know something legal back home is illegal somewhere else. This can happen within a power, not just when traveling between different ones. If there's no law we've broken when we're brought before a judge, he has no authority and the case will be dismissed.

COMMON LAW

Common law derives its name from being common across England among the king's courts, and since Britain's empire spread far, it is now common across a third of the Earth, too, making it the other most widespread legal system (along with civil law). Its primary feature is that a judge will look to past cases that are like the one presented to him. If similar enough, he must abide by the past reasoning when ruling on the current case, as the precedents are considered the law; this principle is called "stare decisis" and is the main difference between this and civil law. If the case is unique, he will be the first one to rule on the matter, his decision henceforth becoming law to be considered by judges thereafter when faced with a similar case. Because of this, if there's no law, a judge can effectively make one. This contrasts with civil law, where a judge would have no authority to do anything.

Another name for this is judge-made or judicial law.

RELIGIOUS LAW

If there's a religious document, such as the Bible or Quran, this will be the source of religious law. Either a god or a prophet (through whom they spoke) may be considered the author of the document, and this sometimes results in the ideas being named accordingly; Mosaic laws were written down by Moses, for example. Such sources are considered the word of a god about ethics and morality. A famous example may be the Ten Commandments. Variations are considerable across religions, which gives us flexibility and frees us from "getting it right." Canon law is the body of laws and regulations that a religious authority creates; these are typically named after a source, such as apostles or a church (or a group of them). As with seemingly everything in religion, these teachings can be interpreted quite differently, resulting in sects and other divisions within the religion, each adopting and applying their own laws. Past cases may or may not be considered;

the interpretations of mankind are less important than the word of a god.

Contrasting Types

Both civil and common systems are unlikely among civilizations that have no written language or which are nomadic, due to the inability to codify the laws or a library in which to store them for reference. Expecting someone to memorize so much is improbable and prone to error, but maybe we have a trusted species with perfect recall or the ability to summon knowledgeable spirits from the afterlife as needed. Without such measures, only civilizations that have advanced to and beyond Roman or medieval times may reasonably be assigned either legal system. We might see elves and dwarves with such a system in fantasy, but probably not ogres and goblins.

By contrast, religious systems may be heavily dependent on fewer texts (at least at the start), which are readily available in churches, with the laws implied or explicitly stated in sermons and other stories that practitioners regularly hear. While not a rule, a religious system may be likely before and during more sophisticated civilizations.

A character who understands the difference between common and civil systems might have a different reaction to being accused of a crime. If he's aware there's no law and finds himself before a judge in a civil system, he might be unconcerned because the judge can't do anything to him. The case will be dismissed. But if he's in a common law system, the judge can invent the law based on this case. He might not feel so confident. In a religious system, it could go either way.

Civil judges must consider any previous cases (known as case law), but this is secondary to interpreting the source of law (constitution or statute). By contrast, in common law systems, previous cases *are* the law the judge follows, and he is highly reluctant to go against precedent.

HOW TO CREATE LAWS

Creating laws is relatively easy if we view them as having two sources: an enforcement or prohibition on values, beliefs, and morals, or to inhibit repetition of a past action, which is viewed negatively. I refer to these as moral and incident laws. While people break laws, the laws exist to inhibit or control behavior. We should keep this in mind and use it to invent ones we can use, and which our characters can break, intentionally or not. It's a good way to get them into trouble, especially in foreign lands. Sometimes a law is both moral and incidental in origin, as we'll see by some examples being reflected in both lists in this section.

What does the ruling authority want to influence? Always consider the form of government, discussed in *Creating Places (The Art of World Building, #2)* because this will impact how much control government is asserting through its legal system.

MORAL LAWS

Whether the system is religious or not, religion often influences laws as values, morals, and beliefs are promoted through restrictions on permissible behavior. Examples would be abortion or whether capital punishment is considered humane. Laws that discriminate are likely to originate in beliefs and values if not morality, as people characterize those who are different poorly. This includes gay, racial, and women's groups. We can extend this to professions such as wizardry or specific types, like witchcraft and necromancy. If we've invented species and worked out their relationships with humans and others, we can envision laws resulting from conflict with or disapproval of another race's values (or perceived values).

In chapter one, we looked at cultural ideas and vision and should leverage this while inventing laws of a moral nature. A society is a sum of its ideas, promoted in part by law, and those of the majority can inversely impact minorities through them. The simplest pronouncement of a law will not include explanation, but the reason for the law can often be inferred, at least by those living within the community. In parenthesis below, a short reason has been added, with an indication of whether it's a value, belief, or moral leading to the law.

Examples of laws based on morals, values, and beliefs:

1. Black magic is forbidden (moral: it requires dealing with unholy forces)
2. Goblins are not allowed near a treasury (belief: they're thieves)
3. Fire wizards must assist with extinguishing public fires (value: they should help)
4. Communication with alien species is prohibited without a permit and government monitoring (morals: solidarity with your species should take precedence over befriending a potential enemy of the state).
5. Wizards may not perform magic on the Holy Day (values/morals: it is reserved for godly shows of such power, as a sign of respect)

6. Ogres may not eat in public places (belief: they're believed to spread disease)

7. Children may not perform magic (belief/morals: it teaches them to rely on this)

8. Capital punishment by being drawn and quartered is forbidden (morals: too barbaric)

9. All residents must pass a biannual swimming test, especially dwarves (value: too many dwarves must be rescued during periodic flooding, hampering efforts to rescue others)

10. Those sentenced to death shall be devoured by dragon (morals/values: it's a quick death and waste not, want not)

11. A knight who flees shall be executed (value/morals: without courage, the knighthood will suffer loss of faith in it)

INCIDENT LAWS

Like the old saying, "shit happens." And sometimes, the ruling authority creates a law to inhibit it from happening again. Examples include restrictions/permits on weapons, pollution, vehicles, building and infrastructure, and many more. What they have in common is an attempt at improving safety and life quality through prohibition. If a building fell down due to an earthquake, a new law may result in better materials being used. People driving too fast or while drunk leads to accidents, injury, and death, and therefore a slew of laws. Most of those aren't particularly glamorous or useful to us and, while they'll exist, we don't need to focus on them. We should focus on what's different about our invented world (magic, tech, lifeforms) and the resulting laws we need to envision.

With technology we've invented, imagine what can go wrong and create incidents proving it. The result can be a character using a weapon that's not up to code because it was invented before a law, and possession and use of it is now illegal, either back home or where they are now. They might be upset to find it confiscated, then even destroyed by the local authority. Magic can lead to many laws, especially if we've decided that our magic system includes the ability for failed spells to still do something (see chapter six). This is a great way to invent small stories, minor characters who were involved (and for whom a law may be named, officially or colloquially), places of interest (where it happened), and some history.

Examples of laws inspired by incidents (with explanations in parenthesis):

1. Black magic is forbidden (it leads to unsavory beings in town and the resulting problems they bring)
2. Goblins are not allowed near a treasury (they robbed several in the neighboring kingdom)
3. Children may not undertake interstellar travel unless accompanied by an adult or guardian (kidnapping risk)
4. Ogres are not allowed in public baths (they're disgusting and cause evacuation)
5. Children may not perform magic (they are too undisciplined)
6. Interstellar travel is only permissible on "Class 5" vessels or above (others are obsolete and do not work with modern docking stations)
7. All residents must pass a biannual swimming test, especially dwarves (over a hundred couldn't be rescued in the last flood and many non-dwarves al-

so perished due to resources diverted to dwarves' rescue)

8. A federal work authorization permit from Earth is permitted to be employed on Mars (illegal immigrants are taking jobs)

9. Inciting Thor's wrath is punishable by death (Thor destroyed a city the last time someone provoked him)

TRIALS

In Earth history, a few trial types warrant mention. We don't mean the staid kind of today, where people calmly apply reason to presented evidence, but events like a trial by combat or ordeal. Some methods were thought to reveal the truth about the accused, even though they didn't. Fighting was physical, of course, but imagine how those with unique powers, like wizards, might conduct these.

A specific form of proof for murders in the medieval period was cruentation, which involved making an accused murderer touch the corpse, which might start bleeding if pressed hard. This indicated guilt and seems ripe for manipulation by the wise (don't press too hard and be exonerated!). We can leverage this to have the body react (or believed to) in different ways and for other crimes, especially with new lifeforms, but audiences will typically scorn such beliefs as nonsense. They may feel contempt for a species or society that practices this, unless it's true. As medical knowledge rose, specifically the understanding of how and when dead bodies naturally emit fluids, this fell out of practice because people realized it was bogus.

Duels

The goal of a duel was not to clear one's name of a crime, but to restore honor besmirched by another. These were originally fought with swords before giving way to firearms; the former continues as the sport of fencing. In both cases, the weapons were to be similar. Established rules governed the engagement. Honor was restored in part by following these rules and by showing that honor meant enough to participants that they'd risk their life over it. Killing the other person was therefore not the goal and could harm the honor of the survivor. Laws against duels led to their elimination, so we should decide whether they're still legal in our setting. Consider the values of each species and whether honor matters this much. They can duel in new ways or achieve "satisfaction" another way.

Trial by Combat

Trial by combat was a duel that had been officially sanctioned, except that instead of honor being the issue, the defendant had been accused of a crime by the person whom they were to fight. This happened when no witnesses or evidence could clear up the matter. The fights took place in public and on special platforms for all to see, like a boxing ring without the ropes. Some were able to decline this combat due to handicap, age (young or old), or other factors that rendered the combat unequal. They were tried by jury instead. Priests or royalty might decline as well. If fighting a woman, men were hampered on purpose to improve equality, such as one arm tied behind the back. Another option was to choose a champion, someone to fight on behalf of the accused or accuser. We could do these if two species we've invented are unmatched physically.

If the defeated didn't die in combat, he might be killed afterward, such as by hanging. In some Earth countries, depending on the crime, we could surrender when defeat was imminent, avoiding death but being dealt a harsh fate, such as slavery. World builders could extend this to include exile or, for a wizard, perhaps permanent removal of magical powers.

TRIAL BY ORDEAL

Variations on trial by ordeal exist and we can, of course, invent our own, especially if using animals or interesting places for them. Many tests were about survival, which indicated innocence, since God had saved the falsely accused. If there's a real god of justice, maybe this trial is accurate (assuming he's paying attention). This association with a deity led to these being carried out in church (maybe so he *is* paying attention!).

One version of a trial by fire was to walk several paces while holding a hot iron bar. Three days later, when the bandages were removed, an innocent person showed signs of healing while a guilty one didn't. Walking over hot coals is a variant. We can raise the drama by using volcanoes or unnatural (magic) fire, even radiation in SF.

Ordeal by water can involve binding the hands and feet and being tossed into water; the guilty floated, the innocent sank. Either might die in the process, but a rope was tied to the accused to bring them up and prevent that. A variant involved retrieving a stone from the bottom of a boiling cauldron, the depth of which corresponded to the severity of the crime; those uninjured by this were innocent. Being submerged in cold water and surviving also indicated innocence.

We can substitute supernatural or scientific elements, such as harmful substances, radiation, or dark matter. If a species is naturally resistant to an element we've devised, this can be used as a test. We can use these Earth analogues as inspiration. There's also no reason earth or air can't be used, too. Maybe those who can survive being buried alive are innocent, or those deprived of oxygen. The latter seems obvious in space, assuming people are spacefaring and yet still this barbaric.

PUNISHMENTS

Inventing punishments is a fun aspect of world building, especially if we're feeling sadistic. We have real world ideas to draw from and can create our own. We can decide later which punishments go with which crimes, but if we're feeling poetic, we can devise penalties that teach a clearer lesson about breaking a specific law. There are typically more laws and crimes than punishments; for example, jail time is used for a wide array of offenses.

We don't need to go overboard inventing punishments, especially ones we aren't going to use. If we invent some, we might benefit from one extreme, horrible, and memorable punishment and several much lesser ones. We want someone to react very seriously to being threatened with the terrible one. But lesser offenses and consequences are far more common, and our characters won't take them seriously, just as a parking ticket is an annoyance and little more. These punishments offer a chance to show the presence of the law (and making our world seem more complete) in ways that don't overtake a story.

Remember to imagine ways characters can resolve, avoid, or minimize a punishment. Sometimes we get a choice of a day in jail or paying a fine, for example. If we're nice to an officer, maybe we get a warning instead of the ticket. In corrupt places, there's always bribery. We're always looking for a way out so give the characters known ways to minimize their punishment; they'll be aware of them unless in a foreign land.

A basic decision is whether capital punishment (i.e., death) is accepted in the society. This is typically reserved for the most serious of offenses, such as murder, rape, treason, war crimes, crimes against the innocent (children), and more. When there is no feasible way to deter criminals from repeating a heinous crime, this led to the death penalty. For example, if we have a wizard who used magic to commit such a crime, and it's possible to prevent them from doing magic ever again, capital punishment is unlikely (removing their access to magic will prevent a repeat). In a nomadic tribe, death may be more common due to the lack of prisons, but an established society with cities may have less need of it.

There are many ways to kill someone in state sponsored execution. The next table lists several:

Title	Description
Boiling Alive	Immersed in boiling liquid of various kinds
Blowing from a Gun	Tied to the end of a cannon, which is then fired through the victim, blowing them to pieces
Blood Eagle	With the victim prone, the ribs are removed and placed to resemble wings
Brazen Bull	Roasted to death inside a brass bull with a fire underneath

Title	Description
Breaking Wheel	Tied to a wheel that slowly breaks all the bones, may slice the skin open
Burning at the Stake	Bound to a stake and burned alive by a fire under and around a person
Charivari	Parading an offender through the streets to mocking jeers of a crowd
Flaying	Skinning someone alive, which leads to slow death
Hung, drawn, and quartered	Dragged behind horse, hanged to near death, disemboweled (sometimes emasculated), beheaded, and finally cut into four pieces, head placed on a pike atop rampart walls
Impalement	Vertically or horizontally shoving a sharpened stake into the body and leaving the victim hanging above the ground on the stake
Keelhauling	Tied to ropes and dragged along rough/sharp bottom of ship
Mazzatello	A blow to the head knocks the victim out, the throat then slit
Sawing	Cutting someone in half with a saw
Schwedentrunk	Forcing copious amounts of foul liquid via funnel into the victim
Slow Slicing	A literal death by a thousand cuts and removal of body parts

Figure 15 Punishments

Exile is another option if value systems inhibit capital punishment.

To invent punishments, we use our imagination and the setting we've created to find uniqueness. People may be modified, such as with chemical castration for sexual crimes; a variant might be eliminating access to magic for wizards or having cybernetic implants removed (or added) in SF. If we've invented unique plants, animals, or locations, we can use them as punishment. The latter are especially useful for either banishment or temporary placement, like a jail. Merely being exposed to a phenomenon that we developed in chapter five might be useful. A plant may be harmful. An encounter with an animal likely to produce death can be used in a trial by combat. What if there's a local monster no one can kill but they're hoping someone can and criminals get the honor of trying? Succeed and go free. Otherwise...

These are ways we can leverage other world building creations. Assigning a punishment to a crime is a matter of matching severity. Harsh governments like an absolute monarchy maybe have the punishment not fit the crime, but others generally strive for fairness, even if what they're doing makes questionable sense, as in the case of some trials by ordeal we previously examined. To people of that time, they were accepted and believed, and this will be true of most within such a society, so consider what this says (to our audience in particular) about how wise they are and their beliefs. As an example, if trial by water and sinking means innocence, the society believes it or wouldn't be following this rule of law. Do we want our readers to roll their eyes about this, or our SF characters that arrive in a less advanced world? And is the idea of God saving the innocent true or essentially superstition? A SF character could scorn this only to discover that it's true. Be sure to consider how our audience and characters will react to punishments they find in other lands.

COMMERCE

We sometimes need to understand how commerce works so we can show it with confidence. Two occasions are if we intend to show any transactions, or what characters need to do to acquire something they need. Without understanding how much an item costs, audiences have less understanding of characters' actions. Are four hours of chopping wood enough to earn a meal, or a rip off? Glossing over it is an option, but showing it adds believability. Writers can experience starting to show a transaction because it feels natural given the unfolding scene, but then hesitate to depict the amount of money being exchanged. Working out commerce solves this.

But sometimes we don't need it. We don't need details on how commerce works to show whether someone is rich, poor or in between. Audiences accept that this happens in society. It's optional to say their job is well or poorly paid, or they inherited wealth, or another factor, but not required. And if we're writing a story where everything is free, or we have a society so barbaric that even trading one thing for another doesn't happen, it won't matter. Otherwise, read on to learn how to determine commerce.

A MONETARY SYSTEM

One challenge of writing stories not taking place on Earth is that we can't say characters are paying with dollars, Euros, or bitcoins. We need a monetary system or to ignore currency altogether. It's standard in fantasy to use metal—platinum, gold, silver, copper, and iron coins—but gems and paper options exist. In SF, we can go with "credits" to keep it simple, even if we call it something else.

The money from a kingdom can and likely will have words and symbols on them, with characters reluctant to use those coins or bills at certain times if they might offend the receiver. Such items can be used to identity where they've recently been, too, though this is prone to misunderstanding; just because we have a coin from a kingdom doesn't mean we've been there; but this depends on whether the item is a unit of weight or of value, as explained next. A unit of weight, such as a measured piece of gold, can be freely traded across kingdoms so that a coin could be in circulation anywhere and we just happened to get it in our last exchange, but a unit of value is specific to a sovereign power and therefore, possessing it does suggest we've been there. An example: if I have a Canadian dollar, I've probably been there, but if I have a gold piece from Canada, the value of gold transcends borders and doesn't mean I've been there. I can't use the Canadian dollar outside Canada, but I can use that gold piece; that it was minted in Canada means nothing, unless they have a reputation for dishonesty and/or the weight is off.

UNITS OF WEIGHT OR VALUE

Money is either a unit of weight or unit of value. For example, paper money has no actual value except for the denomination printed on its surface, which spells out its value. Therefore, bills are a unit of value. On the other hand, the amount (or weight) of gold determines its value, even when fashioned into a coin. Metal is a unit of weight—but not always, because metal can have a value stamped onto it, rendering its weight irrelevant.

In media, we've seen someone handed a coin and then bite it to see if it's really made of the material that it appears to be, like gold, or whether it's only gold-plated. Alternatively, it may be placed on a scale. These matter when the coin is a unit of weight. But it could also matter with coins (of value) if two denominations are the same size. One could be stamped with the value of the other, in theory (counterfeiting). This may influence coins of different values having distinct sizes, but that is done partly to make identification and usage easier. Weighing on a scale can also lead to cheating if improper counterweights are used. These factors can contribute to units of weight falling out of favor in more advanced, established societies.

When a government collapses, so does the value of its currency when it is a unit of *value*. That $100 bill in our hand may now be worth zero if its value was backed by a now defunct government. By contrast, gold is gold. Like other metals (or gems), its value is based on rarity in the world rather than by a sovereign power, and this seldom changes much if at all, which is why, on Earth, it's considered a safe investment—it is largely immune to the impact of a government's collapse. One reason to care about this is that a character who doesn't believe a government will last is unlikely to visit a bank, hand over his gold (a unit of weight) in exchange for bills (a unit of value), and walk away feeling safe.

Doing so seems less likely in fantasy due to the less robust governments that may exist. This robustness, or lack thereof, impacts everything, including police for those robberies, laws and courts to punish offenders, and accountability, which government provides to ensure people believe their state will take care of them and that institutions like banks and other infrastructure work. But if we have an empire, a constitutional monarchy, or a long-established state (over a hundred years), the state may insure banks (just like modern ones on Earth) so that people trust them. This way, even if the bank is robbed, you'll still get your money because that bank is liable.

In SF, the advances in technology (and cooperation) that make activities like space travel possible are likely predicated on sophistication that matches or rivals that of modern-day Earth. Units of value are more likely than units of weight. A collapsing government can cause a rush on financial institutions to transfer that money to an institution in a stable, foreign country, before the value is zero. These people can be gouged by unscrupulous nations or banks who know what to do with desperate people. This can be an excellent way to create a now poor character with a backstory in wealth.

If units of weight are still in use, there's another complication in SF: the value of an ore like gold is based on its rarity. Discovering a new planet where a valuable ore is far more abundant can throw an economy into disarray as the value of that ore plummets. This is what typically happens when a new gold deposit is found: the value of all existing gold drops because greater abundance renders it less valuable. This should be a genuine fear of anyone whose fortune is in precious metals or gems. It's easy to imagine that person being opposed to space exploration – unless they think they can control how much of that ore, found on another planet, makes it to them. If that new planet has civilizations on it, both economies could be disrupted. It's unlikely that the planets have the same composition (or even extraction capabilities). It's also unlikely that a single ore will be different in rarity. While economics isn't a subject that excites, the potential financial disruption that newly discovered planets bring has been successfully overlooked by countless world builders who don't want to worry about it, and audiences accept it because they haven't thought about it, but we should. The introduction of germs and parasites between these two worlds has been featured more often.

OPTIONS

We have multiple options for currency and, just like on Earth today, more than one might exist within a single sovereign power, not to mention the world.

TRADING

Trading means providing two pigs for one chicken, for example, rather than two pigs for a unit of value or weight. It is the oldest form of exchange. While areas of our world may do this, most will be more sophisticated. Nomadic tribes and less technological cultures may not have developed currency or the means to produce it, meaning manipulation of ore into metal. They may not have manufactured swords, for example. Later in this chapter, we'll look at determining the value of items, but it's mostly about supply and demand.

A fictional world means imaginary supply and demand, so we can invent this and never be wrong. That said, an animal that repeatedly produces a commodity, whether wool, milk or eggs has value beyond its own body, which can be used for meat, bone, and more, so take this into account. A plant that can be duplicated (with seeds, for example) is similar. Skilled labor to produce a long-lasting or superior item is also more valuable than, for example, a ram's horn that only had to be broken off a dead ram.

If rams are common, I might need to give you five of their horns for the tanned leather hide you made from a bear. But if ram horns are used to signal in battle and few rams are around, maybe I'm giving you one horn for two hides. A word of explanation like this adds believability and can be invented in the time it takes to write the sentence. Just be consistent: don't show a hugely different number of rams existing four chapters later.

METAL

Coins have been used as money since antiquity. For fantasy worlds, this is our default currency. Long ago, metal had its value because of weight, quality, and material (like 2 oz. of 14k gold). It relied less on a trade valuation at banks and could be melted down and still have [almost] the same value. A sovereign power minted coins in a standardized process to ensure the weight, then stamped them with an official insignia to establish trust in the coin's value. One reason is that metals can be impure by accident or on purpose, whether the latter is intended to defraud the unsuspecting or to reduce the amount of precious metal used as money. This impurity can be checked by use of a touchstone, which is a stone tablet that reveals the alloy of soft metals when those are used to write on it.

In time, metal changed from being a unit of weight into one of value. In some countries, only one type of metal (like gold) was used, with different sizes denoting value. Separate regions have access to different quantities of precious metals. This could make things more realistic and more challenging when characters travel between kingdoms.

An issue with coins is their weight; no one carries around two thousand silver pieces, for example, even when they need to. Our world could have iron, copper, gold, and platinum, too. If one platinum equals a thousand silver, then they only need two coins, assuming they can find and exchange these. We may want a conversion like this example, using American money for clarity:

1 iron piece = 10 cents
10 iron pieces = 1 copper = $1
10 coppers = 1 silver = $10
10 silvers = 1 gold = $100
10 gold = 1 platinum = $1000

Coins are typically round for several reasons. The pointed edges of a square or rectangle will wear down with use, possibly lowering weight and therefore value, while also making the now irregularly shaped coin harder to stack. In production, coins were also struck, causing the metal to push outward in a circular shape, which made this a sensible form. A lucrative business could be had shaving off flat sides of a coin, thereby reducing the weight and value, though milling was added around the edge so that it's easier to tell when the coin's edge has been shaved (the milling would be gone). The absence of these indicates a less sophisticated culture.

Gemstones

Any gem can be used as money, but can they be a unit of weight? Probably not. How much a gem weighs (how many carats) doesn't indicate value by itself because the quality can be so poor as to make it largely worthless. Few people have a specialized magnifier ("loupe") or the training to identify a stone's quality, making gems less viable as a unit of currency. If people can't tell the quality, they'll get manipulated during trading. Despite this, in antiquity, the naked eye was how all gems were appraised, so we can do this, too. Most gem deposits produce low quality stones that will never be fashioned into a jewel. The color and clarity are two elements that determine quality, which can be increased or decreased when the raw stone is carved into a jewel.

An underground race like dwarves would likely mine for gems and minerals, using either one as currency and easily converting values between them. Perhaps one diamond is the equivalent of one platinum piece. Would they have two currencies, or do they represent different spheres of social strata, such as royalty using gems and commoners using coins? A commoner caught with a gem coin might be assumed to be a thief. Maybe every dwarf is given a loupe at birth.

If gems are a unit of value instead, then low grade gems (like amber) can be inscribed with their denomination and function like metal coins. The gems could still be highly polished and look valuable to the naked eye. Even in antiquity, some gems were beautifully carved to show portraits of Roman emperors, including a garland of leaves with the leaf edges clearly visible. They won't need milling because shaving down a jewel doesn't produce useful shavings like it does with metal. The coins need not be round as wear on the edges is unlikely.

Compared to metal, gem coin denominations may challenge audience memories due to this being unusual in fiction and less familiarity with gem values on Earth, not to mention values in a fictitious world. By contrast, we all know gold, silver, and copper are progressively less valuable. Regardless, we can create and use a system like this one, with units of value:

Poor-Quality Stones	High-Quality Stones
1 amber = 10 cents	1 pearl = 10 cents
10 amber = 1 jade = $1	10 pearls = 1 emerald = $1
10 jade = 1 topaz = $10	10 emeralds = 1 sapphire = $10
10 topaz = 1 amethyst = $100	10 sapphires = 1 ruby = $100
10 amethysts = 1 opal = $1000	10 rubies = 1 diamond = $1000

Figure 16 Gems as Currency

BILLS

Paper money is a unit of value and therefore requires trust and the backing of a bank and/or government. Sovereign powers may be too unstable or short lived for trust to develop paper currency, however. In fantasy worlds, the machinery to mass print paper has not usually been invented, but they can be done in smaller quantities by more physical means, just like coins. Paper money can be easily destroyed in fire, water, or by being torn, but it is easier to carry around in large sums than coins, and in some cases, gems. Keep bills simple, such as ones, fives, tens, and so on. Like some Earth countries, we can change the color per denomination. Bills are typically for larger numbers (dollars) than coins (cents), but there's no reason this can't be reversed. They can also be far smaller than what we have on Earth.

CREDIT

Just like today, SF worlds of comparable or superior technology to ours might have credit as currency. This requires official banking by a trusted source, whether a sovereign power on a planet (or elsewhere), a union of powers (possibly across worlds), or an institution that regulates the currency. Today we have bitcoin and other versions of credit, and we can invent more types, but unless we intend to delve into their usage (or the rise and fall of it), we should aim for simplicity. One choice to make is how people access and exchange credit. On Earth we use cards, devices like phones, and computers. What tech might be employed in our world? An iris or face scan? Fingerprints? DNA? An implant?

CURRENCY CONVERSION

When we move between economies/powers, we must convert our money from one currency to another. Several factors influence conversion rates, including differentials in inflation and interest rates, account deficits between countries (how much they owe each other), public debt, trade terms, and economic performance. Does this sound like something an audience wants to read about, or something we want to determine for not one, but two fictional sovereign powers? Probably not. It's reasonable to desire getting it "right," but as is often the case, many details impact this and no one from our fictional world is going to show up and say we're wrong.

Do we need to show conversion and rationales in our work? Not usually. If we're doing a story with sovereign powers having just risen or fallen, or other dramatic changes within our tale, then it's obvious that currency could be disrupted, especially for units of value backed by the government, but most of us can skip it. We don't typically know why our own dollar is rising or falling and audiences certainly won't understand what's happening on a fictitious planet, especially if we don't tell them. Explaining can actually get us accused of having done research and then dropping it into our narrative.

The conversion arguably matters less with units of weight, like gold, because its size and rarity don't change. But it might be differently valued in one place. The exchange is typically transaction by transaction and decided between merchant and customer, as opposed to units of value, where the exchange rate is set by the sovereign power or other governing body and changes by the day (on Earth). A merchant must abide by it, and so do we and our characters. It's simplest to have a character express a reaction to how far their money is going and not focus on details. Being consistent matters less than other subjects because rates change daily anyway.

Relative Value in Currency

We should strive for simplicity in our monetary system, especially in terminology.

Using the U.S. as an example, for paper money, bills come in 1, 2, 5, 10, 20, 100, and 1000. But there's only one name for all of them: "dollar." And yet "dollar" really describes "one" accurately. If I give someone a $100 bill, that's how I say it: "one hundred dollars." Unless I specify which bills I gave, you have no idea what configuration of bills I used. Now imagine that that $100 bill has a name, dellium. Then I could say, "one dellium." The problem here is that the audience has no idea that a dellium is one hundred of something else. Explaining it is a poor use of exposition, it won't be remembered, and it doesn't convey a sense of relative value to other terms we've invented and which the audience also doesn't recall. Using a specific generic term is convenient.

What about coins? Unlike with bills, each coin may have a name (penny, nickel, dime, and quarter) but they can all be referred to with the generic "cents." And that's exactly what people do. I might give someone "seventy-five cents," not say that I gave them "three quarters." Someone not familiar with the U.S. system can infer that a quarter is the one valued at 25 cents, but only because I specified that the three quarters amounted to seventy-five. By contrast, if I say I provided three nickels, do you know if that's three times one ($.03), three times five ($.15), or three times ten ($.30)?

We don't want to do this to an audience. Therefore, two generic words, such as "dollars" and "cents," one denoting whole and another for part of a whole, provide a better sense of relative value and is preferred for fictional monetary systems. Avoid inventing names for denominations (i.e., "penny," "dime"). If we really want to, we can, but use them wisely when writing. For example, "Seeing the price was fifteen cents, he pulled three nickels from a pocket." Contrast that with, "Seeing the price, he pulled three nickels from a pocket." The second tells us nothing about how much he's paying unless we know the value of the denomination; our knowledge of it is *required* to understand. The first tells us what he's paying, with a minor detail of how he did so as an *option*.

With this in mind, we can decide coins, gems, or bills have names and values but still default to generic terms like "dollars" and "cents" to indicate relative value, only rarely specifying which coins, gems, or bills someone used. Or we can just go with two generic terms and be done.

Determining Value

It can be difficult to determine how much anything costs in a fictional world, or the wages people are paid, but this is easier than it seems. Why do we care? Because we may want to show a fantasy character, for example, paying one silver piece for a drink and then three gold pieces for a dragon, and then we wonder if that's on target or ridiculous. There's a simple trick for this: use Earth values from the country where you live, then tweak this.

For example, if I buy prepared food, I know how much things cost in the U.S. Using some made-up numbers, let's say fast food is under $10, a cheap sit-down dinner is under $20, a nicer outing will set me back $30 for just myself, and something above $50 would be expensive, a meal for a rare occasion like a holiday. How does this help?

We're not going to use the words "dollars" or "cents" in a manuscript set on another planet, so let's say I'm writing fantasy and have decided that the generic "coin" is my "one dollar." A turkey leg or steak-on-a-stake (i.e., fast food) might cost me 5 coin, a sit-down meal at a tavern catering to warriors and other working types might run 20 coin, a nice inn or restaurant might set me back 30 coin, and if I'm doing the latter on the eve of a major holiday or buying the most expensive thing on the menu, I'm spending 50 coin. Notice how the numbers are the same as my U.S. analogue.

I don't have to determine value. I borrowed the economics of modern America as a starting point, at least. We can change the numbers, adding a zero so that what's five dollars here is fifty coin there. Or we can multiple or divide by three if we want less relation to our source. We can do the same with wages, products, and services. For something not in use on Earth anymore, substitute an item that *is* in use. Not sure how much a two-handed sword would be worth? Well, it's a pretty big, specialty weapon, so research big, specialty guns (still in use on Earth) and compare them to more ordinary guns to gauge a price. Plausibility is the bar to get over, not being "right."

Don't use the current price of a wagon, because who is using one aside from the Amish? Like cars, wagons come in different sizes, so create a range of values just like cars have. Note that unless a character will buy or lose the use of a wagon in our story, or express pride or dissatisfaction with one, pricing this is unnecessary world building. On the other hand, it adds believability if a farmer goes chasing after our main characters after they're stolen his best one, which cost him a year's earnings, unlike the older, more dilapidated ones. It can also make characters seem less like a jerk when they steal the latter instead.

When something is fictional, we must decide how much value it has. Even if dragons are common, one may be the equivalent of a military jet with fantastic speed, electronics, and weaponry. Those cost millions a piece. This means only a government's military likely has them, but this analogy has a flaw: it costs money to build jets, so is a naturally occurring, living possession like a dragon worth less? Undoubtedly. Training of that dragon, rarity, and possibly equipment like a saddle are the only actual costs (other than lives) of taming one. The cost also doesn't matter if they're not for sale. If you want a dragon, you might have to kill its owner, assuming the dragon lets you or allows you to take ownership. But dragons are a unique subject.

What about something less spectacular, like a flying horse? This would be the most expensive horse, so determine the value of horses (like everything, they come in a range) and raise it. Someone who trains such creatures is unique and likely earns far more, and belongs to a higher social class.

For trading systems, it can be difficult to determine that one knife is worth three cows, for example. There isn't a simple way to determine this, but we can infer that cows are naturally occurring and take no special intervention, whereas a knife, especially a well-made one, does. Therefore the knife is more valuable than a single cow? How much more? Story needs are a good way to determine this; if a character badly needs the knife and to keep the three cows, then this is a pain point for him. Do we need that? A pitfall to avoid is showing characters consuming or using items that aren't local in the absence of trade with other communities. This is a minor detail, but avoid showing an isolated place that has every item available in a city, for example.

We don't need to get value "right." Our world can have gold as common as rocks and therefore gold has no value. Supply and demand means we have significant leeway and only need to be consistent, which matters more when writing a long series in the same world (or region of one). To achieve that, it is best to base our system on Earth values and change the numbers in a consistent manner (such as multiplying everything by three) and using different terms. Besides, even on Earth, rates differ from one place to another. A townhouse in a nice neighborhood might get $500k in one locality, while the money buys a large single-family home with yard and pool in another. No one from our planet is going to show up and tell us we're wrong. All of this applies to SF as well, except that we have even greater leeway due to tech that has never existed here. No one can say how valued it would really be.

LABOR VALUE

We sometimes have a sense of labor's value, but with potential new jobs that exist in SF or fantasy, we may need to be creative. Being plausible is once again our goal. Local conditions will impact this and we can invent that on the fly. Maybe I'll earn a meal by chopping wood for two hours in one place, but it takes four hours in another. Why would this difference occur? The longer time means my labor has less value there. This might happen if there are plenty of potential wood choppers around. Conversely, if this is rare, maybe I'll get by with suggesting only one hour.

Chopping wood isn't unusual labor, but think of unique jobs that might exist in a fantasy setting, given the plants, animals, and existence of magic. What if a wizard needs someone to practice casting a spell on? We'd imagine this quite lucrative, given the risks. Perhaps they need someone to assist as they prepare a potion or summon a demon.

In SF, gadgets and phenomena similarly offer opportunities. Maybe we need to test a device, whether that's dangerous or not. Cleaning radiative sludge somewhere might be needed. Imagine anything dangerous or just unpleasant, depending on how much risk we feel is needed. It's great when the experience changes our character or plot rather than being an aside, such as radiation sickness impacting a character's ability to perform like usual days later when they need to.

In both genres, there could be an animal that must be fed, or watched even though it's in a cage. Plants might need sowing, harvesting, or preparing, which doesn't sound interesting unless there's something special about this. Examples would be harvesting a man-eating plant, or cooking one which produces lethal fumes if not prepared right. Get creative when characters have no money and need something.

If they want to earn money rather than food, lodging, or transportation, we assign a value based on rarity, danger, or story impact. For example, if chopping wood will take two hours, which they have, this doesn't impact the tale (unless they hurt themselves). But if they don't have two hours to spare, this is a problem. We can choose a task and assign a value that will negatively impact them to a degree that seems appropriate. It can also have a positive impact. If chopping wood for a set period of time would earn me two silver pieces and I only need one, I could bargain to reduce the time or just take the extra money.

INFORMATION SYSTEMS

Even in a fantasy setting, we may need an information system. It just won't be technological like SF. Where do people get their news and other intel?

SF

We can modify any real-world technologies in SF. This includes radios, telephones, postal systems, and of course, the internet. But we can also invent new systems. The challenge of doing so is producing a result that's different from what we have. This was easier decades ago than today, when audiences may expect the equivalent of what we have – instant transfer of voice, video, and data across distances as vast as the Earth. There's still a delay across even interplanetary distances, with the speed of light being the upper limit on this. However, we've already seen depictions of almost real-time communication in film and TV.

There's a distinction between the end result (the instant transfer mentioned previously) and the mechanism by which that is achieved. The modern mechanism is the internet, which is comprised of numerous technologies that most of us neither know nor care about. It's possible that our audience has limited interest in any replacements we devise unless their use (and breakdown) impact the story. But do we need to understand how a device works to show the reader that it's failed? Failure can take various forms, such as a battery or connection issues, both of which audiences accept without explanation because it happens now.

If we're inventing an information system and the tech by which is operates, we can approach this similarly to how we'd create items (chapter 7). We'll want new names for the components that comprise our system, basing these on current analogues. Phone systems require a phone, a contact number, and either land lines, towers, or even satellites and other data systems to carry signals, plus the companies that charge us for the privilege. Answering machines, voice dialing, and even fax transmissions are other elements. We can do this same exercise with IT systems, which may need a keyboard, mouse/touch pad, screen, and a computer with ports and wires, etc. When devising our new setup, just replace such elements. When it comes to data storage, we must also decide how much info can be taken with us in portable devices and sources of new and updated contents.

In SF, we should have characters react to the quality and availability of tech at their disposal, because that's what we'd do when confronted with something far better or worse than we're used to. This is when those terms enter our dialogue or narrating. Show them having difficulty controlling the tech by name, jiggling it, giving it a whack, and then asking if anyone has another, then show how they plug it in, turn it on, or synch it. This is how to use this without dumping exposition. All computerized tech lends itself to hacking and other compromises, so be sure to take this into account; people may have to use biometric means to access systems or otherwise be inconvenienced in ways that they gripe about, and this adds realism (and audience empathy).

FANTASY

None of this technology exists in a medieval-like setting, so what did people do on Earth? Notices were sometimes posted on the door of important buildings like a church or town hall, but we can choose any location, like a castle or tower wall. For the townspeople, this requires reading skills, so if education is lax, it may not work or the settlement may have someone, like a priest or guard, assigned to stand there and read it off to anyone who can't. With or without this, a town crier may announce the news in one of several ways, such as wandering through town as needed and repeating it as he goes, or at dawn, noon, and dusk at the town water supply. Especially important announcements might be preceded by a distinctive horn blast, guards even being used to round up everyone and ensure they attend. There may be regular days when less time-sensitive addresses are made, and our ruling class may add levels of pomp and circumstance to conveying information.

We should also consider the role of messengers. Some will travel on foot, others by horse or similar, and some may fly. One that travels by land must gain entrance to the destination, with guards trained on how to deal with them. To prevent gossip, they may instruct a messenger to remain silent about news until escorted to the right person, in private. People will be watching, of course, and may relate that a messenger from a given place has arrived and their state of mind (excited, afraid, calm). Flying messengers can bypass city walls and potentially circumvent all attempts at stopping the intended recipient from getting the message. These couriers may be animals like carrier pigeons or sentient, winged species that have far more discretion in how they go about their work.

All messengers may travel through potentially dangerous lands, so are there protections afforded them, and which wearing a distinctive clothing item, like a sash, promotes? There may be penalties for detaining or interfering with one, especially a king's messenger. They might have the right to accommodations or food, free or reduced. Maybe we get kicked out of our room at a roadside inn because a king's messenger needs it. How are messengers treated where they arrive? Unless someone openly courts war, they will be treated at least decently; only a foolish ruler does otherwise because if messengers are harmed, the flow of information may stop (if from a rival). However, a king killing messengers from cities within his kingdom may not stop them from coming if he can command it, but it's the sort of abuse that leads absolute monarchs into trouble.

There may be mail systems like the Pony Express in the United States. Do ships or stagecoaches carry cargo and mail for ordinary people? They may do so for royalty, which can make them a target of pirates and thieves. As a result, many might be guarded, which could be a sign of a valuable shipment, leading to the guards pretending they aren't guards but other travelers.

Magic also provides a means of spreading information. The crystal ball or magic mirror are two physical examples, but regardless of the manifestation we choose, these can be like either phone or video calls on Earth. We don't need to restrict ourselves to one-on-one communication this way. Perhaps a shimmering image has taken the place of the town crier. Or a spell or clairaudience allows someone to communicate directly with a recipient's mind, and is this one-way or mutual? For this to be a system and not a "one off," we may want items that can be used for this.

WHERE TO START

With all systems, we need to start with our genre. Fantasy and even dystopian SF might have much poorer infrastructure than modern Earth, while other SF might have the same or greater. This and how established the government is will impact that society's ability to create a system, so consider whether it's a new sovereign power or one of several decades or more. While some systems extend throughout the society, some are more localized, so determine the scope of the system that's being invented, such as if it's a city, state, or country. These decisions are the broad strokes we need. Details such as when school starts and ends, or what kind of money is used and how it's configured, are more of a personal preference for our setting. We can decide these at any time based on what we like, more than what's likely.

CHAPTER ELEVEN

CONCLUSION

This chapter concludes *The Art of World Building* series with some final thoughts on our goals, approaches to the work, how to manage files, and ways to partner with others.

GOALS

Having a goal helps reduce both the number of tasks and the depth of world building in which we engage. Otherwise we can spend too much time and energy on activities that don't warrant them. We should always ask ourselves what we are hoping to achieve, and this is typically an enjoyable, immersive, and unique experience for our audience. World building isn't the only way to achieve this, as good storytelling or gameplay can do the same, so world building is one trick in our arsenal – one we shouldn't do at the expense of all others. "Moderation in all things."

Decide on goals by asking yourself some questions:

1. Do I want to focus on storytelling and feel little desire to do world building?
2. Do I plan to write many books or just a few to test the waters?
3. Do I feel creative enough to invent a believable world in some detail? Will the setting be unusual enough to warrant the time spent on it?
4. Do I have the time to do extensive world building, or something less extreme?
5. Do I have the patience to stick with it for months or years?
6. How will I feel if I spend years on a setting only to have rejections from agents and publishers? Am I willing to self-publish?
7. Do I *want* to do this or do I *have* to do this?
8. Do I think it's fun and exciting or a chore and a burden?

Much of what we could do is optional, but certain elements are not. For example, we'll probably need at least one sovereign power, maybe two, plus a few settlements within each. If the characters travel, land features between origin and destination will be encountered unless it's SF and ground features can be bypassed. While we can develop only the areas to be shown in the story, we can suggest a wider world without actually creating it. Most other elements aren't universally required but are project dependent. Most chapters in this series presented a breakdown of how to assess whether or not to invent something, or to what degree, but this is a general reminder to avoid becoming overwhelmed by choosing wisely.

It's also worth mentioning that, while we often invent for a particular setting, sometimes we might not use an idea. If it's not truly integrated with the world, we can reuse it elsewhere. Always be willing to jot down ideas.

ABIDE BY RULES

Modern audiences are especially astute and often notice inconsistency. We should strive to avoid this in world building by following any rules that we've stated for our setting. There are several tricks that can assist with this by providing flexibility.

One is hedging, or using less strict language. Instead of writing that, for example, "wizards must be trained," we state that "wizards must usually be trained." There are other variants on this, such as, "No one knew how else to become skilled without it, and so wizards had to be trained," or "Wizards believed they had to be trained." With each of these, we're giving ourselves a subtle "out" that things might be different than we're saying.

One problem with this is that people don't always read carefully or remember accurately, and if characters are acting like something is an iron-clad rule, this impression can override what we technically said. In both cases, the audience can come to believe it's a bona fide rule and chide us for breaking it. That we did some narrational sleight-of-hand is something we may not have the chance to point out, and even if we do, could be accused of tricking readers. Use this wisely and not too often.

Another ploy is having characters state the supposed fact. They're people, and those are fallible. It's hardly our fault a character passed bad information on to other people, including the reader (of course it's our fault)! To do this, we need either their dialogue or narration that is done in their perspective. In the former, we might put these words in someone's mouth: "Kier, why do wizards have to be trained?" or "Kier, every wizard must be trained!" If the characters to whom this is said accept it as true, so may the audience. We can use their reaction to bolster or weaken the perceived accuracy of the statements.

Whether we want to employ these practices or not, it can be wise to note any statements of absolutism that imply there's a rule. This sometimes happens in the act of storytelling. Develop a sense of this just as we do with any other aspect of writing, such as grammar mistakes. If we don't catch it on writing, hopefully we will on editing our work. When we create or find such a statement, write it down in a file about this setting, appropriately categorizing it. In the above example, it's about wizards, so it goes into the magic file, which should periodically be reviewed while writing this setting or designing games there.

Tying It Together

Creating world building elements that stand isolated from others can make the setting seem poorly designed and lacking depth. There's no quick solution for tying everything together. It pays to have a good memory of what's been invented so far and tweak what we're inventing currently based on this.

Periodically reviewing our world building files is an excellent practice. Put a reminder on a calendar, if you keep one to organize your projects or life. What we'll do is just read through our files. That's it! It might have been months or years since gestation (or repeated refinement) led to the contents of a file. We may have invented many items since and forgotten to intertwine them. Even without that, we may have new ideas or realizations to add. We've also had time away from the invention and our fresher eyes can improve what we've done. Expect and accept that this exercise might lead to additional world building.

Another approach is what I think of as "looping." Choose a land feature, such as a forest, and describe the terrain; details and examples on what to write are discussed in *Creating Places (The Art of World Building #2)*, but we want to discuss how dense the underbrush is, the mood of it, how many roads run through it and their condition, and what plants and animals of interest might be here, in what quantity, and in which areas. If we've invented some lifeforms, we're now merging them with this particular woodland. We can state that a given road is less traveled due to proximity to the territory of one such creature. Rare items might be here; state where they're found and how arduous the journey is. Maybe a nefarious organization has a base within.

Now start the loop. If there are multiple settlements nearby, open the file for one. The inhabitants have a relationship with this place. Describe it. Do they fear it, use it for recreation, or hunt within? How far from the walls is it? They're the one tending a road or letting it be overgrown. Do they see this terrain as protecting them from attack or as a vulnerability? Is there something nasty inside that they fear? What armed forces exist here that are present specifically to deal with such a threat? Are there raids into the woods or from things in the woods? Do knights attend those who venture into this forest? To decide this requires some imagination, and working out the military groups available. Are there useful plants there and major products that result? When we're done updating the settlement file, we need to revisit the one for this forest, updating our description of it to include its relationship with this settlement. We're looping from one file into another and back. If there's another settlement near this forest, repeat the same exercise. Do it with all nearby communities.

Then choose another. Or a mountain range, a lake, a desert, or other features until there's little on a map that's not interwoven. Use the options we discussed in *Creating Places* to ensure no two are alike. While doing this, we may think of additions to non-places and should update those files, too.

For example, if we've imagined new details on our evil organization, perhaps we add a note about their base in these woods and what it's like, and how the nearby settlements impact life there. We might even say that, because a given animal is here, it's been adopted as their symbol, or they specialize in taming or killing it, even cooking it a particular way. The latter can result in a rare treat that people like but are afraid to eat in public due to its association with the group. Now we have to open our files on food and drinks of the world and update that, possibly creating occasions when something is consumed and when it's avoided, or how it's made, its reputation, and whatever else. We might decide that there's another version of it without the bad reputation, as invented by another species, and now we end up in that file jotting down a note about it but leaving the details in our food file.

The same approach is used to integrate species with each other and the world. Work on one and define it according to imagination and the guidance from *Creating Life (The Art of World Building, #1)*, using the provided template for ideas. There's a section on relationships with others. Fill out connections between, for example, your elves and dwarves while in the elven file, and then open the dwarf file and do the same there. To minimize rewrites, I will copy and paste the same text in both files, even though I generally avoid duplication in my notes. Review what's been written about both while doing this because it can trigger ideas.

When we invent an organization or military group, for example, we should define its relations with each species and location (settlements, regions, land features, and sovereign powers) where it is found. We once again want to loop back into the species and location files and update our understanding of them.

The pattern here is periodic review and update. That's the way we integrate elements in the setting. Don't expect it to all be done at once. That's not realistic. I've been updating my Llurien setting for over thirty years now, always improving and refining it. Sometimes it's been a decade since I last read a file. I'm sometimes surprised by what's in one, as I remember many grand scale inventions but often forget details of things I'm not currently using. My duration on this is extreme, but yours needn't be. We can world build many things a few minutes at a time as long as we stay organized.

APPROACHES

There are multiple approaches to world building, such as top-down and bottom-up. All are valid and have their merits and undesirable consequences, which can be mitigated.

TOP DOWN

The top down approach is starting with the big picture and working our way down to smaller elements. For example, when it comes to physically designing the world, we decide how many continents it has and where they are in relation to each other. Next we focus on a single continent, deciding what nations exist and what forest, mountains, and other features exist and where, possibly drawing a map. We would repeat this on other continents. From there, we would choose a nation and decide on where its major cities and towns are and work out their relationships before moving on to other nations.

Regarding life, we would start with creating gods, the reason being that these deities presumably have attributes that affect the species, plants, and animals they created. All of those should be influenced by the land features we've already created. And they should have relationships with each other. The species might have in turn caused supernatural disasters that left residue behind and now everyone avoids that place.

The advantage to such an approach is cohesion. The impression of randomly created pieces slapped together is less likely, as are world building holes (like plot holes). The latter would include something like a river that has no mountain source, but we can't add one because we've already decided that none of the nations near it have a mountain range and their cultures are somehow dependent on that, for example. And maybe we can't get rid of the river, either.

The disadvantage is that world building can feel like a big homework assignment. We're doing this in a specific order and may not have ideas when we need one to continue. Getting stuck can ruin momentum and enthusiasm. We can see a huge to-do list and feel overwhelmed. The process of creation is supposed to be fun; creating things in a freewheeling manner helps with that and also causes interesting ideas to develop.

BOTTOM UP

The bottom up approach means starting at a more localized level, such as the settlement where a story takes place. We may decide some land features are at various distances from here and any impact this causes. Later, we decide what sovereign power type exists, even if this decision changes previous work on the settlements and geography. We might decide that an adjacent sovereign power is needed and invent it, tailoring it to our current needs. We may not have decided which hemisphere this place is or the continent, which means we may not have considered climate much. This matters more with things that don't move (places) because species and animals can be relocated and found in multiple places.

An advantage of the bottom-up way is that it forces us to focus on our immediate setting needs, like a city we'll use. We may skimp on things we won't need yet, saving time. Story can also inspire our inventions. For many of us, it's also easy to envision a city that has specific features or a mood, and we may be unsure how outside factors could contribute, though hopefully this series has changed that.

One problem with this approach, for places, is that the overall picture indelibly impacts the local one. We might decide there are mountains and lush vegetation in a certain direction, then choose a hemisphere only to find out that those mountains would prevent that vegetation. Similar factors could render our work less sensible. Another disadvantage is lack of scope. When we only invent what we need and a little more, our world can seem too tightly focused and like there isn't a broader world out there. This may not matter in a short story or one where characters don't travel, beyond mentioning other places or peoples and things influenced by them, but for more epic uses, we need to at least hint at a broader world.

Random

The random approach means creating individual items and worrying about how they relate to each other later. We can create a species here, a god there, a city elsewhere, doing each on the spur of the moment. There's no quota of species, cities, or gods to create, no obligations. We create whatever seems like a good idea at the time. Only later do we decide that cities are part of a nation, or a god is part of an interconnected pantheon. Or that two species live near each other and are enemies or friends, and why. We might decide a species originates from a given forest, but on later reflection, we realize they'd spread throughout the area and add them to those other regions, both in forests and settlements near. Our concept of them evolves continuously whenever we think of something.

This has the advantage of allowing us to create in an improvised style that will lend itself to rapid creation and exploration without worrying about restrictions we've imposed on ourselves. We can see if we have what it takes for more serious world building. We're focused on a single idea and making it work for its own sake. If there are elements that don't make sense yet, we can fix them later and just try to avoid boxing ourselves into a corner.

The disadvantage is a lack of global cohesion. Maybe we have too many gods, not enough, or they don't make sense as a group. If we haven't worked out how species get along and then use them in scenes together, do they interact in understandable ways?

WHICH TO DO?

If none of these approaches sounds ideal, that's because mixing them is arguably best. To do this, we need a framework, or the "top down" view on the world, establishing some basics about the physical environment, more so than individual gods, species, or other life forms. Then we can fill it in. What follows is a rough order if we're starting with a new setting; authors who already have a setting can see where they might need to backtrack to fill in some of this before forging ahead. These suggestions are just that, so if you disagree, at least it will get you thinking about how you would do this.

START WITH A CONTINENT

It might be called "world building," but many stories take place on a single continent, which is what we start with. Decide which hemisphere it's in so we know whether cold is north or south. This also helps determine whether another continent is north or south of the one we've created; if the world is Earth-like in size, there's probably only one in each hemisphere at that latitude. As discussed in *Creating Places*, this allows us to determine the prevailing winds. This matters because the combination of continent and mountain range placement will determine where vegetation is (and is not). With this done, we can decide where we'd like mountains, which will tell us many of our other land features, including deserts, grasslands, and forests. At a minimum, sketch this on a piece of paper, possibly with arrows pointing off the page to indicate other land masses.

This exercise gives us an overview of a continent with at least a high-level view of where everything lies. If we're not planning to use major areas of it, that's fine. At least we know where they are and have a rough idea of climate there. If we'd like, we can name various regions and land features. For those who want to top-down start, we have a structure we can fill in as we need.

CREATE SETTLEMENTS

Whether we have a map or not, we can start indicating where cities and towns lie. They're typically along major rivers or fresh water sources like a lake, and often where those empty into the sea. For choosing kingdom borders, we can use natural land features like mountains and rivers, even forests, which can become contested areas for resources. Before we go much further, we're going to need names, because it's time to start creating files about our world. This means settlement ones, at the least, and possibly sovereign power files and another about land features on this continent.

FREE REIN

Now that we have a framework, we can create other elements in whatever order. We can fill out basic information for each location in the appropriate file. It's also recommended to create a spreadsheet that works as an overview of all locations; this allows us to determine the age of everywhere, colors, symbols, major products, and population levels. We sense where people congregate, where the oldest and newest places are, and in what direction life spread. This is a cheat sheet to our world.

With this done, we'll be able to work on any other element at our leisure and tie it into our setting according to the "Where to Start" suggestions that conclude nearly every chapter of *The Art of World Building* books. In no particular order, this can mean fleshing out land features, settlements, powers, species and races, plants and animals, gods, magic systems, armed forces, organizations, and ultimately, the cultures. The latter benefits from determining the cultural scope from the top down: power, region, settlement, and social group. Regardless of your decision, be sure to crisscross back and forth between files and periodically update earlier decisions.

FILE STORAGE

We need somewhere to store our ideas. An ideal scenario is to have access wherever we are, whether home, vacation, or work (we never know when an idea will strike). Or the toilet. Some smart phones are even waterproof so that we can work in the pool, a hot tub, or underwater! Depending on location, we have different devices we're likely to have with us, such as a phone, tablet, or laptop. And there's the old-fashioned pen and paper. There's no solution that will work for everyone so here we're just going to look at some options; this is not intended to be comprehensive but guidance on what to consider.

Only some of us make maps, and the programs that allow this usually require installation and a larger screen than a phone provides. Game designers may want to draw creatures that are best done in full-fledged apps as well. World builders are mostly concerned with text, including possibly a few spreadsheets for quick access to information about many places at once; this is what we're examining here. With all tools, we should consider that we may use it for months to years before changing our mind; will we be able to easily move to another working methodology?

HARD DRIVES

We can store our files on a computer hard drive. This will mean always bringing that device with us if we want to work, or taking a copy of files to another computer, which will need any app we use installed. Long ago, I used to bring mine on a writeable CD, then DVD, and finally a thumb drive as tech changed; some carried a significant risk of being lost, which inspired attempts to encrypt them (another hassle). Today I bring nothing because I use Office 365, which we'll discuss later in this chapter.

Since hard drives can fail, it's wise to back up our contents to another device. We once needed a portable drive attached directly to our computer, but there are network accessible ones, some very robust. We can get one with a mirrored drive in a RAID configuration, which means it has two drives and content copied to one is automatically copied to the other. If one fails, our backup is still safe. One scenario this doesn't guard against is our home burning to the ground, destroying both backup drives *and* our laptop, for example. Due to this, it's wise to store files in two locations, such as a relative's house (if they can be trusted not to snoop, should we care) or a safety deposit box.

Hard drives offer few advantages other than a file system that can be backed up with a dragged folder. As we'll see, this can be done with other options. We can also store all types of files, not just world building ones.

WEBSITES

Websites offer the mobility we need to work from anywhere, but they carry a risk that our creative work is on someone's servers and can be compromised. This may expose us to hacking. Our devices, including a laptop (even at home), also face this risk, but it's arguably less likely that we'll be hacked than Google or Microsoft. Several niche sites dedicated to world builders also exist, and they are also less likely to be hacked because the information in them isn't personal enough and there aren't enough users to warrant the effort. However, they are probably much easier to hack. Creative people often worry about their ideas being stolen, and storing and transmitting them over the internet does expose us to more risk. The reality is that "no one" cares about stealing our ideas unless we're famous, but if it matters to you, consider it.

We should read terms of service carefully. Most of us are familiar with the idea that Facebook, for example, can sell our data to advertisers. Any website we use should explicitly state that we own our ideas, not them. I once received a job offer that stated that all work I did once hired belonged to the company, including anything I invented after hours, after I quit, and for the rest of my life. I objected and they admitted it was a mistake and changed the language to be more reasonable. It likely wouldn't have held up in court due to obscene overreach, but why take the chance?

Most sites cost money to operate, which means a potential membership fee for users, whether monthly or annually. This cost may not be necessary; what we're gaining is optional and can usually be achieved via other means. But even apps installed on a device are moving more to a subscription model, versus the old days of installing something and being able to use it indefinitely without paying again. Providers like Microsoft have seen the wisdom of making us pay all the time.

With websites, backing up our data may seem like a concern we don't have, as it's not stored locally on our device. But we should periodically download it, if possible; and if it's not possible, this is a risk. The provider is probably doing backups, but the likelihood of this depends on how professional they are. A company like Google or Microsoft almost certainly is, partly because they have businesses depending on them. But smaller sites run by a few programmers may not. Such sites might be hosted by a genuine hosting company (that does backups) or it might be on a server in the guy's basement. Some sites have already achieved a reputation for crashes that destroy data into being irretrievable. Research any such tool to see what other users are saying.

MICROSOFT OFFICE 365

While we can use installed versions of Microsoft Office, we also have the option to use the online or mobile versions. However, these typically offer a subset of features, being a less robust app. An O365 subscription includes all of them and using a browser to open a file in the desktop program takes a button click. It is fairly seamless to transfer files and folders between devices once we've synched then.

They presumably do robust backups, but if not, the files are also stored locally via Microsoft's OneDrive, which means that, provided the files are synching properly, we have the latest with our device even if we don't have an internet connection. And if we change the files, then the next time we're connected, they will synch.

There are many apps included beyond just the word processor and spreadsheet programs (nearly thirty as of this writing). O365 has the advantage of being unlikely to go away anytime soon. One feature of Word that I use heavily is the "Navigation Pane," pictured next. We can use heading styles to create a hierarchy within our document, then easily collapse or expand it, and jump to a heading by clicking on it. It's only available in the full, installed version of Word, which is one reason why I work there whenever possible.

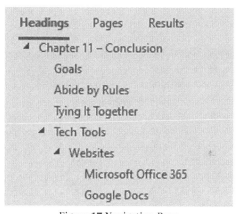

Figure 17 Navigation Pane

O365 has an annual cost. Depending on what we purchase, it may include additional benefits, like the ability to have an email domain. This means that if we have a website, such as randyellefson.com, we also have an email address like mail@randyellefson.com so that we look more professional than using a Gmail one, for example; we can also add multiple addresses. If we're selling books or games, we're in business and this can be deducted as a business expense. These are not world building concerns but ones for our career.

This is what I personally use for not only world building, but for stories, email, calendars, and more. I just log in to O365 via the browser and access everything stored there; I keep many files out of O365 because they're either personal or seldom needed.

My working experience in a day can be like this:

1. Before going to work, via my laptop, I update a file, which autosaves.
2. At work, I open the file via the browser, see my morning changes, and add more.
3. While waiting in line for my lunch order, I pull up the file on the mobile app and add more notes.
4. Back at my desk during some downtime, I use the browser version again.
5. Once home, I work on my main computer and still have everything I've done.
6. Before taking my kids to an afterschool activity where I'll have no internet, I make sure files are synched to a lighter computer, then go, and while they have fun, I work disconnected.
7. At home, I ensure a synch and go back to working via my main laptop.
8. At bedtime, the kids are having trouble sleeping so I grab the lighter computer again and work beside them as they doze off.
9. I go back downstairs and resume working on the main laptop.

Aside from sometimes having to make sure a device has synched files, this is exactly what I wanted.

Google Docs

One of Google's biggest selling points is that it's free. It offers multiple apps online and as mobile ones for a phone or tablet, including word processing and spreadsheets. We can organize our files into folders. They presumably do robust backups. We can also share a file or entire directory with someone, such as a collaborator. We can download entire folders to our computer, then store them offsite if desired, so manual backups are an option. I haven't liked the fonts and, since Microsoft Word is my main program, converting a Google file to Word produces poor results until I manually fix it, so I stopped using this a while back.

World Building Sites

Multiple sites have been created to help world builders create and store their notes. As variations exist between them and we're not diving into each, only general observations are here. For the most up-to-date list, google "world building sites."

These sites are accessible from any device via login. Few if any have a mobile app and therefore, trying to use them via a small device's browser may be unappealing. We're unlikely to know their hosting practices, such as whether it's hosted in their basement or at a professional hosting company. The ability to download our data may not exist, and if it does, we'd have to investigate what format it's in. Can we easily port it to another platform?

Some sites provide writing prompts to help inspire invention. While this is good, that inspiration can come in many other ways that don't pose risks. These sites propose to help with world building, and while they offer advice, that pales in comparison to the depth that books (including this one) offer. Some provide the ability to integrate items for an interactive experience for an audience, which may become of interest if it catches on with them. Until then, no one is expecting it and it might be good to store some amount of material for our fans to enjoy but keep our main files elsewhere.

MY APPROACH

I produce and collect crazy amounts of files of many types and subjects. These include spreadsheets, word processor files, images, image editing files (i.e., Photoshop .psd files), raw and processed podcast and audiobook files, and more. There are PDFs and spreadsheets of sales reports from multiple vendors (Amazon, etc.). There are promotional images, whether final or draft book covers, advertisements, podcast episode images, and more. I run a publishing business, which results in receipts and accounting software files. It is endless. And of course, all of my world building files for each setting, including maps. Never mind all the personal stuff like photos, videos, taxes, and more.

For each book, there are character bios, an outline, random notes, and of course the manuscript. When I hire beta-readers, each returns another file to me. The same happens with an editor. I save all of these in archives, only my final manuscript being a live document on which I work. I also produce eBook files (the program I use to do it and multiple eBook formats). The publishing branch alone produces dozens of files per book.

I typically work on my laptop at home. This is where all of my files are. My fiction (and music, as I'm also a musician) files are currently sorted into four main directories:

1. (Almost) never changes: retired stuff I'll probably never touch. I rarely add to this unless I've ditched another idea or project. I not only don't need to add to this, but I don't need to look at it, but I save everything.

2. Rarely changes: previous year sales reports, published books/albums I'm unlikely to revisit, previous years taxes, old versions of websites, PDFs (they don't change). I seldom add to this and don't work in this directory.

3. Sometimes changes: frequently accessed files that don't often change, like book covers and other images I might need to repost on social media.

4. Regularly changes: my main working directory of stuff actively being worked on, and which likely changes every day. Financial transactions, current and pending book projects, sales reports, and promo materials.

What happens if my laptop's hard drive dies? I lose all of my work. I've been doing creative work for almost forty years now. Can you imagine losing all of it in a hard drive crash? I have a free backup program that runs once a week. It takes each of those directories and creates a single backup file of each, shrinking them down to take less disc space. Literally every Sunday for eons now, you can find me dragging the resulting files to a backup drive on my home network. My backup drive is a RAID setup. What this means is that there are two mirrored drives. What I copy to one gets automatically copied to the other. If one dies, the other one still exists unscathed (and there's always my laptop).

Once a month, I take my files offsite to a trusted location. I keep two identical pen drives. That way I can fill up one at home and exchange it with the other one in one trip. If I only had one drive, I'd have to go get it, come home, fill it up, and then take it back. What happens when I need a new laptop? I buy one, transfer all my files, and then I take apart the old one, get the hard drive out, get a screwdriver to open the drive, find my hammer, and have a fun few minutes destroying the disc.

I sleep like a baby.

GET ORGANIZED

If we choose to use a file system (whether online or not), we'll need to invent a way to organize our files. Otherwise we can forget entire files exist, know that they do but be unable to find them, or not remember which file we entered a note into. As some projects last years, we're going to forget all sorts of things; that's why we wrote them down in the first place, but it doesn't help us when we never see the note we left ourselves again. Knowing how we think is beneficial, so we know where we probably would've put something.

The world building websites typically have an organizational approach chosen for us. This section assumes we must decide. While there are many approaches, a rationale with examples is outlined below. Feel free to alter it to suit your sensibilities. We must always understand where we personally would have put something; I can find the sugar in my pantry faster than someone else because I know how

I think. So if this organization doesn't work for you, used the guiding principles behind it to invent one that does.

FOLDER STRUCTURE

What follows is a possible folder structure, which is presented in non-alphabetic order so that it makes more sense, but a computer will often sort it alphabetically.

1. Name of World
    a. Life
        i. Animals
        ii. Plants
        iii. Monsters
        iv. Supernatural
            1. Gods
            2. Beings
        v. Species
            1. Races
    b. Armed Forces
    c. Continent Name
        i. Maps
        ii. Settlements
        iii. Sovereign Powers
    d. Continent Name
        i. Maps
        ii. Settlements
        iii. Sovereign Powers
2. Books
    a. Fiction
        i. Talon Stormbringer Series
            1. The Ever Fiend
            2. The Screaming Moragul

   b.   Non-Fiction
       i.   The Art of World Building Series
          1.   Creating Life
          2.   Creating Places
          3.   Cultures and Beyond

There are different ways of doing any of this. For example, we could place settlements inside the appropriate sovereign powers folder, but this requires us to remember which one it's in when we're looking for it; also, since powers shrink and expand, it might've changed at some point. It can be easier to just list settlements by name in a single folder because their file is easier to find.

Rather than having a folder for animals with, for example, ten files (one each for ten animals), we could have a single file with all ten animals inside it. The same could be done with armed forces being in one file, species, races, and more. This is an approach I moved to in time to reduce the number of files and because I heavily use the Navigation Pane in MS Word to jump around.

Some of those folders have specific files in them. The "Name of World" folder might be called Llurien for my main planet, and within that are not only the folders above, but the travel and moon orbit calculator spreadsheets like the ones included in *Creating Places*, and a "Planet Llurien" file that details things like how many moons exist. My "Continent Name" folder has the folders listed and files for history, land features, and sovereign powers. If a magic system is specific to a continent, it might go there, but if it's worldwide, it goes higher in the hierarchy.

Regardless of our decision, it's easy to rearrange things in a file system.

SUGGESTED FILES

World building (and authorship) can produce many files that should be structured internally. The downloadable templates included in this series, and shown in each appendix, show ways of doing this but there are some specific instances to cover.

As just mentioned, we may want to include multiple instances in a single file instead of one per file. For example, let's say we have elves and dwarves. Do we create a file for each or one file that has both? This will depend on our use of technology. The Navigation Pane in Microsoft Word makes it easier to jump around within a file. This allows us to place all of our species into one large document, which reduces file clutter and the numbers of windows we have open when working on multiple species at once, a frequent reality the farther into development we get. This happens because they've become so intertwined and updates to one often necessitate updates to another. A problem may be large file size, which can open more slowly, but this is seldom an issue.

Just as some subjects lend themselves to being in one file, others may not. For example, there could be so many settlements, such as more than fifty, that putting them in one file could make the document unwieldy. On the other hand, if we're using the plant template from *Creating Places*, this is short so that having fifty plants in one file is fine. It's all personal preference.

It's recommended to keep a spreadsheet with multiple tabs. The goal is a high-level view of many related items at once. Those fifty settlements can all be listed here, with columns for city colors, symbol, location, year founded, allies, which species founded it, population, which armed forces are here, major products, what it's famous for, and more. This is what I use when determining the age of every settlement at once, since I can see all of them in one place. Another tab can be for the world's gods, with columns for alignment (good or evil), gender, season, element, traits, symbols, which species they relate to, and more. The same can be done with species, plants, animals, and their most important attributes.

We should strive to avoid duplication in our files. With the spreadsheet just mentioned, we might place city colors on that and in a city's file. If we do this (and I do), make a mental note as to which is considered the authoritative source if they get out of sync. In my case, the spreadsheet rules because when changing something like this, I don't want it to resemble another settlement's colors and I'm therefore consulting my spreadsheet. We might also want to get into the habit of updating something everywhere, but lapses will happen.

Another issue is the rabbit hole problem. Sometimes we're busy with writing a story, for example, when we have a world building idea. We may know from experience that if we open a file to write it down more, we'll get sucked into the world building rabbit hole and stop working on our tale. My solution to this is a file with a title akin to "Llurien Changes to Make." This is my temporary location for ideas I'll flesh out and integrate with the setting later when I have time.

But what happens when we're away from that file or don't feel like looking for it? We've all heard of jotting an idea on a napkin. The technological equivalents are the notes app on our phone, or a calendar item, or emailing ourselves. This is fine but at some point, we need to take each of those and move them to that "changes to make file" for one reason: having dozens of pending ideas in a single file is far better than eight in our inbox, seven files on our phone, and the rest in calendar items that are going farther back in time, like emails, with each day. My random world building ideas flow from all of those into that pending changes file and, eventually, become integrated into the world files.

WORLD BUILDING COALITIONS

If all of this seems like far too much work but something we still want to have, we might consider working with one or more partners. This would allow us to divide up the work and even focus on areas we excel at while leaving our weak areas for someone else to do. If all of us are authors, then all of us can write in the resulting setting. One caveat is that we'll have to be very aware of what everyone else is creating, and they might want to do some things that we don't want. One solution is to divide up continents, each of us taking certain kingdoms. One advantage here is that the gods or species can be the same across the world, but we can do different things on the smaller scale.

Tread lightly, however. More than one relationship has been destroyed by disputes over ownership, so if you embark on something like this, you should consult an attorney and draw up a legal document specifying your respective rights. This would include under what conditions someone can leave the partnership. For example, if you leave, you can no longer write books on that setting without getting approval from the remaining members in the partnership because they are still making changes and you must comply with those. This is true while you're in the partnership anyway.

What follows is a thought experiment about how multiple people can participate in a World Building Coalition (WBC). If you and others decide to enter into one, this may lend ideas on how to go about defining roles and responsibilities.

What Is It?

A world building coalition (WBC) is a collection of individuals who've agreed to build a world together, sharing the labor and fruits of that labor. While some items, such as overall world feel, gods, and many life forms will be shared, other items (like kingdoms) will belong to world building owners (WBOs) who have ownership of them, such as say over whether proposed changes are accepted.

Why Do It

World building can take an enormous amount of time depending on how far someone is willing to go. By contrast, skimping on it is likely to produce mediocre results. To mitigate these problems, like-minded individuals can form a coalition, with agreed upon roles, responsibilities, and rights.

Who Does It

Authors are the primary ones likely to create and participate in a WBC. However, gamers, hobbyists, or others who have no intention of ever writing a story can also form a WBC either for entertainment, or to effectively license the use of their world to authors. This can not only free some authors from the need to do world building, but allow those not given to storytelling to do creative work that results in published stories. These WBOs may have written agreements with a given author to share in the profit of any published works, though crafting those agreements lies outside the scope of this book. Interested parties should consult qualified entertainment lawyers.

THE COVENANT

Members of the WBC should agree to a covenant that lays out their rights, roles, and responsibilities, and other things to agree upon, such as terminology (are you going to call elves a species or race?). This includes "severability," meaning what happens when someone leaves and whether they retain their things or have them transferred to someone else. Or even whether they get them back.

WORLD TYPES

There are questions to decide upon at the outset and stick to without alteration. One of these is genre. Is the world intended for fantasy, SF, steampunk, or something else? What kind of world this is should be cast in stone early on. The exception is when the WBC decides that a long history exists and what was a medieval-like fantasy setting two thousand years ago is a space-age SF one today. This allows creators to have variety and even decide that another member of the WBC can author stories in a given time period, provided that they meet the approval of the WBO of that part of the world.

Another decision is about technological level. Does the world have guns? Cars? Spaceships? How technologically advanced is the planet? Some areas can be more advanced than others, such as the Europeans being more advanced than Native Americans when Europeans discovered North America, but generally you'll want some guidelines.

ROLES

WORLD MASTER (WM)

A World Master (WM) is the overriding authority for a planet (or group of them in a solar system, for example). This can also be a called a Universe Master (UM). This person has tie-breaking authority during any voting. Responsibilities include moderating disputes, laying out rules, and general administration of everything in the WBC except what has been delegated to others for ease of management. This person is the "boss." In most instances, the WM will be the one who created the WBC, but if the original WM steps down, another member of the WBC may take his place.

WORLD MASTER BACKUP (WMB)

In the event that the WM is unavailable, such as being on vacation, a backup who has the same level of access should be appointed. The WBC will need to determine how much authority this person has, but generally, the WMB is responsible for ensuring the forward progress of the WBC can continue in the temporary absence of the WM.

WORLD BUILDING OWNER (WBO)

A World Building Owner (WBO) is every member of the WBC. Each should have voting rights, presumably equally. Each must sign the covenant and, if there are any dues for legal fees or hosting of shared files, pay their share.

CONTINENT MASTER (CM)

While sharing a world building project is the point of a WBC, it makes sense for each member to have their own continent, with them as its Continent Master (CM). They are the owner of that continent, responsible for its name and everything on it, from land features to settlements and inhabitants. This allows each member relative freedom to do as they please on their land mass while using shared resources of the WBC/world, such as species, races, plants, animals, and gods.

A CM may carve out a period of their continent's time that belongs exclusively to themselves while allowing other members of the WBC to use or influence the events of their continent with the CM's approval, either in the past, present, or future. This might include others using or inventing history, characters, and items that originate or impact the CM's property. As the CM is the owner, he has final approval over whether such alterations are allowed. It is recommended that this approval take place prior to significant development work by another WBC member, and once approved by the CM, it cannot be rolled back. The CM becomes bound by the invention just as if imagined personally. The CM also then acquires ownership and responsibility of the item.

WBO REGENT

A regent is someone who is temporarily handling another WBO's responsibilities. This optional role must be agreed upon by others in the WBC. Any decisions made by a regent must be honored by others as if the original property owner had made them.

CREATIONS

The WBC must decide what items will be shared and what will belong to each WBO. As suggested by the Continent Master role, it is wise to let each member of the WBC own a continent. However, other divisions can be made, such as Sovereign Power Master or Settlement Master, Forest Master, or even Species Master, Plant Master, and Animal Master. What these have in common is that someone has responsibility and authority for an item and cannot be overridden by other members of the WBC (unless failing in their duties). By contrast, there are shared issues that the entire WBC must decide upon, such as by majority vote. These are often planetary-wide concerns. A potential list of shared items includes:

1. The number of and placement of continents
2. The name of world oceans and bodies of water adjacent to multiple continents
3. The number of gods and basic disposition, if the gods are real and worldwide
4. What species/races exist, especially if worldwide
5. The number and features of moons and other heavenly bodies such as rings, other solar system planets, and sun type

LIFECYCLE

World building can go on forever, but it must start somewhere. This section discusses the reality that some members of the WBC will inevitably leave the coalition. When this happens, ownership of their creations may (and probably should) fall to others. Otherwise, members of the WBC who want to use or suggest changes to the person's possessions cannot get resolution.

The WBC should agree on a rough time frame to complete shared items, such as gods, continent maps, and names of world oceans, for example. Some suggested options for a WBC to decide upon follow. Whether these options exist should be included in the WBC's Covenant.

Option 1 – Perpetuity

In this option, a WBO never loses their rights. No one can alter what they've decided and codified in written world building files.

Option 2 – Transferred

A WBO can transfer their rights to another WBO, whether that person is an existing member of the WBC or a new, replacement one brought in for this purpose. This transfer must be approved by the WBC. The WBO must advise the WM of this request, upon which the WM will help coordinate discussion, voting, and transfer (or rejection), and any appeals or counteroffers by the WBC to the WBO. The WBC should have good, defined reason for rejecting the transfer. These include assessing the new WBO as unskilled or not a good fit personality-wise.

OPTION 3 – SUSPENDED

A WBO might be unable to participate for long periods of time, due to illness, bereavement, loss of interest, or just needing a break. The result might be inability to meet requirements, such as voting on shared resources, another WBO's request to make changes to the WBO's creations, or use them. In these cases, the WBO might intend to return and not lose stake in the WBC. The WBO will suspend their participation, but since this may negatively impact the WBC, the WBO may agree that another WBO, such as the WM, will take over responsibilities in limited fashion as a WBO Regent. Given the possibility of monthly expenses for shared hosting, an WBO might still be required to pay their share or risk expulsion.

OPTION 4 – ABANDONMENT

In the event that a WBO abandons their stake in the WBC, ownership can be assigned or taken by someone else with agreement by the remaining members of the WBC. The definition of abandonment is important and may include a timeframe upon which members are expected to reply to WBC business and failure to do such results in a declaration of abandonment. A three-month window seems plausible. A formal decision by the WBC should follow several written notices to the WBO with adequate time to reply.

OPTION 5 – QUITTING

A WBO can simply quit, permanently forfeiting all rights to their possessions, including using them in any way, such as in stories. To do this, a WBO must submit, in writing, their resignation, which becomes final upon acceptance by the WBC. However, the WBO can ask to come back at a later time at the discretion of the WBC. Another member of the WBC can take over the WBO's territory but must abide by many previous decisions so as not to impact other members of the WBC who were given rights to use material in this WBO's domain.

OPTION 6 – TERMINATED

To protect the WBC's investment of time, energy, and the integrity of the shared world, a WBO's participation in the WBC may be terminated due to violation of the covenant. Termination should be majority, not unanimous, because two WBOs can engage in collusion to violate the world's principles. The terms under which termination may occur should be explicitly stated, as with everything, in the covenant.

OPTION 7 – EXPIRATIONS

A WBC might decide in its covenant that membership in the WBC is automatically renewed annually, provided that each WBO reaffirms their continued interest in remaining.

OPTION 8 – DEATH

The death (or permanent incapacitation) of a WBO automatically transfers all WBO rights to the WBC until such time as the WBC formally votes to assign rights to another WBO. Until such time, any changes to the WBO property requires a simple majority vote of eligible WBC members.

OPTION 9 – DISBANDING

All good things must come to an end, and that can include the WBC, which should prepare for this eventuality and determine what happens. It seems obvious that future world building will not occur, but what about usage of the WBC's properties? This can be permitted for use in stories, for example, provided alteration of the world no longer occurs, unless that alteration is only to territory or items controlled by the former WBO of it.

If shared files are online and require payment for access, this can be achieved via downloading to each former WBC member's personal computers. However, if using sites that do not provide for downloading, continued access could become a problem. Consider the platform that is intended for this purpose at the outset.

COORDINATION

TRACKING

The WBC might find it helpful to keep a running list of decisions that have been made so that everyone stays aware. This will be especially useful if a new WBO joins. Maintaining this list would be the WM's responsibility.

MEETINGS

The WBC should attempt to meet periodically, such as once a month, to discuss group concerns and make decisions. This meeting can be in person or online. A possible agenda might include:

1. Members in attendance
2. Any official business, such as legal, voting, or membership changes
3. Updates of shared WBC items and progress, problems, resolutions
4. Discussion
5. Intended work to be done by next meeting
6. Incoming requests, such as those by authors wishing to write stories there
7. Membership and other dues or changes to them

TOOLS

The WBC will need to share files. This includes documents that everyone can work on, and WBO-specific documents that a WBO has rights to alter but others can only read, to make use of the WBO's work. Google Drive is free and provides both word processor and spreadsheet files. Programs that allow tracking of another's suggested changes may be useful.

LAST WORDS

Many of us will build more than one setting in our career. While this can seem intimidating due to workload, we can often reuse what we've done. For example, one absolute monarchy is much like another in its broad strokes, as is a religion, military group, or countless other elements. A god of war in one world is likely similar to another. We can tweak the details, reusing the basics. Reuse your own work whenever you can, following the Rule of Three, this time for your work instead of an analogue. Just as we don't want the audience to recognize we've modeled a power on Japan, we don't want them to realize our new book has a monarchy that's just like the one in our last book.

I hope you've enjoyed this series and found help, encouragement, and inspiration in it. I've enjoyed writing it and creating its offshoots, like the podcast that has tens of thousands of downloaded episodes. What started as a handful of articles has grown to multiple books totaling at least a quarter million words of advice. If it ever seems too much to take in, remember to do it in pieces and enjoy the process. Above all, never forget that world building is fun!

Please take a moment to review the books online. It's more important than you might think, and if you're an aspiring writer yet to publish, you'll eventually find out just how terribly difficult it is to get a book review. Established authors already know. We creatives must stick together and offer support. I hope I've found yours in the four years it's taken me to author *The Art of World Building*.

So where do you start? Where your heart lies.

Appendix 1
Culture Template

Culture Name

Naming the culture can be used within our work but is also useful for just our world building files, so we can write something like, "The Kiona culture dominates the Illiandor region." This way, we don't have to specify it everywhere, or repeat the details defined here (except when revealing them to the audience, of course).

Cultural Scope

Are we creating a culture for a sovereign power, region, settlement, species/race, or smaller sub group (such as knights, fighter pilots, royalty, etc.)?

Cultural Vision

Determine the morals, values, and beliefs of this culture. Use the government type to influence the decision.

The Body

Eye Contact

How is eye contact handled? Is deference shown? Is a gaze challenging?

Body Language

Do people move stiffly, relaxed, reserved, hunched over, sexy?

Hair Styles

How is hair worn by each gender, child, and professions of importance to the setting? Is hair styled a specific way on certain occasions and does this mean anything to people?

Body Modifications

Do people modify their bodies with piercings, tattoos, or implants? How common is this and what do they and those who don't do this think of the practice?

Gestures

What gestures are common?

Clothing

How do people wear their clothes? What accessories are so common that they're part of typical dress?

GREETINGS AND FAREWELLS

Invent several expressions that are made when greeting peers and superiors. What physical behaviors accompany these?

LANGUAGE

Define the tone of conversations and invent both swear words and expressions, what they mean, their origin, and under what circumstances they tend to be used, and any responses others typically give. What languages are spoken?

DAILY LIFE

DINING

What etiquette is followed? Do people talk with their mouth full? Is dining formal/informal? Are there multiple forks and spoons? Do people double dip? Is the mouth wiped on their sleeve, a napkin, or a tablecloth?

BATHING

How often do people bathe? Do they do alone? Is hot water an option and how often? Do they bathe in a river or a private tub? Is bath water used by multiple people?

SLEEPING

Do people sleep alone? Do married people share a bed? What do people wear while asleep? What kind of beds do they have?

EMPLOYMENT

What is the work week like? How many hours a day, per week? Is there a siesta? Are people paid for days off? Are holidays observed and which ones?

TRANSPORTATION

Is public transportation available and if so, what is it, how good is it, and what's the cost? What is its reputation?

PASTIMES

What do people do for fun?

RITUALS

How are birthdays and similar occasions celebrated? What holidays exist? What ceremonies are undertaken? Are there festivals they participate in?

FOLKLORE

What stories (and their characters or objects) exist? What lesson do they teach?

ARCHITECTURE

What impression do buildings give? What colors and materials dominate? Is there order or chaos?

Appendix 2
Organization Template

Name

Include proper name and nicknames.

Symbol and Colors

The group may not have one in its early stages, but think of something that fits. Is anything given to new members, like a tattoo or pin with the symbol?

Famous For

Summarize in a few sentences what people think of with this group. Details of events and traits are further down. Include legends if they exist.

The Facts

Are there things believed about them and which are false? Are some things true but doubted? Are some things unknown and would they change anyone's opinion of them?

TRAITS

WORLD VIEW

Are there guiding ideas that this group follows, such as the strong shall not prey upon the weak? What is the group's philosophy and how does this affect their actions?

GOALS

What does this group want to achieve? Control objects? Control access to land or who's in control of it? Does it want power to achieve something? How close are they to achieving the goal(s)?

LOCATION

Where are they based and where do they operate? What sort of headquarters do they have, if any? Is it hidden or in plain sight? Is there anything special inside it? Is it guarded and if so, by what?

STATUS

Is the group still operating, defunct, or once gone and being resurrected?

Possessions

Does the group own any shared resources, like ships, a castle, or supernatural items? How is their usage managed?

Relations

With Species

How does this group get along with each of the species? More importantly, are they viewed differently by each species, or famous for different things? What species are in the group and in what numbers?

Humans

Species 1

Enemies

Whether individuals, groups, or kingdoms, who are their enemies?

Friends

Who They Are

Who Rules

Is there one leader or a group? How is the leader(s) selected or changed?

Members

What species make up the group? What kind of people are here regarding skill set (warriors, wizards, etc.)?

Important Members

Are any individuals especially important, besides a leader? Are any of them famous?

History

Origins, Demise, and in Between

Where is the group from and based in now? What formative events made the group exist?

The Deeds

This is it. Tell us what this group does and how.

Appendix 3
Armed Forces Template

Name

Include proper name and nicknames, and any slogans.

Symbol & Colors

Remember to keep symbols easy for the non-artist to create in fantasy, but in SF where machines can create them, we can be more elaborate.

Famous For

What do people think of with this group, and is it accurate?

General Description

The basics on what this military unit is, what it's for, and what types of sovereign powers have them go here.

LOCATION

We can leave this heading blank. Rather than listing here which places they're found, do so in a city/sovereign power file.

TERRAINS

Do they specialize or become hindered in certain terrains? Make a general statement here and tweak in the subheadings. Example: "They are effective over most terrains without vegetation to block horses."

OPEN LAND

Example: "They are especially formidable and feared in open lands, causing many to plan to lure them into other terrain or at least into hilly ground."

FORESTS

Example: "Only thicker forests slow them either with underbrush, closely packed trunks, or due to hiding opponents."

HILLS

MOUNTAINS

Desert

Example: "The horses are slowed in sandy portions of deserts, but as most deserts are harder rock, they aren't slowed but do suffer fatigue from the hard ground and daily mileage suffers."

Swamp

Example: "Being horsemen, they avoid swamps unless an established road exists, though these may be washed out."

Special Sites

Are there any locations they revere, fear, or where something notable happened? Do they have special buildings that cater to their needs and which are found in many locations?

Lore

Invent some famous stories involving them or their members, including an origin story if useful.

History

A generic army, for example, may not need a history, but a more specialized force like the U.S. Marines or a specific knighthood can benefit from one. If we're creating this file not for armies in general, but a specific one, we can add some details.

WORLD VIEW

PLACE IN SOCIETY

Do people respect or fear them, or take them for granted? Are they honored with holidays? Do they get special discounts at stores? Don't just say "yes." Be specific.

LANGUAGES

What languages are they required to know and to what degree? This may change by region due to the inhabitants there, but we can make general statements that they all must have a working knowledge of high-elven, for example. If we're inventing a specific army, then be specific about this one.

CUSTOMS

Use customs to add details to their behavior and expectations. Can they get a seat at a crowded bar every time because someone has to give one up for them? Do people salute? Is there a specific greeting or farewell? Using the "Cultures" chapter to flesh this out.

Relations with Regions, Cities, and Places

Is there a region (including sovereign powers), city, or place where they well received or hated? Save most details for those files, but we can note the most interesting ones below.

Regions

Cities

Places

Those Who Serve

Who Rules

Do they answer to someone outside their organization, like the Prime Minister? This may change with each army, for example, based on the sovereign power, but typically they answer to the head of state. Also decide if they unofficially answer to someone else.

Who They Are

What species or races are accepted, rejected, or in positions of power, typically?

RELATION WITH SPECIES/RACES

For every species/race in the setting, work out how they get along and view each other.

RELATIONS WITH OTHER ARMED FORCES

How do they get along with other military groups? Are they rivals?

IMPORTANT CHARACTERS

FAMOUS MEMBERS

PAST

PRESENT

THE ROAD TO BECOMING ONE

REQUIREMENTS

What must they do before starting training? What sort skills are taught and must be mastered before full acceptance? Is there a way to bypass any of that? Are there well-known training centers or tests that cause fear and respect? Must people pass or die? All of this helps determine how elite they are.

Symbols of Acceptance

Determine what indicates membership. Is it a uniform, pin, weapons or armor no one else gets? How proud are members of these?

Medals, Pins...

Clothing

Arms

Weapons

Armor

In Society

Is there a day when recent graduates are announced? Do they get free drinks or food all day? How does society recognize them? Name on a digital billboard? The town crier yells it?

Ceremony

Is there a public ceremony?

Rank and Advancement

Where using standard ranks or altering them, note that here. Refer to the armed forces chapter.

ARMS

THE WEAPONS

Decide what weapons they use or never use. Much of it will be bestowed and technically owned by the military, but this isn't always true.

REQUIRED

PREFERRED

OTHER

RARE

ARMOR

What are they typically wearing and under what conditions? This detail lets us avoid showing them in the same outfit all the time. We also set scene expectations: someone not expecting battle might not be properly suited up for it.

REQUIRED

Preferred

Other

Combat

Invent some details on how they fight, including any back up skill like hand-to-hand fighting when disarmed. What are they not good at defending against (think a specific martial arts style)?

On Foot

Against Species

Repeat this heading for each species and how they fight them. Tactics against elves may be different from dwarves, for example.

On a Steed

Special Attacks

Special Defenses

Formal

Tournaments & Contests

Do they participate in any? Are those sanctioned or are they told to abstain?

Challenges and Duels

Do they make challenges for single combat? How and under what conditions? Do they respect challenges made by others? What happens during these and is the result highly regarded or disrespected?

War

Their Role

How are they used? In the vanguard? Are they saved for special moments and what are they?

Famous Battles

Missions

Have they been sent on any missions and what was the result? Is it famous? Did they discover anything important along the way? Unknown missions are some of the more fun to create.

Major Accomplishments

General

Inventions and Discoveries

Special, Famous, and Failed Missions

Unknown Missions

Appendix 4
Religion Template

Name

Symbols and Colors

Colors might not be important, but symbols are crucial. Use the history and a prophet's story to create simple symbols average people can draw.

Famous For

What do people immediately associate this religion with? A prophet? Non-violence? Aggressive missionary work? Choose the major aspects you've invented.

World View

Worship Practices

How often must they pray at home or at church? Is it formal? Are any materials or positions required (kneeling)?

Customs

Events and Holidays

Every religion will have an annual holiday and possibly events that take place regularly, such as once a week, month, or seasons.

Place in Society

How do various kinds of sovereign powers view them? Good or bad? Are they influential?

Locations and Holy Sites

Use the prophet's story to create a unique location.

Outreach

Do they perform missionary work and how aggressive are they about it.

Languages

What's the official language? What languages do they typically speak, read, and write? Do they try to be welcoming by learning them or exclusive by rejecting them?

Relations

With Species

With Military

With Other Religions

Do they have conflict with other religions? Most do.

Who They Are

Followers

Are any refused to become practitioners?

Clergy

Which species tend to be clergy and in what capacity?

Important Members

Are any individuals especially important, besides a leader? Are any of them famous?

Sects

This religion might have branches of it that believe and act differently.

History

The history should include the founding and a prophet or other legendary figure we leverage for most elements of this religion.

Combat

Are they allowed to fight or be in the military at all? What do they think of war?

Afterlife(s)

What afterlife do they envision? Is it real? Do they help people prepare?

Supernatural Energy Template

Name

Invent a memorable name and possibly nickname (based on appearance or an event).

Type

Is this magic, radiation, divine power, or something else?

Availability

How often can this force be used or encountered? Are those who harness it taxed in some way, such as with fatigue that limits usage?

Properties

Appearance

This should include not only colors but whether it's invisible or can only be seen with magical sight or specific technologies. Are additional properties only visible that way?

FEEL

This includes its temperature range and whether it gives off heat, cold, or nothing. If the energy can be touched or sensed, what happens to flesh or senses? Is anything heightened or muted?

DURATION

How long does it last when encountered? Does it have phases, like a volcano?

INTENSITY

Is the intensity constant or in a state of flux?

SPECIAL

HISTORY

ORIGINS

Deciding its origins is optional as natural phenomena need no explanation, but did something cause this?

INCIDENTS

Invent a few incidents that have happened with this energy, including when it was first discovered, first contained, or first used as a weapon, especially if these went wrong or had significant impact on events of the time.

USAGE

CONTROLLING IT

Can it be controlled? By who? Is a technology needed? Is there a limit on that control? What happens when control of it is lost?

USES

Do people harness this energy for anything, or would they like to? Using it to power ship engines comes to mind. Can it be weaponized?

SUPERNATURAL LAND TEMPLATE

NAME

Decide on its name and at least one nickname, which may be derived from properties, appearance, and stories of what's taken place here.

LOCATION

ACCESS

How do people enter this land? Are there doorways or portals? Is magic or technology needed? Are entrances and exits guarded or available at only certain times?

REGIONS

Are there definable regions inside, like territories or landscape features (such as a forest)? Such regions might be named for phenomena there.

SETTLEMENTS

Are there any towns inside? What are they like? Do they stay in one place or move? What is their attitude about travelers arriving?

IMPORTANT BUILDINGS

Do any buildings of note exist? What is important about them? Are some like holy ground where evil creatures cannot enter? Do they harbor bad things? Are they a trap?

INHABITANTS

THE RULER

Does anyone or anything claim to be the ruler of this land? Is that accepted or contested (and by whom)?

HORDES

Are there so many creatures of a particular type here that they amount to a horde that people associated with this place and fear? Where do they live? What attracts their attention? How can they be defeated?

MORTALS

Are there any humans (or other species) who've taken up residence here? Was that voluntarily or not? Is anyone rumored to be here but is not? Is anyone found here but no one knows they're here (i.e., presumed dead, for example)?

ANIMALS

Are there any animals that are specific to this place? Use the animal template from volume one to develop them, but indicate their presence here. There may also be animals that have wandered in or been brought here. Are they corrupted by this place in some way?

HISTORY

Have any events taken place here? Are those events known outside this land or not?

ORIGINS

Does anyone know where this land originated? Invent a reason and decide if people know or got it wrong, and how.

DEMISE

Will this place cease to exist at some point? Why and how? How soon is this to happen and what happens to everyone (and everything) still here?

LORE

Are there myths about this place? Stories true and untrue? What place does this hold in the minds of others: somewhere great or feared?

APPENDIX 7
MAGIC SYSTEM TEMPLATE

NAME

This can be the type of magic, such as witchcraft or necromancy.

SYMBOLS AND COLORS

A color is optional, but a symbol is likely. What is it?

FAMOUS FOR

The practitioners will be famous for their basic skills, reputation, impact on society and events, and reputed character. State what these are.

GENERAL DESCRIPTION

What can practitioners do? What can't they?

MAGIC SOURCE

What is the source of magic? The gods or the universe? Who made it possible?

MAGIC ORIGINS

When the spellcaster is summoning power, where does it come from? People? The environment?

LAWS OF MAGIC

What laws of magic govern usage? Can people perform this type and another? Must anything happen first?

PREVALENCE

How common is the ability? How common is a fully trained practitioner?

MAGIC COST

What is the cost of performing a spell? Does it weaken them, age them, cause forgetfulness?

ARE SPELLS NEEDED?

Must practitioners use a spell and what for? What happens when a spell fails?

LOCATIONS

SPECIAL SITES

Are there any sites where magic doesn't work, or where it is augmented?

LORE

Are there any famous stories or myths about a past practitioner or all of them?

HISTORY

Invent several famous practitioners from the past and what they are famous for, such as ending or starting a war, helping royalty, saving the world, or threatening great harm. Some can be known for a smaller scale horror that occurred to them or by them.

WORLD VIEW

PLACE IN SOCIETY

How do most societies view them? Are they beneficial or harmful? Celebrated or shunned? Does family reject them or boast of them?

LANGUAGES

Is there a magic language, or another unique one, that they speak, read, and write? Can others learn it or is magic talent and training required?

CUSTOMS

How do they customarily behave in a wide variety of situations (found in chapter 1 on creating cultures)?

PRACTITIONERS

WHO RULES

Is there a governing body where wizarding practices are codified and abided by, like in the *Harry Potter* books? Who is the head of this and how is such a person chosen?

WHO THEY ARE

Is there a species, race, gender, or other characteristic that influences who becomes a practitioner? What percentage of each does this? What "walk of life" are they from?

RELATIONS WITH SPECIES/RACES

Is there a uniform way they view and interact with any given species or race? And does that species view them a certain way? Have any incidents led to this relationship?

RELATIONS WITH OTHER GROUPS

Are there groups, including military, with whom they have an ongoing relationship? This could be as allies or enemies.

IMPORTANT CHARACTERS

Who are current and former members that have influence?

THE ROAD TO BECOMING ONE

REQUIREMENTS

How does someone acquire the talent and/or ability? Can they lose it and how? If there's a body that administers training in an official way, what must one do to be accepted into training?

SYMBOLS OF ACCEPTANCE

Are they allowed or required to wear specific clothing, pins, metals, or use an item like a staff? Is this required all the time or only at formal events?

RANK AND ADVANCEMENT

Are there any ranks that exist, such as starting on low magic before advancing to high magic? The ranks will have names and skill or power levels associated with them. Define them.

TRAINING

If training is available, what form does it take, what is involved, and what limitations are imposed before graduation? What are the testing criteria, and what restrictions if any exist on those who graduate?

ARMS

Are they allowed to use weapons or wear armor? What restrictions exist? Are laws of magic causing that or laws of "mankind?" In the latter case, we'll want to note that in the location's file more than here.

COMBAT

Are they part of any military group? If so, add them to that file. How do they behave in combat with other practition-

ers of this magic type or another, or physical combatants?
Do they run, subdue, or kill?

Appendix 8
Spell Template

Name

What is the spell called?

Magic Type

For what type of magic is this spell or can more than one do it?

The Spell

Define what the spell does.

Description

Basic description of what the spell does, how, and under what circumstances it can be cast or be effective. What is the spell's reputation?

Difficulty

How hard is the spell to cast? What skill or rank must the caster have achieved?

Duration

For how long does the spell last? How long does it take to cast?

Range

How far from the caster does the spell take effect and for what distance or radius? How close or far must they be from the target?

Targets

Is there a species or race that is more or less affected by it? How so? Describe what they think of this being cast at them. Are they afraid or unimpressed? Are there any tactics that can be used to mitigate the effectiveness?

The Cost

What effect does this spell have on the caster? Fatigue? Memory loss? How does the caster feel about the prospect of casting it (will they be successful? Is the cost of casting it acceptable?)? Do they dread it or look forward to it?

How to Cast

GESTURES

What gestures must they make to cast it? What purpose do they serve? Can the spell be done without them and if so, what impact does that have?

INGREDIENTS

What materials are needed and in what quantity? Define how rare they are and how easy to carry or how something frequently is (such as a vial). Create this like a recipe, with instructions on the order to do everything in and how to handle something, such as rubbing it between fingers, snapping it, throwing it, etc. Be more elaborate if this is about creating a potion or item, for example, rather than a live spell done in battle where speed matters.

WORDS

Are any words needed? What are they in English? What are they in the language of magic? Are they controlling what happens, summoning power, or what?

ITEMS

Can this spell be put into an item or a potion? Are there limitations on it?

Legal Template

This template can be used to create a legal system for any jurisdiction.

System Type

Is this a civil, common, or religious legal system? If the latter, what god?

The Laws

Create a list of laws which are specific to the setting. We can brainstorm here and then move laws to the template for the jurisdiction (city, power, etc.).

Moral Laws

Create laws that originate from morality.

Incident Laws

Create laws that originate from incidents. We can list the incident for our reference and understanding.

TRIALS

Who presides over the court? Who decides innocence or guilt? Are there lawyers?

DUELS

Are duels allowed? What are the rules? Where do they take place? Whether a sovereign power or settlement allows or forbids them will depend upon the location, but we can say how a government type (monarchy, federation) typically looks at them here.

TRIAL BY COMBAT

Is this allowed? What are the rules? Where do they take place?

TRIAL BY ORDEAL

Where do they take place?

PUNISHMENTS

List the available punishments that are unique to this setting, or ones common on Earth if there's something interesting about them, such as jail time in a specific jail.

Appendix 10
Monetary Template

Use this template to determine the monetary system in a sovereign power. An example is below and others are in chapter 10.

Material	Equivalent	U.S. Equivalent
1 iron	1 cent	1 penny
10 iron	1 copper	$1
10 coppers	1 silver	$10
10 silvers	1 gold	$100
10 gold	1 platinum	$1000

Figure 18 Monetary Template

Unit

Is the currency a unit of weight or value? If a unit of value, what is backing it, a power, settlement, or another body?

Form

Is money coins, gems, bills, or credits? Is it made from metal or gems? What does the money look and feel like? Do coins have milling around the edges?

EDUCATION TEMPLATE

SOVEREIGN POWER/SETTLEMENT

For which power or settlement is this education system being defined? Where do these schools tend to exist? Monarchies? Cities but not villages?

TYPE

What types of opportunities exist? Basic education, special education (like college or tech schools), or apprenticeships?

CURRICULUM

Don't create an entire course of study if not needed, but what subjects are taught? What languages must be understood and to what Earth grade level (3rd grade, high school). Which magic/tech subjects exist? Are there unique (and feared) tests?

RESIDENCY REQUIREMENTS

Do students live at home, in boarding school, with their master if an apprentice? For how long does this last, such as the weekdays (weekends at home), a semester, a school year, or until graduation?

FACILITIES

Are libraries, labs, and more on campus, offsite, or off world? What kinds are available and needed?

COST

Is this a public school and there's no cost to attend aside from materials? If a private school, those are expensive. An apprenticeship might mean menial tasks while living with the master. Can students work if their family can't pay? Is a period of service required after graduation?

STUDENT REQUIREMENTS

AGE

At what age must students enroll and when can they leave or graduate?

GENDER

Are genders treated equally? Are classes coed? Dorms? Bathrooms?

Species/Races

Are all species allowed? Who is not and why? Are some favored?

Fame

Are there famous schools and past or current students? What caused their fame? What reputation has this given the school system?

APPENDIX 12
GAME TEMPLATE

NAME

EARTH ANALOGUES

What games does it resemble? It can be more than one.

DETAILS

TYPE

Is this a sport or a tabletop game? Is it only recreational or do professional versions exist?

TEAMS

Are there teams? How many? Can it be done without teams? How many players per team? Can they be substituted and under what conditions and how often? Can a player who leaves the game return?

PLAYERS

What skills do players need? How many positions exist and what are their roles and responsibilities? What sort of training, knowledge, or experience is required? Are species or genders (or anyone else) allowed or forbidden? What social classes play this? Do the elite only watch?

GAME PLAY

Describe how the game is played.

RULES

WHAT ARE THEY?

ITEMS

What items are needed? Balls, baskets, bats, cards, rings, dice? Is a field or court needed and how is it marked? What equipment do players wear or use?

UMPIRES/REFEREES

Do they exist? How many and how good do they tend to be?

PENALTIES

If they exist, how are penalties caused? Are there different levels of infraction? Can one be expelled over them?

SCORING

What are all the ways a point is scored?

VICTORY

How is a victor chosen? First to a score? Highest/lowest score when time runs out? Is a tie possible? Is there overtime if needed?

TOURNAMENTS

Do they exist for this game? Is this at the end of a season? Are there famous ones? What's the prize called and what is it?

ABOUT THE AUTHOR

Randy Ellefson has written fantasy fiction since his teens and is an avid world builder, having spent three decades creating Llurien, which has its own website. He has a Bachelor of Music in classical guitar but has always been more of a rocker, having released several albums and earned endorsements from music companies. He's a professional software developer and runs a consulting firm in the Washington D.C. suburbs. He loves spending time with his son and daughter when not writing, making music, or playing golf.

Connect with me online

http://www.RandyEllefson.com
http://twitter.com/RandyEllefson
http://facebook.com/RandyEllefsonAuthor

If you like this book, please help others enjoy it.

Lend it. Please share this book with others.
Recommend it. Please recommend it to friends, family, reader groups, and discussion boards
Review it. Please review the book at Goodreads and the vendor where you bought it.

JOIN THE RANDY ELLEFSON NEWSLETTER!

Subscribers receive discounts, exclusive bonus scenes, and the latest promotions and updates! A FREE eBook of *The*

Ever Fiend (Talon Stormbringer) is immediately sent to new subscribers!

www.ficiton.randyellefson.com/newsletter

Randy Ellefson Books

Talon Stormbringer

Talon is a sword-wielding adventurer who has been a thief, pirate, knight, king, and more in his far-ranging life.

The Ever Fiend
The Screaming Moragul

www.fiction.randyellefson.com/talonstormbringer

The Dragon Gate Series

Four unqualified Earth friends are magically summoned to complete quests on other worlds, unless they break the cycle – or die trying.

The Dragon Gate

www.fiction.randyellefson.com/dragon-gate-series/

The Art of World Building

This is a multi-volume guide for authors, screenwriters, gamers, and hobbyists to build more immersive, believable worlds fans will love.

Volume 1: Creating Life
Volume 2: Creating Places
Volume 3: Cultures and Beyond
Volume 4: Creating Life: The Podcast Transcripts

Volume 5: Creating Places: The Podcast Transcripts
Volume 6: Cultures and Beyond: The Podcast Transcripts
185 Tips on World Building
The Complete Art of World Building
The Art of World Building Workbook

Visit www.artofworldbuilding.com for details.

RANDY ELLEFSON
MUSIC

INSTRUMENTAL GUITAR

Randy has released three albums of hard rock/metal instrumentals, one classical guitar album, and an all-acoustic album. Visit http://www.music.randyellefson.com for more information, streaming media, videos, and free mp3s.

2004: The Firebard
2007: Some Things Are Better Left Unsaid
2010: Serenade of Strings
2010: The Lost Art
2013: Now Weaponized!
2014: The Firebard (re-release)

Bibliography

"11 Traditional Holiday Dishes From Around The World," *World Strides*, worldstrides.com, Retrieved 3 APR 2018

"A name given to a person at birth or at baptism, as distinguished from a surname", *American Heritage Dictionary*, Archived 11 December 2008

Anderson, Julie, Emm Barnes, and Enna Shackleton. *The Art of Medicine: Over 2, 000 Years of Images and Imagination*: The Ilex Press Limited, 2013.

Barrett, Stephen (2009-01-17). "Quackery: how should it be defined?". *quackwatch.org*. Archived from the original on 2009-02-25. Retrieved 2013-08-09.

"Bloodletting". *British Science Museum*. 2009. Retrieved 2009-07-12.

Burchfield, R. W. (1996). *The New Fowler's Modern English Usage* (3rd ed.): 512

Byron Good. *Medicine, Rationality and Experience: An Anthropological Perspective*, Cambridge University Press, 1994

Campbell, Mike. "Meaning, Origin and History of Names". *Behind the Name*. Retrieved 21 July 2008.

Carpenter, Charles E. (1917). "Court Decisions and the Common Law". *Columbia Law Review*.

"Chambers | Free English Dictionary". *Chambersharrap.co.uk*. Retrieved 10 JUL 2012.

Chauran, Alexandra (2013). *Animal Familiars for Beginners*. Jupiter Gardens Press.

"Colloquialism," *Literary Devices*, literarydevices.com, Retrieved 9 NOV 2018

Davies, Owen (1999). *Witchcraft, Magic and Culture, 1736–1951*. Manchester, England: Manchester University Press

"Death in Early America", Archived December 30, 2010, at the *Wayback Machine*.

D'Este, Madeleine, "The Origins Of 'Touch Wood': Tree Spirits, The True Cross, Or Tag?" *Folklore Thursday*, Folklorethursday.com, Retrieved 18 JUL 2019

DiGiovanna, Jessie Mooney, "Wedding Traditions: Why Is the Wedding Ring Worn on the Left Hand?" *Brides*, Brides.com, Retrieved 9 JUN 2018

"Dining Etiquette," *Etiquette Scholar*, etiquettescholar.com, Retrieved 28 FEB 2018

Faivre, Antoine; Hanegraaff, Wouter. *Western esotericism and the science of religion*. 1995.

"Feudal Japan History," *Legends and Chronicles*, http://www.legendsandchronicles.com, Retrieved 9 JUN 2018

"Fist bumps, high-fives spread fewer germs than handshakes, study says". *Los Angeles Times*. 28 July 2014. Retrieved 7 June 2015.

Forbes, Sophie, "18 gestures that can get you in trouble outside the US," *NY Post*, NYPost.com, Retrieved 15 MAY 2018

Halifax, Joan (1982). *Shaman: The Wounded Healer*. London: Thames & Hudson.

"Handshakes from Around the World," *The Connected Woman*, Theconnectedwoman.com, Retrieved 9 AUG 2019

Hasa, "Difference Between Culture and Custom," *Pediaa*, Pediaa.com, Retrieved 18 AUG 2018

Ingerman, Sandra (2004). *Shamanic Journeying: A Beginner's Guide*. Sounds True

Jackson, William A (2001). "A short guide to humoral medicine". *Trends in Pharmacological Sciences*. 22 (9): 487–489.

Janin, Hunt (2009). *Medieval Justice: Cases and Laws in France, England and Germany, 500-1500*. Jefferson, NC: McFarland.

Jouanna, Jacques (2012), "The Legacy of the Hippocratic Treatise The Nature of Man: The Theory of the Four Humours", *Greek Medicine from Hippocrates to Galen*, Brill, p. 342

Katsev, Igor. "Origin and Meaning." *MFnames.com*. 1 March 2011. Retrieved 5 January 2009.

Kehoe, Alice Beck (2000). *Shamans and religion : an anthropological exploration in critical thinking*. Prospect Heights, Ill.: Waveland Press.

Kumar, Manisha, "Difference Between Morals and Values", *DifferenceBetween.net*, DifferenceBetween.net, Retrieved 10 OCT 2019

Luck, Georg (1985). *Arcana Mundi: Magic and the Occult in the Greek and Roman Worlds; a Collection of Ancient Texts*. Baltimore, Maryland: Johns Hopkins University Press.

"Mage." *Online Etymology Dictionary*. Etymonline.com. Retrieved 10 NOV 2019

Marriott, John, Dr., "What causes people to lose their faith?" *Church Times*, Churchtimes.co.uk, Retrieved 5 MAY 2019

Melton, J. Gordo, ed. (2001). "Black Magic". *Encyclopedia of Occultism & Parapsychology*. Vol 1: A–L (Fifth ed.). Gale Research Inc.

Mircea Eliade, *Shamanism, Archaic Techniques of Ecstasy*, Bollingen Series LXXVI, Princeton University Press 1972, pp. 3–7.

Murray, M. A., *Divination by Witches' Familiars*. Man. Vol. 18 June 1918.

Nasaw, Daniel, "When did the middle finger become offensive?" *BBC*, BBC.com, Retrieved 9 DEC 2019

"Necromancy". Merriam-Webster's *Collegiate Dictionary (11th ed.)*. Springfield, MA: Merriam-Webster. April 2008.

Needham, Joseph. *Science & Civilisation in China: Chemistry and chemical technology. Spagyrical discovery and invention: magisteries of gold and immortality.* Cambridge. 1974

Neubauer, David W., and Stephen S. Meinhold. *Judicial Process: Law, Courts, and Politics in the United States.* Belmont: Thomson Wadsworth, 2007.

"Officer (armed forces)." *Wikipedia*, Wikipedia.com. Retrieved 1 SEP 2019.

Offit, Paul A. (2013). *Do you believe in magic? : the sense and nonsense of alternative medicine.* New York: HarperCollins.

Ovid. *Metamorphoses, Book IV, Fable VII*, Lines 440–464.

Palmer, Kim, "Hue Believers," *Stir*, Sherman-Williams.com, Retrieved 8 AUG 2019.

Pappas, Stephanie, "Thirteen common (but silly) superstitions to save," *Nbcnews.com*, Nbcnews.com, Retrieved 6 MAY 2019

Pereira, Michela (2018). "Alchemy". *Routledge Encyclopedia of Philosophy.* Routledge

Post, Emily (1922). *Etiquette in Society, in Business, in Politics and at Home.* New York: Funk & Wagnalls.

Rank, Scott Michael, "Crime and Medieval Punishment," Historyonthenet.com, Retrieved 6 JUL 2019

Russell, Jeffrey Burton (1972). *Witchcraft in the Middle Ages*. Ithaca, New York: Cornell University Press.

Sanderson, Brandon. "Sanderson's First Law." Brandon-Sanderson.com. Retrieved 8 NOV 2019.

Segal, Ph.D., Jeanne; Smith, M.A., Melinda; Robinson, Lawrence; Boose, Greg, "Nonverbal Communication," *Help Guide*, helpguide.com, Retrieved 9 FEB 2019

Seigworth, Gilbert R. (1980). "Bloodletting Over the Centuries". New York State Journal of Medicine.

Sem, Tatyana. "Shamanic Healing Rituals". Russian Museum of Ethnography.

"Significance of Tattoos in Different Cultures," *Tattoo Splendor*, Tattoosplendor.net, Retrieve 8 SEP 2018

Singh, Manvir (2018). "The cultural evolution of shamanism". *Behavioral and Brain Sciences*. 41: e66: 1–61.

Social Law Library, Common Law or Civil Code?, Boston Mass.

Thomas, Keith (1997). *Religion and the Decline of Magic*. Oxford, England: Oxford University Press.

Twin, Alexandra, "6 Factors That influence Exchange Rates." *Investopedia*, Investopedia.com. Retrieved 20 MAY 2019.

"What is social class?" udel.edu, Retrieved 8 APR 2019

"Why do some countries drive on the left and others on the right?" *World Standards*, Worldstandards.eu, Retrieved 10 JAN 2018

"Why fair tests are needed". jameslindlibrary.org. 2009. Retrieved January 8, 2017.

Wilbert, Johannes; Vidal, Silvia M. (2004). Whitehead, Neil L.; Wright, Robin (eds.). *In Darkness and Secrecy: The Anthropology of Assault Sorcery and Witchcraft in Amazonia*. Durham, NC: Duke University Press.

Made in the USA
Monee, IL
30 March 2021